C000299131

YOU'LL NEVER WALK ALONE

LIVERPOOL
FOOTBALL CLUB

EST·1892 ®

LIVERPOOL FC
THE OFFICIAL GUIDE
2011

Sport Media
A Trinity Mirror Business

HONOURS

LEAGUE CHAMPIONSHIP (18)
1900/01, 1905/06, 1921/22, 1922/23, 1946/47, 1963/64, 1965/66, 1972/73, 1975/76, 1976/77, 1978/79, 1979/80, 1981/82, 1982/83, 1983/84, 1985/86, 1987/88, 1989/90

DIVISION TWO WINNERS (4)
1893/94, 1895/96, 1904/05, 1961/62

FA CUP WINNERS (7)
1964/65, 1973/74, 1985/86, 1988/89, 1991/92, 2000/01, 2005/06

LEAGUE CUP WINNERS (7)
1980/81, 1981/82, 1982/83, 1983/84, 1994/95, 2000/01, 2002/03

EUROPEAN CUP/UEFA CHAMPIONS LEAGUE WINNERS (5)
1976/77, 1977/78, 1980/81, 1983/84, 2004/05

UEFA CUP WINNERS (3)
1972/73, 1975/76, 2000/01

EUROPEAN SUPER CUP WINNERS (3)
1977/78, 2001/02, 2005/06

FA CHARITY SHIELD WINNERS/FA COMMUNITY SHIELD WINNERS (15)
1964 (SHARED), 1965 (SHARED), 1966, 1974, 1976, 1977 (SHARED), 1979, 1980, 1982, 1986 (SHARED), 1988, 1989, 1990 (SHARED), 2001, 2006

SCREEN SPORT SUPER CUP WINNERS (1)
1986/87

LANCASHIRE LEAGUE WINNERS (1)
1892/93

INTRODUCTION

Welcome to the **Liverpool FC : The Official Guide**, the essential club publication for 2011. We have again sought to provide you with the very best there is to celebrate about the club, be it on the pitch and off it, keeping you in touch with what has happened in the previous 12 months – as well as looking ahead to a brand new era.

There is a slightly different feel to this year's edition, with new content, analysis and sectioning as the yearbook naturally evolves. We have lost the cup section, which has been included in each previous edition – the decision being made to allow space for fresh content elsewhere. If you are seeking full results records in domestic cup competitions, these can be found in earlier editions. We have also included an International Section 'For Club, For Country' to looking back on the 2010 World Cup, while also noting Liverpool players' records on the international stage. 'Reds In League' combines Football League and Premier League achievement, including club and player records – while there is reflection on Rafael Benitez's six-year tenure coming to an end in 2010, as well as lauding previous men at the Anfield helm in the 'Managers' section.

Once again our gratitude to Ged Rea and Dave Ball, who have again been instrumental in providing up-to-date, accurate statistics, whil also suggesting the inclusion of various landmark achievements created since the fifth edition.

We hope you continue to find this publication of interest and a major reference point, balancing as it does the best of Liverpool FC in the past, present and future, whilst also utilising some of the best pictures available celebrating the club's rich pedigree at home and abroad.

WRITERS

Ged Rea and Dave Ball are official statisticians for the official Liverpool FC matchday programme, and weekly club magazine. Ged's Liverpool FC records are the most accurate available, while Dave is a key researcher for long-running BBC TV show *A Question of Sport*. James Cleary has overseen the editorial, design, research and writing of the publication.

Executive Editor: KEN ROGERS Senior Editor: STEVE HANRAHAN
Senior Production Editor: PAUL DOVE Senior Art Editor: RICK COOKE
Editor: ROY GILFOYLE Sub Editors: JAMES CLEARY, ADAM OLDFIELD
Design Team: BARRY PARKER, COLIN SUMPTER, GLEN HIND, LEE ASHUN, ALISON GILLILAND,
JAMIE DUNMORE, JAMES KENYON, LISA CRITCHLEY
Liverpool FC Writers: CHRIS McLOUGHLIN, JOHN HYNES, SIMON HUGHES, WILLIAM HUGHES
Sport Media Marketing Executive: CLAIRE BROWN

All Rights Reserved. No part of this publication may be reproduced, stored in a retrieval system, or transmitted in any form, or by any means, electronic, mechanical, photocopying, recording or otherwise without the prior permission in writing of the copyright holders, nor be otherwise circulated in any form of binding or cover other than in which it is published and without a similar condition being imposed on the subsequent publisher. Liverpool FC logo and name are registered trademarks of The Liverpool Football Club and Athletics Grounds Ltd and are reproduced under license.

ISBN 978 1 9068 02547
Photographs: PA Photos, Trinity Mirror, Liverpool FC & AG Ltd
Printed and finished by Korotan

CLUB CONTACT NUMBERS

Main Switchboard   0151 263 2361

Customer Services   0843 170 5000
International callers   + 44 (0)151 907 9399

Ticket Office   0843 170 5555
International Ticket Office   + 44 (0)843 170 5555

Mail Order Hotline (UK)   0844 800 4239
International Mail Order Hotline   + 44 1386 848247
Club Store (Anfield)   0151 264 2368
Club Store (Williamson Square - City Centre)   0151 330 3077
Club Store (Liverpool One - City Centre)   0151 709 4345
Club Store (Chester)   01244 344608
Conference and Banqueting (for your events at Anfield)   0151 263 7744
Corporate Sales   0151 263 9199
Community Department   0151 432 5689
Museum & Tour Centre   0151 260 6677
Membership Department   0843 170 5000
Public Relations (including all charity requests)   0151 432 5671
Press Office   0151 230 5721
Digital Media (online, TV and mobile)   0151 263 2361

BECOME A MEMBER OF **ALL RED**, the LFC Official Membership Scheme.
To join, visit www.liverpoolfc.tv/ALLRED or call 0844 499 3000.

SUBSCRIBE TO THE OFFICIAL **LFC PROGRAMME AND WEEKLY MAGAZINE**
To take out a subscription please call: 0845 1430001

LIVE AND BREATHE LFC 24/7
Official Club Media

Online – visit the official club website at **www.liverpoolfc.tv** for breaking news,
views, match reports, interviews, statistics, history and more.

Watch goals, highlights, interviews, press conferences, reserve matches, classic matches and
listen to commentary of every game with a subscription to LFCTV Online – visit
www.liverpoolfc.tv/video

TV – the official TV channel (LFC TV) is broadcast every day from the heart of your club. Available by
satellite, cable and online – visit **www.liverpoolfc.tv/tv**

Mobile – take LFC wherever you go. Download player animations, videos, games and our new
iPhone app or get the news as it happens with SMS alerts – visit **www.liverpoolfc.tv/mobile**

CONTENTS

Analysis of Liverpool FC's previous men in charge, while also providing an overview of Rafael Benitez's six season in charge.

Includes full profiles of the 2010/11 squad, a look at new manager Roy Hodgson and his coaching staff, the 2010 summer diary plus first team, reserves and Under-18s fixtures.

An in-depth look back at the campaign, including news, quotes, results, six of the best of the season, appearances, goals and the player of the season. We also focus on the seasons enjoyed by the reserves, Under-18s and ladies teams.

A detailed overview of the 2009/10 European season in the Champions and Europa Leagues, together with a complete record of the Reds' European results. The 1977/78 European Cup-winning campaign is revisited, along with a whole host of updated facts and statistics related to the club's – and players' – achievements in overseas competition.

Updated facts, figures and statistics concerning Liverpool's Football League and Premier League performances since 1893 – including team and player records.

World Cup and international achievements, including caps and honours won by players while representing the club.

A compilation of Liverpool records and achievements, including the complete first-team record. Goalscoring and appearance record holders are noted, as are notable landmarks – super subs, old/young Liverpool first-teamers, goalkeeping records and long-serving Reds.

A guide to Liverpool FC's Barclays Premier League opponents in 2010/11.

All the club information you need – from ticket prices to Anfield details and club tours, the work of each department, soccer schools, store information and LFC media.

FOREWORD

This is the sixth edition of the Guide, the most authoritative annual publication of one of England's most successful clubs. We are now at the beginning of what will be another exciting period in the club's history as we welcome our eighth manager since the legendary Bill Shankly.

Once again we have endeavoured to highlight the story of the 2009/10 season as well as updating the statistics of our proud history. One of the enjoyable aspects of our work is to compare the records of different periods since Liverpool FC's formation as well as comparisons with the other leading clubs in England. Although 2009/10 proved to be somewhat disappointing, it is still pleasing to record many positives which it is hoped can be carried over to the current campaign.

Last season we witnessed a 27th successive scoring league game, a Premier League record for the club and the second best-ever sequence of 37 consecutive Anfield games in all competitions. Strangely the side which ended that run was Fulham – then managed by a certain Roy Hodgson in April 2010. In Europe the Reds reached their 16th semi-final – a record for a British club – four more than Manchester United and six more than Chelsea.

Individually the honours went to Steven Gerrard, Pepe Reina and Fernando Torres. The captain became the highest scoring British player in Europe with his 33rd goal, scored against Unirea Urziceni, overtaking the previous best of Alan Shearer. Reina broke the club record for most clean sheets in his first 150 league games, as well as keeping the same amount of clean sheets as Golden Glove winner Petr Cech – the Chelsea keeper netting the prize only by virtue of playing fewer matches. Torres reached 50 league goals in the quickest time for Liverpool – just 72 games.

We also take an extended look at the 2010 World Cup and its history. Although it was a more than disappointing venture for England, we should applaud the exploits of Fernando Torres and Pepe Reina in winning the competition and Dirk Kuyt and Ryan Babel, whose Dutch team provided the opposition in the Soccer City Final.

The main part of the Guide chronicles the records of the club in both domestic and world competitions and we are sure that it is far better for supporters of Liverpool Football Club as well as the more studious members to have the information in one source rather than to scour the internet to identify any facts that are needed.

The ultimate intention of all concerned in this publication is that in years to come this Guide will be as relevant to Liverpool supporters as the Rothmans/Sky Sports annual is to the wider audience. We hope you will enjoy the book, and if you would like us to include certain information in future editions please feel free to contact Sport Media.

Ged Rea & Dave Ball

KEY DATES 2010/11

(Dates are subject to change)

August 2010

6	UEFA Europa League 4th qualifying round draw
14	Barclays Premier League kick-off
27	UEFA Europa League group stage draw
28	Carling Cup third-round draw
31	Transfer window closes

September 2010

3	England v Bulgaria, Euro 2012 qualifier (Wembley Stadium, London)
	Liechtenstein v Spain, Euro 2012 qualifier (Rheinpark Stadium, Vaduz)
	San Marino v Holland, Euro 2012 qualifer (Stadio Olimpico, Serravalle)
	Portugal v Cyprus, Euro 2012 qualifier (D. Afonso Henriques Stadium, Guimaraes)
	Faroe Islands v Serbia, Euro 2012 qualifier (Torsvollur, Torshavn)
7	Switzerland v England, Euro 2012 qualifier (St Jakob-Park, Basel)
	Holland v Finland, Euro 2012 qualifer (De Kuip, Rotterdam)
	Denmark v Iceland, Euro 2012 qualifier (Parken Stadium, Copenhagen)
	Norway v Portugal, Euro 2012 qualifier (Ullevaal Stadium, Oslo)
	Serbia v Slovenia, Euro 2012 qualifier (Red Star Stadium, Belgrade)
16	UEFA Europa League group stage matchday 1
21/22	Carling Cup third round
25	Carling Cup fourth-round draw
30	UEFA Europa League group stage matchday 2

October 2010

8	Spain v Lithuania, Euro 2012 qualifier (Estadio El Helmantico, Salamanca)
	Moldova v Holland, Euro 2012 qualifier (Zimbru Stadium, Chisinau)
	Portugal v Denmark, Euro 2012 qualifier (Estadio do Dragao, Porto)
	Serbia v Estonia, Euro 2012 qualifier (Red Star Stadium, Belgrade)
12	England v Montenegro, Euro 2012 qualifier (Wembley Stadium, London)
	Scotland v Spain, Euro 2012 qualifier (Hampden Park, Glasgow)
	Holland v Sweden, Euro 2012 qualifier (Amsterdam Arena, Amsterdam)
	Denmark v Cyprus, Euro 2012 qualifier (Parken Stadium, Copenhagen)
	Iceland v Portugal, Euro 2012 qualifier (Laugardalsvollur, Reykjavik)
	Italy v Serbia, Euro 2012 qualifier (Stadio Luigi Ferraris, Genoa)
21	UEFA Europa League group stage matchday 3
26/27	Carling Cup fourth round
30	Carling Cup quarter-final draw

November 2010

4	UEFA Europa League group stage matchday 4
17	Portugal v Spain, international friendly (TBC)
30	Carling Cup quarter-finals

December 2010

1	UEFA Europa League group stage matchday 5
1/7/8	Carling Cup quarter-finals
15/16	UEFA Europa League group stage matchday 6
17	UEFA Europa League last 32 and last 16 draw
TBC	Carling Cup semi-final draw

KEY DATES 2010/11
(Dates are subject to change)

January 2011

1	Transfer window re-opens
8/9	FA Cup third round
11/12	Carling Cup semi-finals, first leg
25/26	Carling Cup semi-finals, second leg
29/30	FA Cup fourth round

February 2011

2	Transfer window closes
17	UEFA Europa League last 32, first leg
19/20	FA Cup fifth round
24	UEFA Europa League last 32, second leg
27	Carling Cup Final (Wembley Stadium, London)

March 2011

10	UEFA Europa League last 16, first leg
12/13	FA Cup quarter-finals
17	UEFA Europa League last 16, second leg
18	UEFA Europa League quarter-finals and semi-finals draw
25	Spain v Czech Republic, Euro 2012 qualifier (TBC)
	Hungary v Holland, Euro 2012 qualifier (TBC)
	Serbia v Northern Ireland, Euro 2012 qualifier (TBC)
26	Wales v England, Euro 2012 qualifier (TBC, Cardiff)
	Norway v Denmark, Euro 2012 qualifier (TBC)
29	Lithuania v Spain, Euro 2012 qualifier (TBC)
	Holland v Hungary, Euro 2012 qualifier (Amsterdam Arena, Amsterdam)
	Estonia v Serbia, Euro 2012 qualifier (TBC)

April 2011

7	UEFA Europa League quarter-finals, first leg
14	UEFA Europa League quarter-finals, second leg
16/17	FA Cup semi-finals
28	UEFA Europa League semi-finals, first leg

May 2011

5	UEFA Europa League semi-finals, second leg
14	FA Cup Final (Wembley Stadium, London)
18	UEFA Europa League Final (Aviva Stadium, Dublin, Republic of Ireland)
22	Barclays Premier League final day
28	UEFA Champions League Final (Wembley Stadium, London, England)

June 2011

4	England v Switzerland, Euro 2012 qualifier (Wembley Stadium, London)
	Iceland v Denmark, Euro 2012 qualifier (Laugardalsvollur, Reykjavik)
	Portugal v Norway, Euro 2012 qualifier (TBC)

THE LIVERPOOL MANAGERS

Roy Hodgson's became not only Liverpool Football Club's 17th full-time manager in the summer of 2010 – but also the club's oldest. The full record, dates of appointment/departure and respective ages upon appointment, are noted below.

THE COMPLETE LIST 1892-2010

MANAGER	APPOINTED–DEPARTED
Roy Hodgson	July 2010-
Rafael Benitez	June 2004-June 2010
Gerard Houllier	November 1998-May 2004
Roy Evans (joint manager with Gerard Houllier)	July 1998-November 1998
Roy Evans	January 1994-November 1998
Graeme Souness	April 1991-January 1994
Ronnie Moran (caretaker)	February 1991-April 1991
Kenny Dalglish	May 1985-February 1991
Joe Fagan	July 1983-May 1985
Bob Paisley	July 1974-May 1983
Bill Shankly	December 1959-July 1974
Phil Taylor	May 1956-November 1959
Don Welsh	March 1951-May 1956
George Kay	August 1936-February 1951
George Patterson	March 1928-May 1936
Matt McQueen	February 1923-February 1928
David Ashworth	December 1919-December 1922
Tom Watson	August 1896-May 1915
John McKenna	August 1892-August 1896

OLDEST LIVERPOOL MANAGERS

	D.O.B.	DATE APPOINTED	AGE
Roy Hodgson	09/08/1947	01/07/2010	62 years, 326 days
Joe Fagan	12/03/1921	01/07/1983	62 years, 111 days
Matt McQueen	18/05/1863	13/02/1923	59 years, 271 days
Bob Paisley	23/01/1919	26/07/1974	55 years, 184 days
David Ashworth	na/na/1868	17/12/1919	approx. 51 years
Gerard Houllier	03/09/1947	16/07/1998*	50 years, 316 days
Bill Shankly	02/09/1913	01/12/1959	46 years, 90 days
Roy Evans	04/10/1948	31/01/1994	45 years, 119 days
George Kay	21/09/1891	06/08/1936	44 years, 320 days
Rafael Benitez	16/04/1960	16/06/2004	44 years, 61 days
George Patterson	na/na/1887	07/03/1928	approx. 41 years
Don Welsh	25/02/1911	05/03/1951	40 years, 8 days
Phil Taylor	18/09/1917	May 1956	approx. 38 years, 8 months
Graeme Souness	06/05/1953	16/04/1991	37 years, 345 days
Tom Watson	09/04/1859	17/08/1896	37 years, 130 days
John McKenna	03/01/1855	15/03/1892	37 years, 72 days
Kenny Dalglish	04/03/1951	30/05/1985	34 years, 87 days

* date appointed as joint-manager

MANAGER RECORDS

The complete statistical league record for every Liverpool boss, in chronological order, up until and including the end of the 2009/10 season.

THE COMPLETE LIVERPOOL MANAGERS' LEAGUE RECORD							
MANAGER	**P**	**W**	**D**	**L**	**F**	**A**	**WIN %**
John McKenna	88	51	16	24	234	120	57.95
Tom Watson	678	297	128	253	1123	980	43.81
David Ashworth	127	65	37	25	203	109	51.18
Matt McQueen	210	83	57	70	327	290	39.52
George Patterson	348	129	83	136	639	672	37.07
George Kay	321	121	88	112	489	469	37.69
Don Welsh	220	76	56	88	373	411	34.55
Phil Taylor	143	73	31	39	283	201	51.05
Bill Shankly	609	319	152	138	1034	622	52.38
Bob Paisley	378	212	99	67	648	298	56.08
Joe Fagan	84	44	25	15	141	67	52.38
Kenny Dalglish	224	136	56	32	437	187	60.71
Ronnie Moran (caretaker)	9	4	1	4	20	15	44.44
Graeme Souness	115	47	34	34	164	133	40.87
Roy Evans	172	83	46	43	280	173	48.26
Roy Evans/Gerard Houllier	12	4	4	4	19	14	33.33
Gerard Houllier	216	108	54	54	354	212	50.00
Rafael Benitez	228	126	55	47	371	183	55.26

Liverpool managers past and present: Kenny Dalglish (left) and Roy Hodgson

MANAGER RECORDS

A statistical breakdown of Liverpool managers' records when in charge of the club in the First Division or the Premier League – in chronological order.

LIVERPOOL MANAGERS' TOP-FLIGHT LEAGUE RECORD							
MANAGER	P	W	D	L	F	A	WIN %
John McKenna	30	7	8	15	51	70	23.33
Tom Watson	644	270	124	250	1030	955	41.93
David Ashworth	127	65	37	25	203	109	51.18
Matt McQueen	210	83	57	70	327	290	39.52
George Patterson	348	129	83	136	639	672	37.07
George Kay	321	121	88	112	489	469	37.69
Don Welsh	136	39	40	57	196	252	28.68
Bill Shankly	504	260	129	115	802	491	51.59
Bob Paisley	378	212	99	67	648	298	56.08
Joe Fagan	84	44	25	15	141	67	52.38
Kenny Dalglish	224	136	56	32	437	187	60.71
Ronnie Moran (caretaker)	9	4	1	4	20	15	44.44
Graeme Souness	115	47	34	34	164	133	40.87
Roy Evans	172	83	46	43	280	173	48.26
Roy Evans/Gerard Houllier	12	4	4	4	19	14	33.33
Gerard Houllier	216	108	54	54	354	212	50.00
Rafael Benitez	228	126	55	47	371	183	55.26

Reds boss Bill Shankly (centre) watches on with Liverpool bootroom and future managerial and coaching talent (from left to right) Ronnie Moran, Joe Fagan and Bob Paisley on the bench

MANAGER RECORDS

The record for the men in charge at Anfield after 150 and 200 games is noted below, again in chronological order.

LIVERPOOL MANAGERS' LEAGUE RECORD (FIRST 150 GAMES)

MANAGER	P	W	D	L	F	A	WIN %
Tom Watson	150	66	29	55	232	192	44.00
Matt McQueen	150	58	43	49	214	193	38.67
George Patterson	150	56	39	55	281	276	37.33
George Kay	150	54	40	56	243	254	36.00
Don Welsh*	150	44	42	64	226	282	29.33
Bill Shankly*	150	77	33	40	307	195	51.33
Bob Paisley	150	79	42	29	220	119	52.67
Kenny Dalglish	150	87	39	24	289	123	58.00
Roy Evans	150	72	39	39	239	148	48.00
Gerard Houllier	150	81	35	34	258	142	54.00
Rafael Benitez	150	81	35	34	230	121	54.00
* Not all in top flight							
** Shankly top-flight record	150	75	29	46	279	198	50.00

LIVERPOOL MANAGERS' LEAGUE RECORD (FIRST 200 GAMES)

MANAGER	P	W	D	L	F	A	WIN %
Tom Watson	200	86	45	69	301	242	43.00
Matt McQueen	200	79	56	65	310	268	39.50
George Patterson	200	75	48	77	373	391	37.50
George Kay	200	75	51	74	316	326	37.50
Don Welsh*	200	66	55	79	337	380	33.00
Bill Shankly*	200	106	40	54	414	256	53.00
Bob Paisley	200	113	51	36	320	148	56.50
Kenny Dalglish	200	120	50	30	391	168	60.00
Gerard Houllier	200	101	48	51	331	199	50.50
Rafael Benitez	200	114	46	40	334	161	57.00
* Not all in top flight							
** Shankly top-flight record	200	103	43	54	365	248	51.50

Early pioneer Tom Watson (left), and the great Bob Paisley

MANAGER RECORDS

The following table highlights the speed in which Liverpool managers have made an impact – specifically how quickly they reached the landmark 100 league wins.

Note that the only change in the table if relating statistics to the top flight is in Bill Shankly's record – he took 193 games to reach 100 wins, claiming the century in 1967.

FASTEST TO 100 LEAGUE WINS AS LIVERPOOL MANAGER

MANAGER	NUMBER OF GAMES TAKEN	YEAR OF 100TH LEAGUE WIN
Kenny Dalglish	167	1989
Bob Paisley	179	1978
Rafael Benitez	181	2009
Bill Shankly	184	1964
Gerard Houllier	197	2004
Tom Watson	227	1903
George Kay	262	1949
George Patterson	271	1934
CONTEMPORARY COMPARISIONS		
Arsene Wenger	179	2001
Sir Alex Ferguson	231	1992

Kenny Dalglish is noted statistically as the club's most successful manager, certainly in league games, and this table below, in 'success' order highlights the respective records of LFC bosses in charge for 250+ games.

MANAGERS' RECORD AFTER 250 GAMES IN CHARGE OF LIVERPOOL

MANAGER	SEASON OF 250 GAMES	P	W	D	L	F	A	WIN %
Kenny Dalglish	1989/90	250	152	61	37	493	204	60.8
Rafael Benitez	2008/09	250	145	50	55	410	207	58.0
Bob Paisley	1978/79	250	140	62	48	419	192	56.0
Gerard Houllier	2002/03	250	134	57	59	424	239	53.6
Bill Shankly	1964/65	250	133	54	63	502	307	53.2
Tom Watson	1902/03	250	110	55	85	391	314	44.0
George Kay	1948/49	250	100	63	87	400	376	40.0
George Patterson	1933/34	250	94	58	98	462	486	37.6

Rafael Benitez is above the legendary Bob Paisley and Bill Shankly at No 2 in the above list of success in all competitions, and we've compiled the statistical breakdown for his first 250 games at the helm below.

RAFAEL BENITEZ'S RECORD AFTER 250 GAMES IN CHARGE OF LIVERPOOL

COMPETITION	P	W	D	L	F	A	WIN %
Premier League	158	87	37	34	240	123	55.1
FA Cup	12	8	1	3	33	17	66.7
League Cup	14	10	0	4	27	21	71.4
European Competition	63	38	12	13	105	44	60.3
FA Community Shield	1	1	0	0	2	1	100.0
World Club Championship	2	1	0	1	3	1	50.0
TOTAL	**250**	**145**	**50**	**55**	**410**	**207**	**58.0**

MANAGER RECORDS

Since Liverpool's first foray into Continental competition in 1964, seven men have resided over European campaigns. Their respective records – in success order – are noted here.

BIGGEST WIN RATIO ENJOYED BY LIVERPOOL MANAGERS IN EUROPEAN COMPETITION

MANAGER	P	W	D	L	F	A	WIN %
Joe Fagan	19	14	2	3	34	10	73.7
Bob Paisley	61	39	11	11	140	49	63.9
Rafael Benitez	85	49	16	20	114	54	52.3
Bill Shankly	65	34	13	18	78	45	50.0
Gerard Houllier	52	26	17	9	24	16	50.0
Roy Evans	16	8	5	3	24	16	50.0
Graeme Souness	12	6	0	6	26	16	50.0
Roy Evans/Gerard Houllier	4	2	2	0	10	2	50.0

Rafael Benitez, tasted success in European competition

BENITEZ RECORD

In recognition of Rafael Benitez's six seasons at Liverpool FC, the following pages offer a statistical breakdown of his tenure.

RAFAEL BENITEZ'S OVERALL LIVERPOOL RECORD 2004-2010

COMPETITION	P	W	D	L	F	A	PTS	WIN %
Premier League	228	126	55	47	371	183	433	55.26
FA Cup	17	9	3	5	38	22	–	52.94
League Cup	17	11	0	6	31	27	–	64.71
FA Community Shield	1	1	0	0	2	1	–	100.00
UEFA Champions League	76	43	16	17	123	60	–	56.58
Europa League	8	5	0	3	14	7	–	62.50
European Super Cup	1	1	0	0	3	1	–	100.00
Club World C'ship	2	1	0	1	3	1	–	50.00
TOTAL	**350**	**197**	**74**	**79**	**585**	**302**	**–**	**56.29**

LANDMARK RAFAEL BENITEZ GAMES

GAME	DATE	OPPOSITION	COMPETITION	VENUE
1	10/08/04	AK Graz	Champions League	Away
50	09/04/05	Manchester City	Premier League	Away
100	01/02/06	Birmingham City	Premier League	Home
150	09/12/06	Fulham	Premier League	Home
200	10/11/07	Fulham	Premier League	Home
250	01/10/08	PSV Eindhoven	Champions League	Home
300	16/09/08	Debrecen	Champions League	Home
350	09/05/10	Hull City	Champions League	Away

BENITEZ RECORD

The season-by-season breakdown, including all competitions the first team played in under Rafael Benitez from August 2004 to May 2010.

RAFAEL BENITEZ'S OVERALL LIVERPOOL RECORD SEASON-BY-SEASON

SEASON	P	W	D	L	F	A	WIN %
2004/05 League	38	17	7	14	52	41	44.74
2004/05 FA Cup	1	0	0	1	0	1	0
2004/05 League Cup	6	5	0	1	10	4	83.33
2004/05 Champions Lge	15	9	3	3	20	10	60.00
2004/05 Overall	**60**	**31**	**10**	**19**	**82**	**56**	**51.67**
2005/06 League	38	25	7	6	57	25	65.78
2005/06 FA Cup	6	6	0	0	20	8	100.00
2005/06 League Cup	1	0	0	1	1	2	0
2005/06 Champions Lge	14	8	3	3	20	7	57.14
2005/06 Euro. Super Cup	1	1	0	0	3	1	100.00
2005/06 Club World Ch.	2	1	0	1	3	1	50.00
2005/06 Overall	**62**	**41**	**10**	**11**	**104**	**44**	**66.13**
2006/07 League	38	20	8	10	57	27	52.63
2006/07 FA Cup	1	0	0	1	1	3	0
2006/07 League Cup	3	2	0	1	8	9	66.67
2006/07 FA Comm. Shield	1	1	0	0	2	1	100
2006/07 Champions Lge	15	9	2	4	22	12	60.00
2006/07 Overall	**58**	**32**	**10**	**16**	**90**	**52**	**55.17**
2007/08 League	38	21	13	4	67	28	55.26
2007/08 FA Cup	4	2	1	1	12	5	50.00
2007/08 League Cup	3	2	0	1	6	5	66.67
2007/08 Champions Lge.	14	8	3	3	34	12	57.14
2007/08 Overall	**59**	**33**	**17**	**9**	**119**	**50**	**55.93**
2008/09 League	38	25	11	2	77	27	65.78
2008/09 FA Cup	3	1	1	1	3	2	33.33
2008/09 League Cup	2	1	0	1	4	5	50.00
2008/09 Champions Lge	12	7	4	1	22	12	58.33
2008/09 Overall	**55**	**34**	**16**	**5**	**106**	**46**	**61.82**
2009/10 League	38	18	9	11	61	35	47.37
2009/10 FA Cup	2	0	1	1	2	3	0
2009/10 League Cup	2	1	0	1	2	2	50.00
2009/10 Champions Lge	6	2	1	3	5	7	33.33
2009/10 Europa League	8	5	0	3	14	7	62.50
2009/10 Overall	**56**	**26**	**11**	**19**	**84**	**54**	**46.43**
TOTAL	**350**	**197**	**74**	**79**	**585**	**302**	**56.29**

BENITEZ RECORD

The player nationalities and contributions of players during Rafael Benitez's tenure are noted below, with the top 10 games played and goalscorers in games under the Champions League-winning boss' management taking into account **Premier League games only.**

NATIONALITIES OF PLAYERS UNDER RAFA

COUNTRY	PLAYERS
England	22
Spain	13
France	7
Argentina	6
Holland	4
Republic of Ireland	4
Brazil	3
Italy	3
Czech Republic	2
Switzerland	2
Australia	1
Chile	1
Croatia	1
Denmark	1
Finland	1
Germany	1
Greece	1
Israel	1
Mali	1
Morocco	1
Norway	1
Poland	1
Senegal	1
Slovakia	1
Ukraine	1
USA	1
Wales	1

Jamie Carragher – Rafa regular

TOP 10 APPEARANCES UNDER RAFA

PLAYER	GAMES
Jamie Carragher	230
Steven Gerrard	208
John Arne Riise	201
Steve Finnan	186
Sami Hyypia	184
Xabi Alonso	172
Pepe Reina	166
Peter Crouch	134
Luis Garcia	121
Dirk Kuyt	106

TOP 10 GOALSCORERS UNDER RAFA

PLAYER	GOALS
Steven Gerrard	72
Peter Crouch	42
Fernando Torres	36
Luis Garcia	30
Dirk Kuyt	27
Djibril Cisse	24
John Arne Riise	17
Xabi Alonso	14
Milan Baros	13
Sami Hyypia	12
Fernando Morientes	12
Robbie Fowler	12

BENITEZ RECORD

The 83 players – and their respective records – during the course of Rafael Benitez's 350 games in charge.

PLAYERS TO PLAY FOR LIVERPOOL UNDER RAFAEL BENITEZ

PLAYER	APPS	GOALS	PLAYER	APPS	GOALS
Jamie Carragher	326	3	Andrea Dossena	31	2
Steven Gerrard	292	104	Robbie Keane	28	7
Pepe Reina	259	0	Antonio Nunez	27	1
Xabi Alonso	210	19	Alberto Aquilani	26	2
John Arne Riise	201	17	Sotirios Kyrgiakos	21	1
Sami Hyypia	200	14	Jan Kromkamp	18	0
Dirk Kuyt	200	51	Darren Potter	17	0
Steve Finnan	186	1	Maxi Rodriguez	17	1
Javier Mascherano	138	3	Neil Mellor	16	5
Yossi Benayoun	134	29	Vladimir Smicer	16	1
Peter Crouch	134	42	Salif Diao	14	1
Ryan Babel	129	20	Chris Kirkland	14	0
Luis Garcia	121	30	Philipp Degen	13	0
Lucas Leiva	121	5	Manuel Pellegrino	13	0
Fernando Torres	116	72	Scott Carson	9	0
Daniel Agger	115	7	Anthony Le Tallec	9	0
Fabio Aurelio	110	4	Diego Cavalieri	8	0
Alvaro Arbeloa	98	2	Gabriel Paletta	8	1
Harry Kewell	90	5	Damien Plessis	8	1
Momo Sissoko	87	1	Danny Guthrie	7	0
Jermaine Pennant	81	3	Charles Itandje	7	0
Djibril Cisse	79	24	Daniel Pacheco	7	0
Martin Skrtel	79	1	Jay Spearing	7	0
Dietmar Hamann	75	1	John Welsh	7	0
Stephen Warnock	67	1	Zak Whitbread	7	0
Djimi Traore	66	0	Daniel Ayala	5	0
Emiliano Insua	62	1	Stephen Darby	5	0
Fernando Morientes	61	12	Jack Hobbs	5	0
David Ngog	56	11	Stephane Henchoz	4	0
Albert Riera	56	5	Martin Kelly	4	0
Jerzy Dudek	53	0	Sebastian Leto	4	0
Milan Baros	47	13	Lee Peltier	4	0
Bolo Zenden	47	2	David Raven	4	0
Florent Sinama-Pongolle	43	7	Nathan Eccleston	2	0
Craig Bellamy	42	9	Richie Partridge	2	0
Andriy Voronin	40	6	Antonio Barragan	1	0
Robbie Fowler	39	12	Daniel Padelli	1	0
Mark Gonzalez	36	3	Jack Robinson	1	0
Igor Biscan	35	2	Miki Roque	1	0
Glen Johnson	35	3	James Smith	1	0
Josemi	35	0	Mark Smyth	1	0
Nabil El Zhar	32	1			

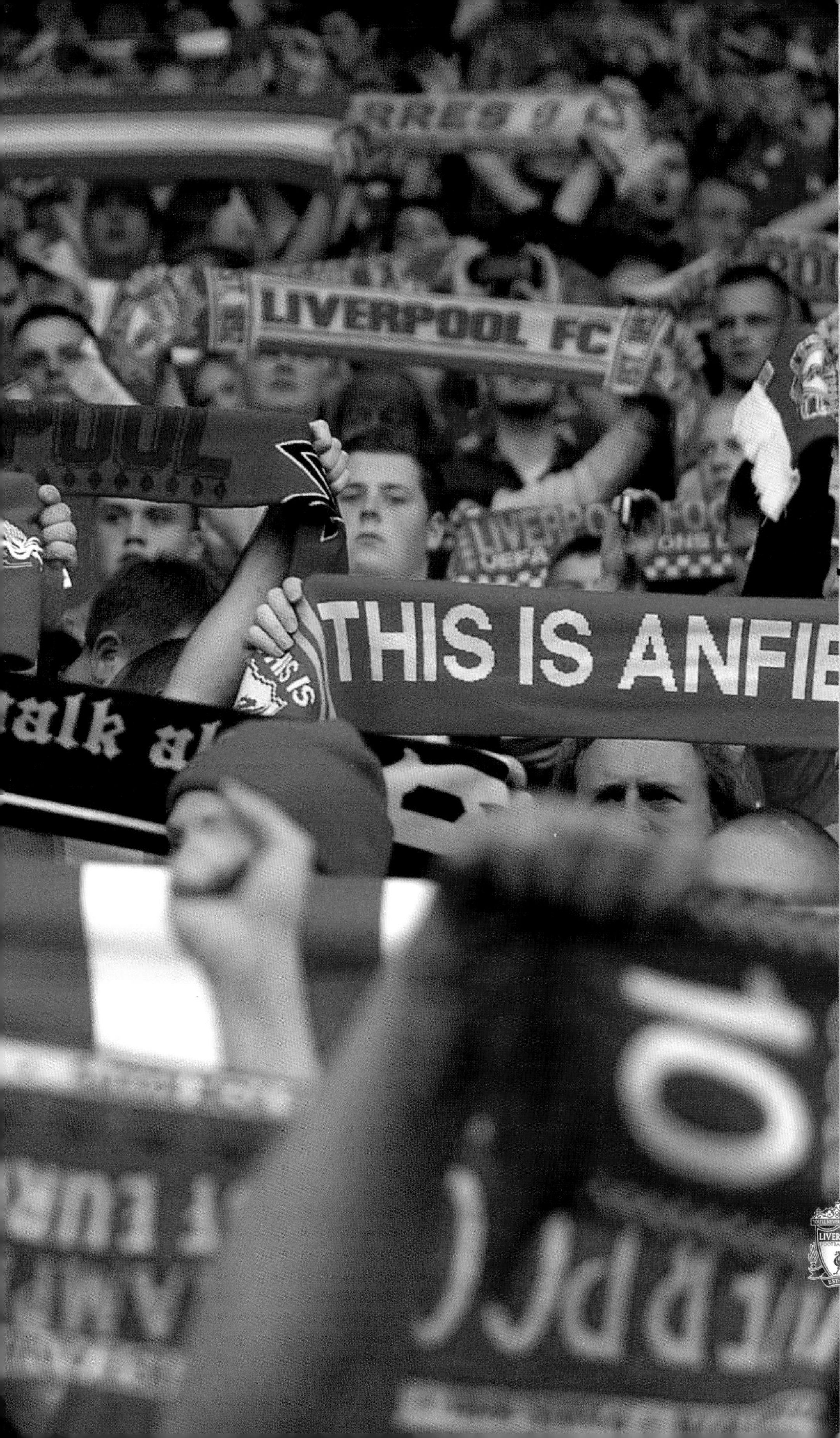
LIVERPOOL FC
THIS IS ANFIE

THE SQUAD 2010/11

LFC stats correct before start of 2010/11 Premier League season

Peter Gulacsi - Squad number 42

Positions	Goalkeeper
Born	Budapest, Hungary
Age (at start of 10/11)	20
Birth date	06/05/1990
Height	6ft 3ins
Other clubs	MTK,
	Hereford United,
	Tranmere Rovers
Liverpool debut	–
Liverpool appearances	–
Liverpool goals	–
International caps	0

Martin Hansen - Squad number 41

Positions	Goalkeeper
Born	Glostrup, Denmark
Age (at start of 10/11)	20
Birth date	15/06/1990
Height	6ft 2ins
Other club	Brondby
Honours	2007 FA Youth Cup
Liverpool debut	–
Liverpool appearances	–
Liverpool goals	–
International caps	0

Brad Jones - Squad number 1

Positions	Goalkeeper
Born	Armadale, Australia
Age (at start of 10/11)	28
Birth date	19/03/1982
Height	6ft 2ins
Other clubs	Middlesbrough,
	Stockport County,
	Rotherham United,
	Blackpool,
	Sheffield Wed.
Liverpool debut	–
Liverpool appearances	–
Liverpool goals	–
International caps	2 (0 goals)

Pepe Reina – Squad number 25

Position	Goalkeeper
Born	Madrid, Spain
Age (at start of 10/11)	27
Birth date	31/08/1982
Height	6ft 2ins
Other clubs	Barcelona, Villarreal
Honours	2004, 2005 UEFA Intertoto Cup, 2005 European Super Cup, 2006 FA Cup, 2006 FA Community Shield
Liverpool debut	13/07/05 v TNS
Liverpool appearances	259
Liverpool goals	0
International caps	20 (0 goals)
International honours	2008 Euro C'ships, 2010 World Cup

Daniel Agger – Squad number 5

Positions	Left/Central Defence
Born	Hvidovre, Denmark
Age (at start of 10/11)	25
Birth date	12/12/1984
Height	6ft 3ins
Other clubs	Rosenhoj, Brondby
Honours	2005 Denmark League, 2005 Denmark Cup, 2006 FA Comm. Shield
Liverpool debut	01/02/06 v Birmingham
Liverpool appearances	108 + 8 as substitute
Liverpool goals	7
International caps	36 (3 goals)

Fabio Aurelio – Squad number 6

Positions	Left Defence/ Midfield
Born	Sao Carlos, Brazil
Age (at start of 10/11)	30
Birth date	24/09/1979
Height	5ft 8ins
Other clubs	Sao Paulo, Valencia
Honours	1998, 2000 Sao Paulo State C'ship, 2002, 2004 Spain League, 2004 Euro. Super Cup, 2006 FA Community Shield
Liverpool debut (first)	13/08/06 v Chelsea
Liverpool appearances	77 + 33 as sub.
Liverpool goals	4
International caps	0

Daniel Ayala – Squad number 40

Position	Central Defence
Born	Seville, Spain
Age (at start of 10/11)	19
Birth date	07/11/1990
Height	6ft 3ins
Other club	Sevilla
Liverpool debut	16/08/09 v Tottenham Hotspur
Liverpool appearances	2 + 3 as substitute
Liverpool goals	0
International caps	0

Jamie Carragher – Squad number 23

Positions	Right/Central Defence
Born	Bootle, Liverpool
Age (at start of 10/11)	32
Birth date	28/01/1978
Height	6ft 1ins
Honours	2001, 2006 FA Cup, 2001, 2003 Lge Cup, 2001 UEFA Cup, 2001, 2005 European Super Cup, 2001, 2006 FA Community Shield, 2005 Champions League
Liverpool debut	08/01/97 v Middlesbrough
Liverpool appearances	610 + 21 as substitute
Liverpool goals	5
International caps	38 (0 goals)

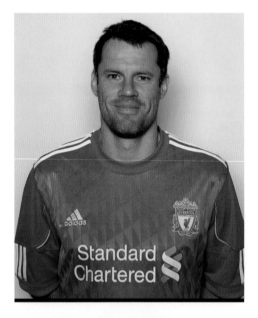

Stephen Darby – Squad number 32

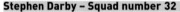

Position	Right Defence
Born	Liverpool
Age (at start of 10/11)	21
Birth date	06/10/1988
Height	5ft 8ins
Other club	Swindon Town
Honours	2006 FA Youth Cup, 2007, 2008 FA Premier Reserve League
Liverpool debut	12/11/08 v Tottenham Hotspur
Liverpool appearances	2 + 4 as substitute
Liverpool goals	0
International caps	0

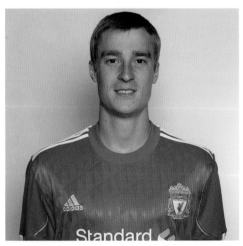

Glen Johnson – Squad number 2

Position	Right Defence
Born	Greenwich
Age (at start of 10/11)	25
Birth date	23/08/1984
Height	5ft 11ins
Other clubs	West Ham, Millwall, Chelsea, Portsmouth
Honours	2005 FA Premier League, 2005 League Cup, 2008 FA Cup
Liverpool debut	16/08/09 v Tottenham Hotspur
Liverpool appearances	34 + 2 as substitute
Liverpool goals	3
International caps	27 (1 goal)

Martin Kelly – Squad number 34

Position	Central Defence
Born	Whiston
Age (at start of 10/11)	20
Birth date	27/04/1990
Height	6ft 3ins
Other club	Huddersfield Town
Honours	2008 FA Premier Reserve League
Liverpool debut	09/12/08 v PSV Eindhoven
Liverpool appearances	3 + 3 as substitute
Liverpool goals	0
International caps	0

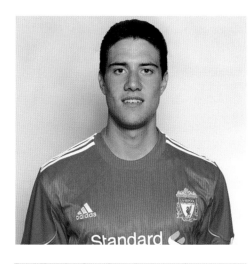

Paul Konchesky – Squad number 3

Position	Left Defence
Born	Barking
Age (at start of 10/11)	29
Birth date	15/05/1981
Height	5ft 10ins
Other clubs	Charlton Athletic, Tottenham Hotspur, West Ham United, Fulham
Liverpool debut	–
Liverpool appearances	–
Liverpool goals	–
International caps	2 (0 goals)

Sotirios Kyrgiakos – Squad number 16

Position	Central Defence
Born	Trikala, Greece
Age (at start of 10/11)	31
Birth date	23/07/1979
Height	6ft 3ins
Other clubs	Panathinaikos, Agios Nikolaos, Rangers, Eintracht Frankfurt, AEK Athens
Honours	2004 Greece Lge & Cup, 2005 Scottish League, 2005 Scottish Lge Cup
Liverpool debut	29/08/09 v Bolton
Liverpool appearances	19 + 3 as substitute
Liverpool goals	1
International caps	60 (4 goals)

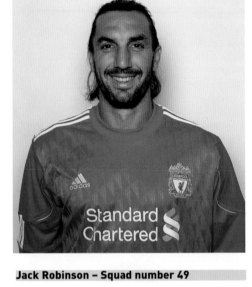

Jack Robinson – Squad number 49

Positions	Left Defence/Midfield
Born	Warrington
Age (at start of 10/11)	16
Birth date	01/09/1993
Height	6ft 1ins
Liverpool debut	09/05/10 v Hull City
Liverpool appearances	0 + 1 as substitute
Liverpool goals	0
International caps	0

Martin Skrtel – Squad number 37

Position	Central Defence
Born	Handlova, Slovakia
Age (at start of 10/11)	25
Birth date	15/12/1984
Height	6ft 3ins
Other clubs	FK AS Trencin, Zenit St. Petersburg
Honours	2007 Russian Premier League
Liverpool debut	21/01/08 v Aston Villa
Liverpool appearances	73 + 8 as substitute
Liverpool goals	1
International caps	42 (5 goals)

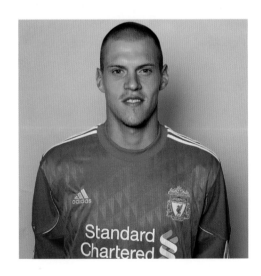

Danny Wilson – Squad number 22

Position	Central Defence
Born	Edinburgh
Age (at start of 10/11)	18
Birth date	27/12/1991
Height	6ft 1ins
Other club	Rangers
Honours	2009 Scottish Cup, 2010 Scottish Prem. Lge & League Cup
Liverpool debut	–
Liverpool appearances	–
Liverpool goals	–
International caps	0

Joe Cole - Squad number 10

Positions	Midfield/Forward
Born	London
Age (at start of 10/11)	28
Birth date	08/11/1981
Height	5ft 9ins
Other clubs	West Ham United, Chelsea
Honours	2005, 2006, 2010 Prem Lge, 2007, 2010 FA Cup, 2005, 2007 Lge Cup, 2005, 2009 FA Community Shield
Liverpool debut	05/08/10 v FK Rabotnicki
Liverpool appearances	1 + 0 as substitute
Liverpool goals	0
International caps	56 (10 goals)

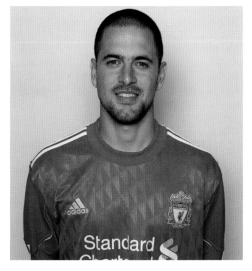

Steven Gerrard MBE – Squad number 8

Positions	Central/Right Midfield or Forward
Born	Whiston
Age (at start of 10/11)	30
Birth date	30/05/1980
Height	6ft 0ins
Honours	2001, 2006 FA Cup, 2001, 2003 Lge Cup, 2001 UEFA Cup, 2001 Euro Super Cup, 2001, 2006 FA Comm Shield, 2005 Champions League
Liverpool debut	29/11/98 v B'burn
Liverpool appearances	489 + 44 as sub.
Liverpool goals	133
International caps	85 (19 goals)

Steven Irwin – Squad number 36

Positions	Defence/Midfield
Born	Liverpool
Age (at start of 10/11)	19
Birth date	29/09/1990
Height	5ft 8ins
Honours	2007 FA Youth Cup
Liverpool debut	-
Liverpool appearances	-
Liverpool goals	-
International caps	0

Milan Jovanovic - Squad number 14

Positions	Left Midfield/Forward
Born	Bajina Basta, Serbia
Age (at start of 10/11)	29
Birth date	18/04/1981
Height	6ft 0ins
Other clubs	Vojvodina, Shakhtar Donetsk, Lokomotiv Moscow, Standard Liege
Liverpool debut	29/07/10 v FK Rabotnicki
Liverpool appearances	2 + 0 as substitute
Liverpool goals	-
International caps	30 (10 goals)

Lucas Leiva – Squad number 21

Position	Central Midfield
Born	Dourados, Brazil
Age (at start of 10/11)	23
Birth date	09/01/1987
Height	5ft 10ins
Other club	Gremio
Honours	2005 Brazilian Serie B, 2006, 2007 Rio Grande do Sul State Championship, 2008 FA Prem Reserve Lge
Liverpool debut	28/08/07 v Toulouse
Liverpool appearances	88 + 35 as substitute
Liverpool goals	5
International caps	4 (0 goals)
International honours	2008 Olympics Bronze Medal

Raul Meireles - Squad number 4

Position	Central Midfield
Born	Porto, Portugal
Age (at start of 10/11)	27
Birth date	17/03/1983
Height	5ft 10ins
Other clubs	Aves, Boavista, Porto
Honours	2006, 2007, 2008, 2009 Portugal Lge, 2006, 2009, 2010 Portugal Cup, 2006, 2009, 2010 Portugal Super Cup
Liverpool debut	–
Liverpool appearances	–
Liverpool goals	–
International caps	38 (6 goals)

Christian Poulsen - Squad number 28

Position	Central Midfield
Born	Asnaes, Denmark
Age (at start of 10/11)	30
Birth date	28/02/1980
Height	6ft 0ins
Other clubs	FC Copenhagen, Schalke 04, Sevilla, Juventus
Honours	2001 Denmark League, 2006 European Super Cup, 2007 UEFA Cup
Liverpool debut	–
Liverpool appearances	–
Liverpool goals	–
International caps	77 (6 goals)

Maxi Rodriguez - Squad number 17

Positions	Right/Left Midfield
Born	Rosario, Argentina
Age (at start of 10/11)	29
Birth date	02/01/1981
Height	5ft 11ins
Other clubs	Newell's Old Boys, Real Oviedo, Espanyol, Atletico Madrid
Liverpool debut	16/01/10 v Stoke City
Liverpool appearances	14 + 4 as substitute
Liverpool goals	1
International caps	41 (12 goals)

Jonjo Shelvey - Squad number 33

Position	Central Midfield
Born	Romford
Age (at start of 10/11)	18
Birth date	27/02/1992
Height	6ft 0ins
Other club	Charlton Athletic
Liverpool debut	-
Liverpool appearances	-
Liverpool goals	-
International caps	0

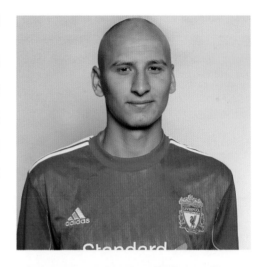

Jay Spearing – Squad number 26

Position	Central Midfield
Born	Wirral
Age (at start of 10/11)	21
Birth date	25/11/1988
Height	5ft 6ins
Other club	Leicester City
Honours	2006, 2007 FA Youth Cup, 2008 FA Premier Reserve League
Liverpool debut	09/12/08 v PSV Eindhoven
Liverpool appearances	4 + 5 as substitute
Liverpool goals	0
International caps	0

David Amoo – Squad number 46

Positions	Right/Centre Forward
Born	London
Age (at start of 10/11)	19
Birth date	13/04/1991
Height	6ft 0ins
Other club	Millwall
Liverpool debut	29/07/10 v FK Rabotnicki
Liverpool appearances	1 + 0 as substitute
Liverpool goals	0
International caps	0

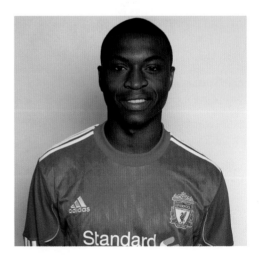

Ryan Babel – Squad number 19

Positions	Midfield/Forward
Born	Amsterdam, Holland
Age (at start of 10/11)	23
Birth date	19/12/1986
Height	6ft 0ins
Other club	Ajax
Honours	2005, 2006 Dutch Super Cup, 2006, 2007 Dutch Cup
Liverpool debut	11/08/07 v Aston Villa
Liverpool appearances	58 + 71 as substitute
Liverpool goals	20
International caps	39 (5 goals)
International honours	2010 World Cup runner-up

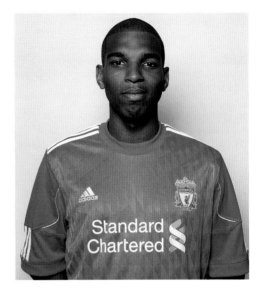

Nathan Eccleston – Squad number 39

Position	Forward
Born	Manchester
Age (at start of 10/11)	19
Birth date	30/12/1990
Height	5ft 10ins
Other club	Huddersfield Town
Honours	2007 FA Youth Cup
Liverpool debut	28/10/09 v Arsenal
Liverpool appearances	0 + 3 as substitute
Liverpool goals	0
International caps	0

Dirk Kuyt – Squad number 18

Positions	Right/Centre Midfield or Forward
Born	Katwijk, Holland
Age (at start of 10/11)	30
Birth date	22/07/1980
Height	6ft 0ins
Other clubs	FC Utrecht, Feyenoord
Honours	2003 Dutch Cup
Liverpool debut	26/08/06 v West Ham United
Liverpool appearances	173 + 27 as substitute
Liverpool goals	51
International caps	69 (16 goals)
International honours	2010 World Cup Runner-up

David Ngog – Squad number 24

Position	Centre Forward
Born	Gennevilliers, France
Age (at start of 10/11)	21
Birth date	01/04/1989
Height	6ft 3ins
Other club	Paris Saint-Germain
Honours	2008 French League Cup
Liverpool debut	31/08/08 v Aston Villa
Liverpool appearances	25 + 33 as substitute
Liverpool goals	14
International caps	0

Daniel Pacheco – Squad number 12

Position	Forward
Born	Malaga, Spain
Age (at start of 10/11)	19
Birth date	05/01/1991
Height	5ft 6ins
Other club	Barcelona
Honours	2008 FA Premier Reserve League
Liverpool debut	09/12/09 v Fiorentina
Liverpool appearances	1 + 7 as substitute
Liverpool goals	0
International caps	0

Fernando Torres – Squad number 9

Position	Centre Forward
Born	Madrid, Spain
Age (at start of 10/11)	26
Birth date	20/03/1984
Height	6ft 1ins
Other club	Atletico Madrid
Honours	2002 Spanish Second Division
Liverpool debut	11/08/07 v Aston Villa
Liverpool appearances	102 + 14 as substitute
Liverpool goals	72
International caps	80 (24 goals)
International honours	2008 Euro C'ships, 2010 World Cup

OTHER PLAYERS ON LOAN
2010/11

Alberto Aquilani

Position	Central Midfield
Born	Rome, Italy
Age	26
Birth date	07/07/1984
Height	6ft 1ins
Club	Juventus
Loan spell	One year
Honours	2007, 2008 Italian Cup, 2007 Italian Super Cup
International caps	11 (2 goals)

Philipp Degen

Positions	Right Defence/Midfield
Born	Holstein, Switzerland
Age	27
Birth date	15/02/1983
Height	6ft 1ins
Club	VfB Stuttgart
Loan spell	One year
Honours	2002, 2004, 2005 Swiss League, 2003 Swiss Cup
International caps	32 (0 goals)

Nabil El Zhar

Position	Forward
Born	Ales, France
Age	24
Birth date	27/08/1986
Height	5ft 6ins
Club	PAOK
Loan spell	One year
International caps	7 (2 goals) – for Morocco

Emiliano Insua

Position	Left Defence
Born	Buenos Aires, Argentina
Age	21
Birth date	07/01/1989
Height	5ft 8ins
Club	Galatasaray
Loan spell	One year
Honours	2008 FA Premier Reserve League
International caps	1 (0 goals)

THE MANAGEMENT

Roy Hodgson – Manager

Appointed	01/07/2010
Born	Croydon
Birth date	09/08/1947
Other clubs managed	Halmstad, Bristol C, Orebro, Malmo, N. Xamax, I. Milan, Blackburn Rovers, Grasshopper, C'hagen, Udinese, Viking, Fulham
Honours (senior manager)	1976, 1979, 1986, 1987, 1988, 1989 Swedish Lge, 1986, 1989 Swedish Cup, 2001 Danish Lge, 2001 Danish S. Cup
Other countries managed	Switzerland, UAE, Finland

Sammy Lee – Assistant-manager

Appointed	16/05/2008
Born	Liverpool
Birth date	07/02/1959
Coaching career	Liverpool, England, Bolton Wanderers
Clubs (player)	Liverpool, QPR, Osasuna, Southampton, Bolton
Honours (player)	1979, 1980, 1982 FA Charity Shield, 1981, 1984 European Cup, 1981, 1982, 1983, 1984 League Cup, 1982, 1983, 1984 Division 1

John McMahon – Reserves manager

Appointed	June 2009
Born	Manchester
Birth date	07/12/1949
Coaching career	Tranmere Rovers, Shrewsbury Town
Clubs (player)	Preston North End, Southend United, Chesterfield, Crewe Alexandra

BACKROOM STAFF
2010/11

John Achterberg – GK Coach

Appointed	June 2009
Born	Utrecht, Holland
Age	39
Birth date	08/07/1971
Other clubs (player)	NAC Breda, Eindhoven, Tranmere Rovers

Dr. Peter Brukner – Head of Sports Med./Sci.

Appointed	July 2010
Born	Australia
Other posts	Melbourne (AFL), Collingwood (AFL), Australia (football, swimming, hockey, athletics)

Rob Price – Physiotherapist

Appointed	September 2005
Born	Oldham
Age	37
Birth date	31/10/1972
Previous role	Football Association

Eduardo Macia – Chief Scout

Appointed	June 2006
Born	Valencia, Spain
Age	36
Birth date	07/05/1974
Other club	Valencia

Sammy Lee and Roy Hodgson at Melwood flanked by Head of Sports Medicine and Science Peter Brukner (left) and Darren Burgess, Head of Fitness and Conditioning

SUMMER DIARY 2010

A look back at what went on - and when - during the summer months involving Liverpool FC.

JUNE

1 Jamie Carragher, Glen Johnson and Steven Gerrard are in England's World Cup squad. Dirk Kuyt is on target in Holland's 4-1 friendly victory over Ghana.

3 Manager Rafael Benitez's six-year spell with the club comes to an end.

4 Injury to England captain Rio Ferdinand means that Steven Gerrard will take over as England's World Cup captain.

8 European champions Inter Milan confirm Rafael Benitez as Jose Mourinho's successor.

11 Rafael Benitez donates £96,000 to the Hillsborough Family Support Group.

12 Steven Gerrard opens the scoring – but England are pegged back to draw 1-1 with the USA following Robert Green's goalkeeping howler at the World Cup. Glen Johnson started while Jamie Carragher came on as a substitute for Ledley King.
Captain Javier Mascherano and sub Maxi Rodriguez help Argentina defeat Nigeria 1-0.

14 Dirk Kuyt scores Holland's second goal as they defeat Daniel Agger's Denmark 2-0.

16 Spain – for whom Fernando Torres comes on as a second-half substitute – are shocked 1-0 by Switzerland, while Martin Skrtel's Slovakia are held to a 1-1 draw by New Zealand following a last-gasp equaliser.

17 Liverpool will host Arsenal on the opening weekend of the new Premier League season. Sotirios Kyrgiakos is recalled to the Greece side as they score their first goals and earn their first World Cup win, 2-1 against Nigeria.
Javier Mascherano and Maxi Rodriguez play in Argentina's 4-1 victory over South Korea.

18 Steven Gerrard, Glen Johnson and Jamie Carragher all play in England's disappointing 0-0 draw with Algeria.

19 Dirk Kuyt and Ryan Babel's Holland qualify for the last 16 following a 1-0 win over Japan, while Daniel Agger's Denmark claim a 2-1 comeback defeat of Cameroon.

20 Martin Skrtel plays in Slovakia's 2-0 defeat to Paraguay.

21 Fernando Torres starts in Spain's 2-0 victory over Honduras.

22 Sotirios Kyrgiakos' Greece bow out following their 2-0 defeat to Argentina.

23 Glen Johnson and skipper Steven Gerrard help England reach the knockout phase following a 1-0 win over Slovenia.

24 Martin Skrtel helps Slovakia shock Italy 3-2 to knock the world champions out of the World Cup, but there's disappointment for Daniel Agger, as his Denmark side bow out.

25 Fernando Torres plays nearly an hour as Spain defeat Chile 2-1 to go through.

27 There's disappointment for Gerrard, Johnson and Carragher as England slump 4-1 to bow out of the World Cup at the hands of Germany.
Javier Mascherano and Maxi Rodriguez start in Argentina's 3-1 win over Mexico.

28 Dirk Kuyt sets up the crucial second goal as Holland reach the last eight with a 2-1 victory over Slovakia.

29 Spain – for whom Fernando Torres lasts an hour – see off Portugal 1-0.

JULY

1 Roy Hodgson is appointed Liverpool's new boss, signing a three-year contract.

2 Yossi Benayoun completes his move to Chelsea.
Holland come from behind to shock World Cup favourites Brazil 2-1, reaching the semi-final for the first time in 12 years.

3 Jamie Carragher reveals his total commitment to Liverpool having briefly come out of international retirement to play for England at the World Cup.
Spain reach the semi-finals of the World Cup, defeating Paraguay 1-0.

6 Dirk Kuyt sets up the decisive third goal as Holland reach the World Cup final for the first time since 1978 following a 3-2 victory over Uruguay.

7 Fernando Torres comes on as a second-half substitue to help European champions Spain overcome Germany 1-0 to set up a World Cup final against the Dutch.

SUMMER DIARY 2010

A look back at what went on - and when - during the summer months involving Liverpool FC.

JULY

9	Forward Milan Jovanovic completes his Bosman free transfer move.
11	Pepe Reina and Fernando Torres taste World Cup success as Spain defeat Holland 1-0 after extra time.
13	It is announced that the Reds are top seeds ahead of the Europa League draw.
14	Fernando Torres' thigh injury, picked up in the World Cup final, is not as serious as first feared – and he could return for the start of the new season.
	Francisco Duran and goalkeeper Nikolay Mihaylov are released.
16	The Europa League draw sees the Reds drawn to face Macedonian side FK Rabotnicki.
17	The first pre-season game in Switzerland is called off due to a waterlogged pitch.
19	England international Joe Cole agrees to join the club on a four-year contract.
20	Scottish Young Player of the Year Danny Wilson becomes Roy Hodgson's third major signing, the defender moving from SPL champions Rangers.
21	An inexperienced side draw 0-0 with Grasshoppers in the Reds' first pre-season game.
24	Albert Riera completes his move to Greek champions Olympiakos.
	Milan Jovanovic makes his first-team bow as the Reds go down 1-0 to Kaiserslautern.
29	David Ngog scores twice in the Europa League as Roy Hodgson wins his first competitive game in charge, Liverpool earning a 2-0 win at FK Rabotnicki.
31	Fabio Aurelio re-signs for the club on a two-year deal.

AUGUST

1	Joe Cole makes his first appearance in a Liverpool shirt in the 1-0 friendly defeat to Borussia Moenchengladbach in Germany.
2	It's revealed that ex-defender and reserve coach Gary Ablett is battling blood cancer.
5	Joe Cole impresses on his full debut in the 2-0 home victory over FK Rabotnicki thanks to goals from David Ngog and Steven Gerrard, progressing 4-0 on aggregate.
6	Turkish side Trabzonspor are next up for Liverpool in the Europa League play-off.
7	Steven Gerrard and Glen Johnson are in Fabio Capello's first post-World Cup squad.
9	Philipp Degen joins German Bundesliga side VfB Stuttgart on a season-long loan deal.
10	Martin Kelly celebrates his England Under-21 bow with a goal in a win over Uzbekistan.
11	Captain Steven Gerrard scores both goals as England come from behind to defeat Hungary 2-1 at Wembley Stadium.
12	Denmark international midfielder Christian Poulson signs from Juventus.
15	A late Pepe Reina own goal denies 10-man Liverpool a winning start to the season, a game in which Joe Cole was sent off on his league debut.
17	Australian goalkeeper Brad Jones completes his move from Middlesbrough.
18	Martin Skrtel pens a two-year contract extension.
19	Christian Poulson makes his debut in the 1-0 Europa League win over Trabzonspor.
21	Alberto Aquilani returns to his homeland, signing a year's loan with Juventus.
23	The Reds suffer a first league defeat of the season, 3-0 at Manchester City.
26	Reserve striker Krisztian Nemeth joins Olympiakos.
	Progress to the Europa League groups is confirmed after a 2-1 victory at Trabzonspor.
27	Napoli, Steaua Bucharest and FC Utrecht are drawn in Liverpool's Europa group.
28	Liverpool complete the signing of Portugal midfielder Raul Meireles, a replacement for Barcelona-bound Javier Mascherano.
	The Carling Cup pairs Liverpool with League Two side Northampton Town.
29	Fernando Torres fires the only goal in victory over West Brom – his 50th at Anfield.
31	Transfer deadline day ends with Paul Konchesky joining from Fulham – Lauri Dalla Valle and Alex Kacaniklic heading in the other direction. Youngsters Suso and Adam Hajdu are also signed, from FC Cadiz and MTK respectively while Emiliano Insua, Damien Plessis, Nabil El Zhar and Vincent Weijl also make moves to overseas clubs.

FIRST-TEAM FIXTURE LIST 2010/11

July 2010

29	FK Rabotnicki **(E. League Q)**	(A)	–	7.45pm

August 2010

5	FK Rabotnicki **(E. Lge Q)**	(H)	–	7.45pm
15	Arsenal	(H)	–	4pm
19	Trabzonspor **(E. Lge P-O)**	(H)	–	7.45pm
23	Manchester City	(A)	–	8pm
26	Trabzonspor **(E. Lge P-O)**	(A)	–	7.30pm
29	West Bromwich Albion	(H)	–	3pm

September 2010

12	Birmingham City	(A)	–	4pm
16	Steaua Bucharest **(E. Lge)**	(H)	–	8.05pm
19	Manchester United	(A)	–	1.30pm
22	Northampton Town **(C. Cup)**	(H)	–	8pm
25	Sunderland	(H)	–	3pm
30	FC Utrecht **(E. Lge)**	(A)	–	6pm

October 2010

3	Blackpool	(H)	–	3pm
17	Everton	(A)	–	1.30pm
21	Napoli **(E. Lge)**	(A)	–	6pm
24	Blackburn Rovers	(H)	–	3pm
26/27	CARLING CUP 4			
31	Bolton Wanderers	(A)	–	1.30pm

November 2010

4	Napoli **(E. Lge)**	(H)	–	8.05pm
7	Chelsea	(H)	–	4pm
10	Wigan Athletic	(A)	–	7.45pm
13	Stoke City	(A)	–	5.30pm
20	West Ham United	(H)	–	5.30pm
28	Tottenham Hotspur	(A)	–	4pm

December 2010

2	Steaua Bucharest **(E. Lge)**	(A)	–	6pm
5	Aston Villa	(H)	–	3pm
7/8	CARLING CUP QUARTER-FINALS			
11	Newcastle United	(A)	–	3pm
15	FC Utrecht **(E. Lge)**	(H)	–	8.05pm
18	Fulham	(H)	–	3pm
26	Blackpool	(A)	–	3pm
28	Wolverhampton Wanderers	(H)	–	3pm

FIRST-TEAM FIXTURE LIST 2010/11

January 2011

1	Bolton Wanderers	(H)	–	3pm
5	Blackburn Rovers	(A)	–	8pm
8/9	FA CUP THIRD ROUND			
11/12	CARLING CUP SEMI-FINALS, FIRST LEG			
15	Everton	(H)	–	TBC
22	Wolverhampton Wanderers	(A)	–	3pm
25/26	CARLING CUP SEMI-FINALS, SECOND LEG			
29/30	FA CUP FOURTH ROUND			

February 2011

2	Stoke City	(H)	–	8pm
5	Chelsea	(A)	–	3pm
12	Wigan Athletic	(H)	–	3pm
19/20	FA CUP FIFTH ROUND			
26	West Ham United	(A)	–	3pm
27	CARLING CUP FINAL			

March 2011

5	Manchester United	(H)	–	TBC
12/13	FA CUP QUARTER-FINALS			
19	Sunderland	(A)	–	3pm

April 2011

2	West Bromwich Albion	(A)	–	3pm
10	Manchester City	(H)	–	3pm
16	Arsenal	(A)	–	3pm
16/17	FA CUP SEMI-FINALS			
23	Birmingham City	(H)	–	3pm
30	Newcastle United	(H)	–	3pm

May 2011

7	Fulham	(A)	–	3pm
14	FA CUP FINAL			
15	Tottenham Hotspur	(H)	–	3pm
18	UEFA EUROPA LEAGUE FINAL			
22	Aston Villa	(A)	–	4pm
28	UEFA CHAMPIONS LEAGUE FINAL			

Copyright © The FA Premier League Ltd and The Football League Ltd 2010.
Compiled in association with Atos Origin. All fixtures and kick off times subject to change.
Home UEFA Europa League group matches matches kick off at 8.05pm.
FA Cup and Carling Cup kick off times to be confirmed.
Potential Europa League dates in 2011 can be found on pages 10-11.
All information correct at time of press - August 2010.

Please note all fixtures, kick-off times and dates are subject to change

FA PREMIER RESERVE LEAGUE NORTHERN SECTION FIXTURES 2010/11

SEPTEMBER

01	Wigan Athletic	(H)
07	Newcastle United	(A)
14	Wolverhampton Wanderers	(H)
27	Chelsea	(A) – 2pm KO

OCTOBER

05	West Ham United	(H)
12	Manchester City	(A)
19	Blackburn Rovers	(A)

NOVEMBER

02	Sunderland	(A)
16	Blackpool	(H)
23	Everton	(A)

DECEMBER

13	West Bromwich Albion	(H)

JANUARY

11	Sunderland	(H)

JANUARY

26	Blackpool	(A) – 2pm KO

FEBRUARY

15	Everton	(H)

MARCH

01	Blackburn Rovers	(H)
15	Arsenal	(A)
22	Manchester United	(H)

APRIL

04	Aston Villa	(A)
12	Bolton Wanderers	(H)

FINAL DATES

NGF   North Group final to be played on April 27
F   North v South final to be played on May 4

All fixtures 7pm unless stated,
subject to change.

Copyright © and Database Right 2010 The FA Premier League Ltd. All rights reserved. Compiled in association with Atos Origin.
Home fixtures to be played at Prenton Park, Tranmere Rovers FC, subject to change.
Please check on our website www.liverpoolfc.tv for up-to-date information on whether the match is still being played on the above scheduled date.

Nathan Eccleston stretches the FK Rabotnicki defence in the Europa League qualifier

FA PREMIER ACADEMY LEAGUE
FIXTURES 2010/11

AUGUST

| 21 | Aston Villa | (A) – 12pm KO |
| 28 | Bristol City | (H) |

SEPTEMBER

04	Sunderland	(A)
11	Derby County	(H)
18	Leeds United	(A) – 12pm KO
25	Stoke City	(A)

OCTOBER

02	Crewe Alexandra	(H)
09	Blackburn Rovers	(A)
16	West Bromwich Albion	(H)
30	Manchester United	(A)

NOVEMBER

06	Bolton Wanderers	(A)
13	Everton	(H)
20	Manchester City	(A)

DECEMBER

| 04 | Wolves | (H) |
| 11 | West Bromwich Albion | (A) – 12pm KO |

JANUARY

08	Manchester United	(H)
15	Bolton Wanderers	(H)
22	Everton	(A)

FEBRUARY

05	Manchester City	(H)
12	Wolves	(A) – 11.30am KO
19	Stoke City	(H)
26	Crewe Alexandra	(A)

MARCH

05	Blackburn Rovers	(H)
12	Huddersfield Town	(H)
19	Newcastle United	(A)
26	Nottingham Forest	(H) – 12pm KO

APRIL

| 09 | Sheffield Wednesday | (H) – 12pm KO |
| 30 | Sheffield United | (A) – 12pm KO |

MAY – FINAL DATES

| 07 | Play-Off Semi-Final |
| 14 | Play-Off Final |

FA YOUTH CUP DATES

R3	To be played by December 11
R4	To be played by January 15
R5	To be played by January 29
R6	To be played by February 12
SF1	To be played by March 5
SF2	To be played by March 19
F1&2	TBC

All fixtures 11am unless stated,
subject to change.

**Academy product Jack Robinson made his
Premier League debut in May 2010**

THE 2009/10 SEASON

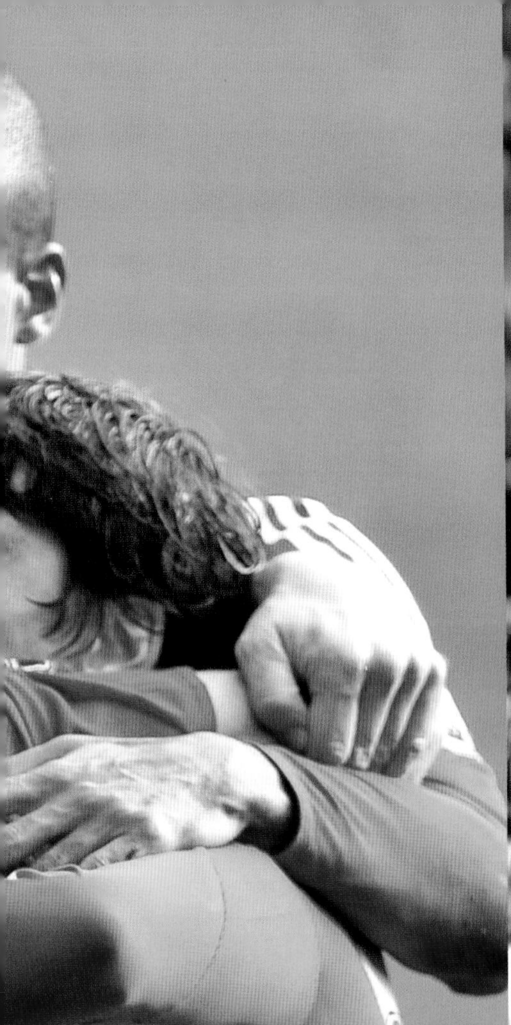

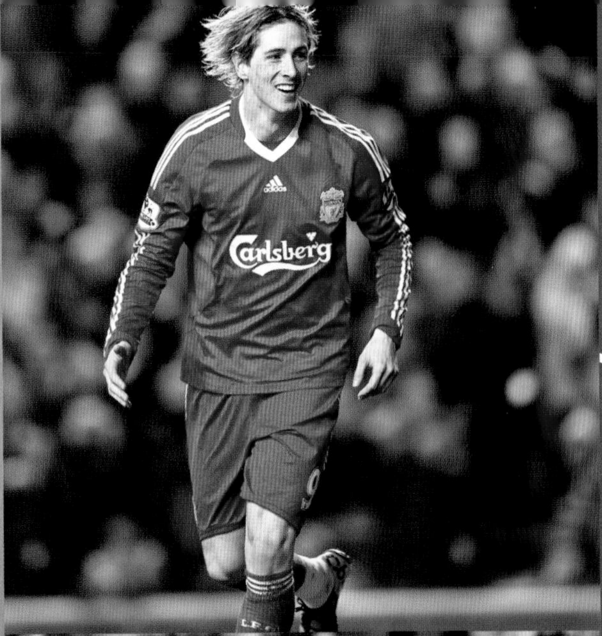

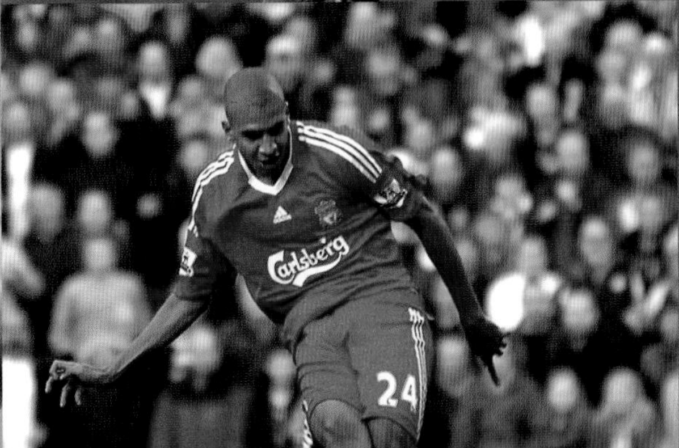

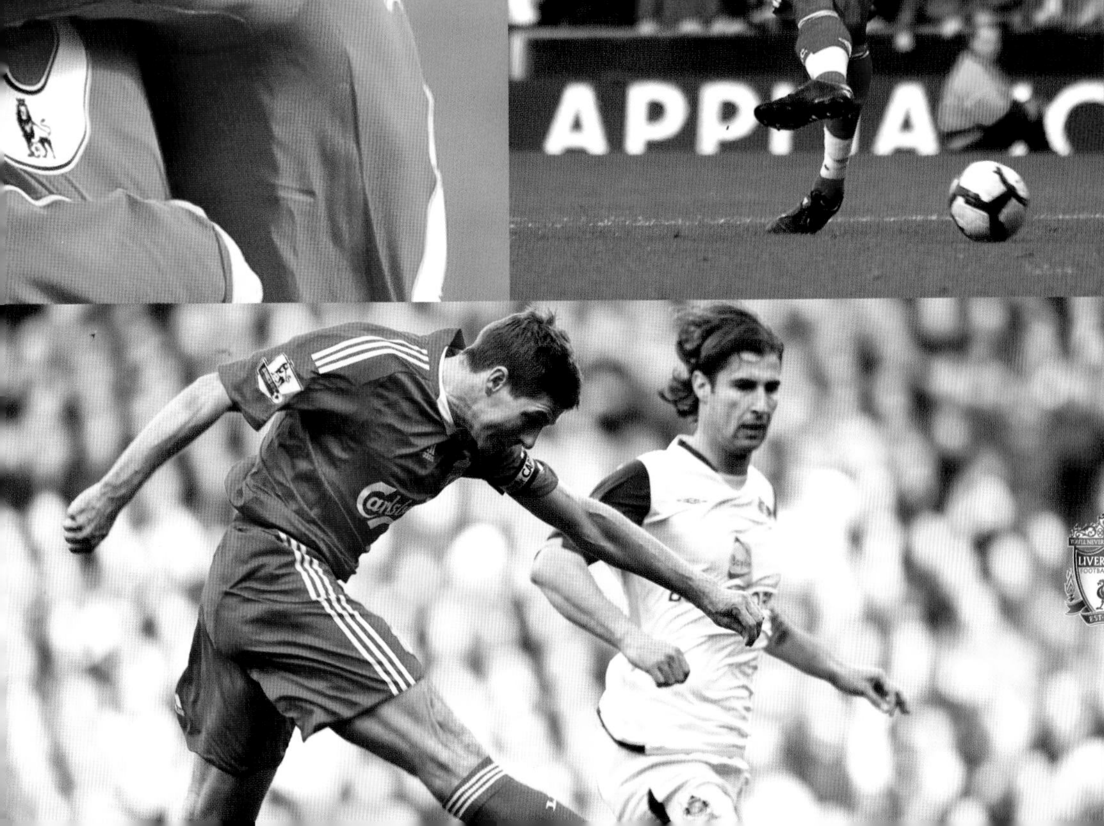

THAT WAS THEN

August

2   The Reds go down 3-0 at Espanyol in a friendly to mark the opening of the Barcelona club's new stadium.

4   Reserve striker Nathan Eccleston is handed a new three-year deal.

5   Xabi Alonso hails Liverpool fans after completing his big-money move to Real Madrid.
Andriy Voronin and David Ngog are on target in the 2-0 friendly win at FC Lyn.

8   Italy international midfielder Alberto Aquilani completes his move from AS Roma.
Atletico Madrid run out 2-1 winners at Anfield in the club's last pre-season friendly.

10   Barnsley complete the signing of reserve midfielder Adam Hammill.

11   A groin injury forces Steven Gerrard out of the England squad to face Holland.
Reserve striker Craig Lindfield, a member of the FA Youth Cup-winning sides of 2006 and 2007, is released.

12   Daniel Pacheco pens a new three-year deal.
Dirk Kuyt is on target as Holland and England draw 2-2 in Amsterdam.
Fernando Torres and Albert Riera net as Spain come back from two goals down to defeat Macedonia 3-2 in a friendly international.

15   Fernando Torres pens his new five-year contract.
Mikel San Jose returns to Athletic Bilbao on a season-long loan deal.

16   A Steven Gerrard penalty fails to prevent a 2-1 opening-day defeat at Tottenham.

17   The club skipper is nominated for UEFA's Club Footballer of the Year award.

19   Glen Johnson nets on his home debut as Liverpool cruise to a 4-0 victory over Stoke.

20   Prospects Peter Gulacsi and Krisztian Nemeth sign new deals.

21   Greece international defender Sotirios Kyrgiakos completes his move from AEK Athens.
Defender Robbie Threlfall joins Northampton Town on an initial one-month loan.

24   Aston Villa earn a shock 3-1 win at Anfield in the Barclays Premier League.

25   Hungarian duo Krisztian Nemeth and Andras Simon go out on loan for the season, to AEK Athens and Cordoba CF respectively.

27   The Reds are paired with Lyon, Fiorentina and Debrecen in the Champions League.

29   The Carling Cup third-round draw sees the club travel to Leeds United.
A late Steven Gerrard strike ensures a 3-2 victory at 10-man Bolton Wanderers.

31   Goalkeeper Charles Itandje joins Greek club Kavala FC on loan for the season.

Quotes of the month:

"Winning the league here would be like winning the European Championship with Spain. A player wants to be remembered for what he has won, for what he has given his club. Ten years after you stop playing you want to have medals, trophies. You may have a fantastic car and home but it's not the same."

Fernando Torres outlines his playing ambitions

"The players wanted to impress. We have quality and when we play at our level, we can beat anyone."

Rafael Benitez

"I am very grateful to Liverpool fans, they were very warm during my five years. It will be really difficult to match their appreciation."

Real Madrid-bound Xabi Alonso salutes the Anfield faithful

AUGUST

THE GAMES

16	Tottenham Hotspur	A	1-2	Gerrard 56 (pen)
19	Stoke City	H	4-0	Torres 4, Johnson 45, Kuyt 78, Ngog 90
24	Aston Villa	H	1-3	Torres 72
29	Bolton Wanderers	A	3-2	Johnson 41, Torres 56, Gerrard 83

WHERE THEY STOOD

4	Stoke City
5	Arsenal
6	Manchester City
7	**Liverpool**
8	Sunderland
9	Burnley
10	West Ham United

JAMIE CARRAGHER:

'There's no better strike pairing than Gerrard and Torres. They are our most important players.'

THAT WAS THEN

September

5   Steven Gerrard and Glen Johnson start in England's 2-1 friendly victory over Slovenia.

9   Two goals from Steven Gerrard help England to a 5-1 victory over Croatia, confirming qualification for the 2010 World Cup finals in South Africa. Amongst the other Liverpool players in international action, Martin Skrtel helped Slovakia to a 2-0 win in Northern Ireland which all but seals their passage to the finals.

12   Yossi Benayoun's third hat-trick for the club helps the Reds to a 4-0 victory over Burnley.

14   A record four-year sponsorship with banking giant Standard Chartered is announced, starting in the summer of 2010.

15   Ryan Flynn, on loan at Falkirk, pens a permanent deal with the Scottish club.

16   Dirk Kuyt's 12th European Cup goal – putting him joint third in the all-time Liverpool charts – helps the Reds get off to a winning start in the Champions League, courtesy of a 1-0 win over Debrecen.

    Southend United prospect Michael Ngoo, 16, joins the club after a successful trial.

19   Fernando Torres' double earns a hard-fought 3-2 victory at West Ham.

22   A weakened side earns a place in the last 16 of the Carling Cup thanks to a 1-0 win at Leeds United.

26   Liverpool are drawn to travel to Arsenal in the Carling Cup fourth round.

    Hull City are swept aside 6-1 at Anfield, Liverpool's sixth win in a row, with Fernando Torres helping himself to his fourth hat-trick for the club.

27   Emiliano Insua receives his first call-up to the Argentina squad for crucial World Cup qualifiers against Peru and Uruguay.

29   Two first-half goals condemn the Reds to Champions League defeat at Fiorentina. Daniel Agger makes his comeback for the reserves following a back problem.

Quotes of the month:

"Everybody knows we have already lost two times, but the way we beat Bolton where we came from behind twice gives us a much more positive feeling. I still believe we have a great chance. As long as we start winning our own games from this stage I am sure we will be up there."

Dirk Kuyt

"Glen is a quality player and he has added something to us. What we try to do is recruit quality and we have done that with Glen. He has come here and has been willing to listen and learn. For someone who is an established England international that's great and long may it continue."

Sammy Lee

"It was a good day for me and great to score three. I started on the right but Rafa told me to move around and get in between the lines. Every time I did that I found space so I could turn and go forward. I was lucky the team provided me with good passes to score. It was the perfect day."

Yossi Benayoun

"We can achieve whatever we want. We go out to achieve maximum points, or get through the cup tie, whatever is relevant. We go out on the pitch with the same determination as we have ever done to be successful. We've never shouted our mouth off, we've just got on with our work."

Kenny Dalglish

"We all have 100 per cent confidence in him and we trust him. He is always working hard for the team and he always creates space for the other players to allow them to score."

Pepe Reina on Fernando Torres

SEPTEMBER

THE GAMES

12	Burnley	H	4-0	Benayoun 27, 61, 82, Kuyt 41
16	Debrecen	H	1-0	Kuyt 45
19	West Ham United	A	3-2	Torres 20, 75, Kuyt 41
22	Leeds United	A	1-0	Ngog 66
26	Hull City	H	6-1	Torres 12, 28, 47, Gerrard 61, Babel 88, 90
29	Fiorentina	A	0-2	

WHERE THEY STOOD

1 Manchester United
2 Chelsea
3 **Liverpool**
4 Tottenham Hotspur
5 Arsenal
6 Manchester City
7 Aston Villa

RAFAEL BENITEZ:

'Six goals is fantastic, it could have been even better...that's another positive, the mentality going forward.'

THAT WAS THEN

October

4   A second successive 2-0 defeat, this time at the hands of Chelsea.

5   Former defender Steve Staunton takes over at League Two strugglers Darlington.

6   Glen Johnson and Steven Gerrard are included in the England squad for the last two World Cup qualifiers against Ukraine and Belarus.

9   Former Reds John Barnes and his assistant Jason McAteer are sacked by Tranmere Rovers after only 11 games in charge.

10   World Cup qualifying action sees defender Emiliano Insua make his Argentina debut in their dramatic 2-1 win over Peru. Daniel Agger plays as Denmark qualify for the finals courtesy of victory over Sweden.

14   The final round of World Cup qualifying in Europe sees Martin Skrtel's Slovakia qualify for their first ever finals courtesy of a win in Poland.

16   Fernando Torres is named Barclays and PFA Player of the Month for September. David Martin joins Tranmere Rovers on a month's loan.
Fears that Sotirios Kyrgiakos will be out for six months subside after the knee injury picked up playing for Greece in midweek is found not to be as serious as first thought.

17   Without the injured Steven Gerrard and Fernando Torres, the Reds see a stray beach ball inadvertently help guide Darren Bent's shot past Pepe Reina as Sunderland claim a 1-0 win at the Stadium of Light.

19   Steven Gerrard and Fernando Torres are confirmed on the shortlist for the 2009 European Footballer of the Year award.
The World Cup play-offs in Europe sees Sotirios Kyrgiakos and Andriy Voronin go head-to-head as Greece face Ukraine for a place in South Africa.

20   An injury to Steven Gerrard and a late Lyon winner make it a bad Champions League night for Liverpool as they go down 2-1 at Anfield.

21   Alberto Aquilani makes his reserve bow, a 15-minute run-out in a win over Sunderland.

25   Fernando Torres hits his ninth goal in nine league games and David Ngog clinches victory as the Reds end a four-game losing streak in style by beating Manchester United.

27   Uncapped Fabio Aurelio and Lucas Leiva earn call-ups for Brazil's Middle East tour.

28   Alberto Aquilani makes his bow as a second-half sub but despite Emiliano Insua's first goal for the club, Liverpool, captained by Dirk Kuyt for the first time, bow out of the Carling Cup at Arsenal.

30   Gerrard and Torres are announced as contenders for the FIFA World Player of the Year.

31   Without the injured Johnson, Aquilani, Gerrard and the rested Agger and Aurelio, the nine-man Reds suffer a 3-1 setback at Fulham – Degen and Carragher seeing red.

Quotes of the month:

"We take the plaudits when things are going well so you have to take the criticism when it's not going well. I know I need to improve myself and we also need to improve as a team."

Jamie Carragher

"It is my ambition to score at the Kop. I've thought about it a lot during my rehab here. I can't wait to play in front of that crowd."

Alberto Aquilani

"It's a bad situation for us that the [beach] ball was in the middle and was influential."

Rafael Benitez reflects on 'that' goal at Sunderland

"This was a fantastic moment for me and the team – it's my best moment in football. I have always dreamed of scoring for Liverpool against Manchester United."

David Ngog, in buoyant mood post-Manchester United

OCTOBER

THE GAMES

4	Chelsea	A	0-2	
17	Sunderland	A	0-1	
20	**Lyon**	**H**	**1-2**	Benayoun 41
25	Manchester United	H	2-0	Torres 65, Ngog 90
28	**Arsenal**	**A**	**1-2**	Insua 26
31	Fulham	A	1-3	Torres 42

WHERE THEY STOOD

2	Manchester United
3	Arsenal
4	Tottenham Hotspur
5	**Liverpool**
6	Manchester City
7	Aston Villa
8	Sunderland

FERNANDO TORRES:

'This was a massive, massive win, so important. We knew we needed nothing less than a win.'

THAT WAS THEN

November

4   A last-minute Lisandro Lopez goal denies Liverpool victory in Lyon, leaving their hopes of Champions League progress firmly in the balance.

9   Sub Steven Gerrard's second-half penalty rescues a point in the 2-2 draw with Birmingham. Fernando Torres is again ruled out due to injury, although there is a home debut for late sub Alberto Aquilani.

10   Ex-Red Vladimir Smicer is appointed team manager of the Czech Republic.

11   Glen Johnson and Daniel Agger withdraw from their national squads for upcoming friendly matches.

13   Daniel Ayala agrees a new deal, keeping him with the club until the summer of 2012.

14   Sotirios Kyrgiakos' Greece draw 0-0 in their World Cup play-off first leg against Ukraine – who did not call Andriy Voronin up to their squad. Javier Mascherano, Dirk Kuyt, Ryan Babel, Philipp Degen and Martin Skrtel are all involved in friendly action for their respective countries.

18   Greece's 1-0 second-leg victory over Ukraine means Sotirios Kyrgiakos will perform in next summer's World Cup in South Africa. Pepe Reina, Dirk Kuyt, Ryan Babel and Martin Skrtel also feature in friendly international action.

21   Martin Skrtel scores his first Liverpool goal in the Reds' 2-2 draw with Manchester City, Yossi Benayoun equalising almost immediately after City had come from behind in the second half to lead.

24   Despite a 1-0 win at Debrecen, Fiorentina's 1-0 victory over Lyon condemns Liverpool to third place in their Champions League group – and a place in the Europa League.

27   Goalkeepers David Martin and Dean Bouzanis agree loan moves to Leeds United and Accrington Stanley respectively.

29   Javier Mascherano's deflected strike off Joseph Yobo and a late Dirk Kuyt goal earn a hard-fought 2-0 win at Everton.
The FA Cup third-round draw sees the Reds drawn to face Championship side Reading at the Madejski Stadium.

30   Steven Gerrard is confirmed on the 10-man shortlist for the European Footballer of the Year award.

Quotes of the month:

"Rafa has improved me. I've learnt a lot at this club and the manager has given me a lot of confidence. I thank him for that and now I have to give my best for him. I just want to score and do my best for the team, and I know I have the qualities to do these things."

David Ngog

"England have always had individually strong players and I am a huge fan of Stevie Gerrard. He has the heart of a lion and is the icon of the modern footballer with his ability to attack and defend."

Kaka

"We did our job but we cannot change things. If you analyse the games, two late goals against Lyon were a massive difference. We had chances in all of the games – we could have won all of them."

Rafael Benitez, post Debrecen

"We're really happy with the result. It's one of the most important games of our season and to beat Everton always gives you a special feeling. I'm really happy for the team and the supporters. A derby is more important than almost every other game, and to win this means a lot for us. The result is more important than the performance in a derby. You know it's going to be hard to play football and you need to show character."

Dirk Kuyt, post-derby

NOVEMBER

THE GAMES

4	**Lyon**	A	1-1	Babel 83
9	Birmingham City	H	2-2	Ngog 4, Gerrard 71 (pen)
21	Manchester City	H	2-2	Skrtel 50, Benayoun 77
24	**Debrecen**	A	1-0	Ngog 4
29	Everton	A	2-0	Mascherano 12, Kuyt 80

WHERE THEY STOOD

2	Manchester United
3	Tottenham Hotspur
4	Arsenal
5	**Liverpool**
6	Aston Villa
7	Manchester City
8	Sunderland

JAVIER MASCHERANO:

'This season some people have criticised my shooting, but I am trying hard to improve it.'

THAT WAS THEN

December

1   Steven Gerrard is 10th in the European Footballer of the Year standings as Barcelona's Lionel Messi claims the honour ahead of Real Madrid's Cristiano Ronaldo.

5   The Reds are held to a 0-0 draw at Blackburn Rovers.

8   Fernando Torres' spectacular strike against Blackburn in April is amongst the nominations for FIFA's Goal of 2009 award.

9   Alberto Aquilani makes his first Liverpool start and Fernando Torres returns after injury as the Reds end their Champions League campaign with defeat, Alberto Gilardino's injury-time goal ensuring a 2-1 defeat. The result also means the club will be unseeded in the Europa League draw as one of the four third-ranked teams with the weakest record in their Champions League group.

13   In a game of two halves, the Reds surrender a half-time advantage to go down 2-1 to Arsenal at Anfield.

16   David Ngog and sub Fernando Torres (on his 100th Liverpool appearance) goals help cap a memorable Shankly tribute night at Anfield in a 2-1 victory over Wigan.

18   Liverpool are drawn to face Romanian champions Unirea Urziceni in the last 32 of the Europa League. Should the club progress, they would meet the winners of the Lille v Fenerbahce tie next.

19   Javier Mascherano is sent off as the Reds go down 2-0 at Portsmouth.

22   Steven Gerrard and Fernando Torres are named in FIFA's World Team of the Year.

26   Second-half goals from Steven Gerrard and Yossi Benayoun earn a 2-0 victory over 10-man Wolves at Anfield.

29   Fernando Torres nets his 50th league goal for the club in injury time as Liverpool secure a vital 1-0 win at fellow Champions League candidates Aston Villa. It also makes the Spanish star the fastest player to score 50 league goals for the club – taking him only 72 games.

Quotes of the month:

"If we get back to our full-strength team, and we get people fit, we're confident we are good enough. Torres' return is massive for everyone. He's the main man, our top scorer and we need him back firing. If that happens I'm sure we'll move back up the league."

Steven Gerrard on Fernando Torres

"If we can stay together, we have quality enough to win trophies. The people of Liverpool deserve to play in finals, whether it be in Europe or England. It is a long time since we played in a final and they deserve it, they deserve more trophies."

Fernando Torres

"Liverpool are a good side and when they get their confidence back they can beat anyone. With Gerrard and Torres back and Aquilani starting to play, many teams will drop points (at Anfield)."

Arsene Wenger

"To be at one club for such a long time and play 600 games is amazing. He has improved every single year. He is a top professional. That is the difference between him and others. Some have different qualities but he analyses, he reads the games well and he can adapt to different situations. He is one of the best defenders in England – and I'm sure he will continue to do well."

Rafael Benitez on Jamie Carragher

"It was different to anything I have experienced, it was so quick, the football we played was so fast."

Alberto Aquilani after making his full league home debut against Wolves

DECEMBER

THE GAMES

5	Blackburn Rovers	A	0-0	
9	**Fiorentina**	**H**	**1-2**	Benayoun 43
13	Arsenal	H	1-2	Kuyt 41
16	Wigan Athletic	H	2-1	Ngog 9, Torres 79
19	Portsmouth	A	0-2	
26	Wolverhampton W.	H	2-0	Gerrard 62, Benayoun 70
29	Aston Villa	A	1-0	Torres 90

WHERE THEY STOOD

4	Tottenham Hotspur
5	Manchester City
6	Aston Villa
7	**Liverpool**
8	Birmingham City
9	Fulham
10	Sunderland

STEVEN GERRARD:

'It's important to build on this. I'm sure we'll gain a lot of confidence from this.'

WHAT HAPPENED WHEN?

January

2   An equaliser from Steven Gerrard earns an FA Cup third-round replay with
         Championship side Reading.

6   Former favourite Patrik Berger, latterly of Sparta Prague, hangs up his boots at the age
         of 36.

7   Reserve goalkeeper Dean Bouzanis extends his loan deal at Accrington Stanley for
         another month.

8   Andrea Dossena completes a move back to his home country by joining Napoli.
         The club's Premier League home game with Tottenham is called off due to the
         dangerous freezing conditions around Anfield. The weekend sees only two top-flight
         fixtures fulfilled.

11   Three new directors are elected in a boardroom reshuffle – namely Casey Coffman,
         Philip Nash and Ian Ayre.
         Andriy Voronin completes his switch to Dynamo Moscow.

13   Argentina winger Maxi Rodriguez completes his move from Atletico Madrid.
         The Reds, who saw Steven Gerrard and Fernando Torres suffer injuries, fall to a shock
         extra-time defeat to Reading in the FA Cup third-round replay, going down 2-1 after the
         Royals had levelled in injury time.

16   A late Robert Huth equaliser denies the Reds victory at Stoke City after Sotirios
         Kyrgiakos had netted his first goal for the club.

20   Alberto Aquilani starts his first home game as a Dirk Kuyt double defeats fellow
         Champions League chasers Tottenham 2-0 at Anfield. The game also sees Lucas
         Leiva make his 100th Liverpool appearance.

26   Steven Gerrard returns from injury as a point is gained from a 0-0 draw at Wolves.

28   Reserve striker Nathan Eccleston joins Huddersfield Town on a month's loan.

30   Dirk Kuyt scores his ninth goal of the season as Liverpool move to within a point of
         Tottenham in fourth by beating Bolton 2-0. They are now unbeaten in six games, a run
         that has seen them keep five clean sheets.

Quotes of the month:

"I want to keep breaking records so I am always in the books and in the memories of the people. I am just doing my job and I want to keep breaking records and keep making people happy."

Fernando Torres, eyeing more LFC landmarks

"The mentality among us is really good and we want to take Liverpool to the place it deserves."

Javier Mascherano

"You never get an easy game here. You stand out there and hear the crowd sing – it's the most amazing sight in football and it lifts the players."

Harry Redknapp

"Carra has been a big influence...he shouts at me, he tells me where to stand and what to do. He is very important for us and also for me. Sometimes when you are behind a man, you have a better view of what is going on. This is very good and helps me a lot."

Philipp Degen, grateful to Jamie Carragher

"When every player is fit, including me, it will bring the best out of me, and the fans will see the real player. I am happy at Liverpool and am already completely settled. It is clear it is a family club and I am grateful for the way I have been treated – and I now want to repay that kindness."

Alberto Aquilani

JANUARY

THE GAMES

2	**Reading**	A	**1-1**	Gerrard 36
13	**Reading**	H	**1-2 aet**	Bertrand 45 (o.g.)
16	Stoke City	A	1-1	Kyrgiakos 57
20	Tottenham Hotdpur	H	2-0	Kuyt 6, 90 (pen)
26	Wolverhampton W.	A	0-0	
30	Bolton Wanderers	H	2-0	Kuyt 37, Davies 70 (o.g.)

WHERE THEY STOOD

2	Manchester United
3	Arsenal
4	Tottenham Hotspur
5	**Liverpool**
6	Aston Villa
7	Manchester City
8	Birmingham City

RAFAEL BENITEZ:

'The fans are amazing... sometimes you have bad moments and now is the time we have to show character.'

THAT WAS THEN

February

1   Fulham complete the signing of young German defender Christopher Buchtmann, who had played for the Reds' youth sides.

Goalkeepers Dean Bouzanis and David Martin plus striker Nathan Eccleston, extend their loan stays at Accrington, Leeds and Huddersfield respectively.

5   Steven Gerrard is confirmed as England vice-captain after former skipper John Terry's demotion from the role.

6   Ten-man Liverpool complete a derby double by earning a 1-0 win over Everton at Anfield. Dirk Kuyt heads the winner early in the second half after the Reds had seen Sotirios Kyrgiakos dismissed after half-an-hour.

10   The club confirm the signing of Standard Liege forward Milan Jovanovic on a three-year deal, the Serbian international set to join in the summer.

The Reds go down to a first defeat in eight league games, 1-0 at Arsenal.

18   A late David Ngog header earns a 1-0 victory over Urinea Urziceni in the Europa League last 32 first leg.

21   A point in the 0-0 draw at Manchester City leaves the club sixth, a point behind Tottenham in fourth.

23   Reserve defender Robbie Threlfall joins Bradford City on a month's loan.

25   Steven Gerrard hits his 33rd goal in European competition – a record for an English-born player – as Liverpool come from behind to beat Unirea Urziceni 3-1, 4-1 on aggregate.

27   The Reds win the signature of QPR's England youth international Raheem Sterling.

28   Fernando Torres scores on his return to the side after injury as the Reds hold off Blackburn 2-1 at Anfield. Steven Gerrard's opener also means the side have now scored in 28 successive home games – the best sequence for 41 years.

Quotes of the month:

"Liverpool has always had speculation about managers, players, players coming, players going and it's the same as managers. That's part of being part of a big club, you always have that type of thing. People always want to talk about the club, whether it is positively or negatively, and if you play for Liverpool you have got to get used to that as part of the job."

Jamie Carragher, business as usual

"It isn't in the character of any of us to turn our backs and run somewhere else when times are tough. For me, if the club offered a five, six or seven-year contract right now, I'd sign it with my eyes closed. Where else is there to go? Being anywhere else would be a step down."

Albert Riera

"We should be up at the top and winning games. We aren't happy about where we are, but we have to keep on going and try and get as high up the table as possible."

Jamie Carragher

"Rafa Benitez is the best manager I have played for. I enjoy working for him and have learned a lot from playing for Rafa. We want to play well in every game for him and this club."

Sotirios Kyrgiakos

FEBRUARY

THE GAMES

6	Everton	H	1-0	Kuyt 55
10	Arsenal	A	0-1	
18	Unirea Urziceni	H	1-0	Ngog 81
21	Manchester City	A	0-0	
25	Unirea Urziceni	A	3-1	Mascherano 29, Babel 40, Gerrard 57
28	Blackburn Rovers	H	2-1	Gerrard 20, Torres 44

WHERE THEY STOOD

3	Arsenal
4	Tottenham Hotspur
5	Manchester City
6	**Liverpool**
7	Aston Villa
8	Birmingham City
9	Fulham

STEVEN GERRARD:

'That's what derbies are all about – passion, commitment, fight...we beat a good side with 10 men.'

THAT WAS THEN

March

1   The club complete the signing of QPR's England youth international Raheem Sterling.

3   Steven Gerrard skippers England in their 3-1 friendly victory over African champions Egypt. In other international games, Dirk Kuyt and Yossi Benayoun are on target as they help their respective countries, Holland and Israel, to wins.

8   Glen Johnson makes his first appearance of the year as a second-half substitute as the Reds suffer a shock 1-0 defeat at Wigan Athletic.

11   Liverpool are forced to rue missed opportunities as Lille win 1-0 thanks to a late goal in the first leg of the Europa League last 16 clash in France.

12   Reserve-team skipper Stephen Darby (the rest of the season) and goalkeeper David Martin (one month) join Swindon Town and Derby County respectively on loan.

15   The 4-1 victory over Portsmouth is the Reds' first in a Monday night home match since November 1999. The game also sees Alberto Aquilani score his first goal for the club, at the Kop end.

18   Fernando Torres scores twice for the second consecutive game as Liverpool overcome their first-leg deficit to beat Lille 3-0 at Anfield and progress to the quarter-final of the Europa League. They will meet Portuguese champions elect Benfica.

21   An early Fernando Torres header proves in vain as Manchester United claim a 2-1 win at Old Trafford.

24   Midfielder Jay Spearing agrees a loan deal with Leicester until the end of the season.

28   There is another brace for Fernando Torres, taking his tally to 20 for the season and seven in four matches, in the 3-0 win over Sunderland at Anfield.

30   Martin Kelly is ruled out for the rest of the season after tearing his meniscus knee ligament in training.

Quotes of the month:

"This has been a special season because I've played many games in a row. It has given me a lot of confidence that I can do the job. This season will help me for the future and give me experience."

Emiliano Insua

"There is a massive hunger. The boys are very determined, professional and focused. We never prepare for failure. There have been certain disappointments along the way [this season], and we know we're not firing on all cylinders, but it's a case of getting some momentum going and we believe we have. If everything clicks into place, then who knows?"

Sammy Lee

"The desire is there. We still have things to fight for and I'm with the lads every day so I know for sure they have a desire to win."

Glen Johnson

"I feel good because I've scored my first goal after a really long time. I'm also really happy because of the result - we needed that. The goal is even more special because I scored it in front of the Kop. I said when I arrived that I wanted to score in front of the Kop and that moment has arrived."

Alberto Aquilani

"There is lot more to come from Fernando. He is world class, it's as simple as that. When he is playing, it doesn't just give the crowd a lift. It lifts us and it causes the players he comes up against to think twice about how they deal with him."

Steven Gerrard on Fernando Torres

MARCH

THE GAMES

8	Wigan Athletic	A	0-1	
11	Lille	A	0-1	
15	Portsmouth	H	4-1	Torres 26, 77, Babel 28, Aquilani 32
18	Lille	H	3-0	Gerrard 9 (pen), Torres 49, 90
21	Manchester United	A	1-2	Torres 5
28	Sunderland	H	3-0	Torres 3, 60, Johnson 32

WHERE THEY STOOD

2	Chelsea
3	Arsenal
4	Tottenham Hotspur
5	**Liverpool**
6	Manchester City
7	Aston Villa
8	Everton

RAFAEL BENITEZ:

'Maxi is a very good signing – he has quality, experience and is a very good professional.'

THAT WAS THEN

April

1   Ryan Babel sees red in the first half as Liverpool lose 2-1 at Benfica in the first leg of the Europa League quarter-final – having led through Daniel Agger's early strike.

4   Steven Gerrard's goal isn't enough to secure three points as Birmingham hit back to earn a 1-1 draw.

6   Brazilian Vitor Flora returns home having struggled to break into the club's reserves.

8   A stirring second-leg showing sees Liverpool defeat Benfica 4-1 to book a Europa League semi against Atletico Madrid. Fernando Torres' two goals meant it was the first time a Liverpool player had scored two goals a game in four successive home fixtures.

9   Goalkeeper Pepe Reina pens a new six-year contract, potentially keeping him at the club until 2016.

11   Fernando Torres misses out through injury as Fulham hold the Reds to a 0-0 draw.

14   The first pre-season friendly of 2010/11 is confirmed at Borussia Moenchengladbach on July 31. The game, against the side the Reds defeated in the 1977 European Cup final, has been arranged as part of the German club's 110th anniversary celebrations.

16   Chairman of British Airways, Martin Broughton, is brought in as new chairman.

17   Goalkeeper Peter Gulacsi joins Tranmere Rovers on an emergency seven-day loan.

18   Fernando Torres is ruled out for the rest of the season having been forced to undergo knee surgery on a torn cartilage.

19   The Reds ease to a 3-0 victory over lowly West Ham – their 10th successive home win – keeping their faint Champions League qualification hopes alive.

21   Liverpool's squad arrive in Madrid after a mammoth 2,600 trip overland caused by the flight ban over much of northern Europe. They travelled by train and coach, staying overnight in Paris before flying in from Bordeaux.

22   An early Diego Forlan goal means Liverpool must come from behind in the second leg at Anfield to reach the Europa League final.

25   Steven Gerrard scores twice and Maxi Rodriguez gets his first for the club as a 4-0 win at Turf Moor relegates Burnley.

26   Ian Rush returns to the club as Soccer Schools Ambassador.

28   The club confirm the signing of Charlton Athletic's England Under-17 midfielder Jonjo Shelvey, with the deal set to be completed at the end of the season.

29   A Diego Forlan strike in extra time proves decisive as the Reds miss out on a Europa final spot against Fulham after bowing out on away goals against Atletico Madrid.

Quotes of the month:

"We know the season hasn't been great. It hasn't been good enough. We should have done better. It was always going to be difficult to repeat the 86 points, as that was a massive achievement and the league was always going to be tougher. But we have had one bad season. English football is not easy. We were so close last season, that's why we have been so disappointed this season."

Pepe Reina on disappointment in 2009/10

"It was a great home performance and a massive result for us against a very good side. Almost every goal was of the highest quality. When we play well as a team and work hard for each other you can see we are a very good team and a tough side to beat."

Dirk Kuyt post-Benfica second leg

"It hurts because we controlled the game, more or less. We made one mistake and they scored. It's frustrating when you know you are so close to a trophy and in the end it's gone. It's disappointing."

Ryan Babel, post-Atletico

"Someone said we needed four or five players. I would more or less agree with that."

Rafael Benitez looking ahead

APRIL

THE GAMES

1	Benfica	A	1-2	Agger 9
4	Birmingham City	A	1-1	Gerrard 47
8	Benfica	H	4-1	Kuyt 28, Lucas 34, Torres 59, 82
11	Fulham	H	0-0	
19	West Ham United	H	3-0	Benayoun 19, Ngog 29, Green 59 (o.g.)
22	Atletico Madrid	A	0-1	
25	Burnley	A	4-0	Gerrard 52, 59, Maxi 74, Babel 90
29	Atletico Madrid	H	2-1 aet	Aquilani 44, Benayoun 95

WHERE THEY STOOD

4	Tottenham Hotspur
5	Aston Villa
6	Manchester City
7	**Liverpool**
8	Everton
9	Birmingham City
10	Sunderland

FERNANDO TORRES:

'If I had been thinking about the World Cup I would have asked for a change...I wanted to get to the final with my team.'

THAT WAS THEN

May

2   Chelsea edge closer to the Premier League title after winning 2-0 at Anfield.

4   Defender Sotirios Kyrgiakos is named in Greece's 30-man pre-World Cup squad.

7   Everton are confirmed as the opposition for Jamie Carragher's testimonial on September 4. Past and present Liverpool stars are set to turn out, with all money raised going towards Jamie's 23 Foundation charity.

9   Liverpool end the season with a 0-0 draw at relegated Hull City. The result means the Reds finish seventh and must now play a Europa League qualifier in July. The game is marked by a debut for substitute Jack Robinson, who becomes the club's youngest-ever player aged 16 years and 250 days.

11   Jamie Carragher comes out of international retirement and is named in England's 30-man pre-World Cup squad, along with Glen Johnson and Steven Gerrard. Pepe Reina and Fernando Torres are also named in Spain's squad.

12   Holland include Dirk Kuyt and Ryan Babel in their 30-man World Cup squads.

14   Reserve goalkeeper David Martin is set to re-join MK Dons when his contract expires.

19   Second-string skipper Stephen Darby hits the decisive penalty to help loan club Swindon Town to the League One Play-Off final at Wembley.
Former defender Markus Babbel is appointed boss of Hertha Berlin.

20   Javier Mascherano and Maxi Rodriguez are confirmed in Argentina's World Cup 23.

21   Spanish defender Mikel San Jose completes a permanent move to Athletic Bilbao.
Pepe Reina and Fernando Torres make the cut for Spain's World Cup squad.

24   Glen Johnson scores his first international goal – while Jamie Carragher makes a sub appearance – in England's 3-1 victory over Mexico.

25   It is confirmed that Fabio Aurelio will leave the club at the end of his contract.

26   The club unveil a plaque at Anfield remembering the 39 Heysel Stadium victims.
Reserve players Robbie Threlfall and Chris Oldfield are released.

29   On-loan Stephen Darby is on the losing side as Swindon lose to Millwall in the League One Play-Off final at Wembley.

30   Glen Johnson, Jamie Carragher and Steven Gerrard all feature in England's 2-1 win over Japan in their final friendly before the World Cup.

Quotes of the month:

"Liverpool is a great club and I enjoy it but a lot of things are happening. If it depended on me, I would stay here and retire in Liverpool. The fans are the best in the world."

                           Yossi Benayoun

"He was training with us one day, so we felt he could be an option. We knew he was a young player. I am really pleased. He is now clutching his shirt and doesn't want to give it to anyone."

                     Rafael Benitez on youngster Jack Robinson

"We have to learn from mistakes. We've got to push next season and be bouncing from the start."

                     Dirk Kuyt's reflections on the season

"The World Cup and Champions League are the highest levels of football. I'm not getting any younger and I am keen to work under Fabio Capello."

                     Jamie Carragher on his England U-turn

"We have tried to bring in British players with the right mentality and the passion for the club. We are trying to do what is best for the club. We have a long-term plan and we try to follow that."

                           Rafael Benitez

MAY

THE GAMES

2	Chelsea	H	0-2
9	Hull City	A	0-0

WHERE THEY FINISHED

4	Tottenham Hotspur
5	Manchester City
6	Aston Villa
7	**Liverpool**
8	Everton
9	Birmingham City
10	Blackburn Rovers

DIRK KUYT:

'If we can buy a few more players we will be close again. We just need a bit more luck and a bit more quality.'

2009/10

Game played   Goal scored
Substituted player   Used Sub
Unused sub   Substituted sub

Players (columns 1–19): Diego Cavalieri, Glen Johnson, Alberto Aquilani, Daniel Agger, Steven Gerrard, Fernando Torres, Andriy Voronin, Albert Riera, Fabio Aurelio, Yossi Benayoun, Sotirios Kyrgiakos, Maxi Rodriguez, Dirk Kuyt, Ryan Babel

DATE	OPPONENTS		RES	ATT
Sun 16 Aug	Tottenham Hotspur	A	1-2	35,935
Wed 19 Aug	Stoke City	H	4-0	44,318
Mon 24 Aug	Aston Villa	H	1-3	43,667
Sat 29 Aug	Bolton Wanderers	A	3-2	23,284
Sat 12 Sep	Burnley	H	4-0	43,817
Wed 16 Sep	Debrecen (CL group match 1)	H	1-0	41,591
Sat 19 Sep	West Ham United	A	3-2	34,658
Tue 22 Sep	Leeds (Carling Cup 3rd round)	A	1-0	38,168
Sat 26 Sep	Hull City	H	6-1	44,392
Tue 29 Sep	Fiorentina (CL group match 2)	A	0-2	33,426
Sun 04 Oct	Chelsea	A	0-2	41,732
Sat 17 Oct	Sunderland	A	0-1	47,327
Tue 20 Oct	Lyon (CL group match 3)	H	1-2	41,562
Sun 25 Oct	Manchester United	H	2-0	44,188
Wed 28 Oct	Arsenal (Carling Cup 4th rd)	A	1-2	60,004
Sat 31 Oct	Fulham	A	1-3	25,700
Wed 04 Nov	Lyon (CL group match 4)	A	1-1	39,180
Mon 09 Nov	Birmingham City	H	2-2	42,560
Sat 21 Nov	Manchester City	H	2-2	44,164
Tue 24 Nov	Debrecen (CL group match 5)	A	1-0	41,500
Sun 29 Nov	Everton ^	A	2-0	39,652
Sat 05 Dec	Blackburn Rovers	A	0-0	29,660
Wed 09 Dec	Fiorentina (CL group match 6)	H	1-2	40,863
Sun 13 Dec	Arsenal	H	1-2	43,853
Wed 16 Dec	Wigan Athletic	H	2-1	41,116
Sat 19 Dec	Portsmouth	A	0-2	20,534
Sat 26 Dec	Wolves	H	2-0	41,956
Tue 29 Dec	Aston Villa	A	1-0	42,788
Sat 02 Jan	Reading (FA Cup 3rd round)	A	1-1	23,656
Wed 13 Jan	Reading (FA Cup 3rd rd replay) ^	H	1-2*	31,063
Sat 16 Jan	Stoke City	A	1-1	27,247
Wed 20 Jan	Tottenham Hotspur	H	2-0	42,016
Tue 26 Jan	Wolverhampton Wanderers	A	0-0	28,763
Sat 30 Jan	Bolton Wanderers ^	H	2-0	43,413
Sat 06 Feb	Everton	H	1-0	44,316
Wed 10 Feb	Arsenal	A	0-1	60,045
Thu 18 Feb	Unirea Urziceni (EL last 32 1st)	H	1-0	40,450
Sun 21 Feb	Manchester City	A	0-0	47,203
Thu 25 Feb	Unirea Urziceni (EL last 32 2nd)	A	3-1	25,000
Sun 28 Feb	Blackburn Rovers	H	2-1	42,795
Mon 08 Mar	Wigan Athletic	A	0-1	17,427
Thu 11 Mar	Lille (EL last 16 1st leg)	A	0-1	17,931
Mon 15 Mar	Portsmouth	H	4-1	40,316
Thu 18 Mar	Lille (EL last 16 2nd leg)	H	3-0	38,139
Sun 21 Mar	Manchester United	A	1-2	75,216
Sun 28 Mar	Sunderland	H	3-0	43,121
Thu 01 Apr	Benfica (EL quarter-final 1st leg)	A	1-2	62,629
Sun 04 Apr	Birmingham City	A	1-1	27,909
Thu 08 Apr	Benfica (EL quarter-final 2nd leg)	H	4-1	42,377
Sun 11 Apr	Fulham	H	0-0	42,331
Mon 19 Apr	West Ham United ^	H	3-0	37,697
Thu 22 Apr	Atletico Madrid (EL semi 1st)	A	0-1	50,000
Sun 25 Apr	Burnley	A	4-0	21,553
Thu 29 Apr	Atletico Madrid (EL semi 2nd)	H	2-1*	42,040
Sun 02 May	Chelsea	H	0-2	44,375
Sun 09 May	Hull City	A	0-0	25,030

*AET

^ Own goal v Everton (J Yobo)   ^ Own goal v Bolton (K Davies)
^ Own goal v Reading (R Bertrand)   ^ Own goal v West Ham (R Green)

	Emiliano Insua	Jamie Carragher	David Ngog	Pepe Reina	Jay Spearing	Philipp Degen	Damien Plessis		Nabil El Zhar	Stephen Darby		Martin Kelly	Steven Irwin	Martin Skrtel	Robbie Threlfall	Nathan Eccleston	Daniel Ayala	Martin Hansen	Peter Gulacsi	Dean Bouzanis	Alex Kacaniklic	David Amoo	Daniel Pacheco	Gerardo Bruna	Jack Robinson	Andrea Dossena
22	23	24	25	26	27	28	29	30	31	32	33	34	36	37	38	39	40	41	42	43	45	46	47	48	49

6 50 of the best

Fernando Torres became the quickest player to reach the 50-goal mark for the club with a dramatic injury-time winner at Aston Villa in December 2009.

5

Golden Gloves

Pepe Reina marked another consistent season by finishing runner-up for the Golden Gloves award in the Premier League. He kept 17 clean sheets in an ever-present season in the Liverpool goal, only missing out on the award due to playing more games than Chelsea's Petr Cech.

4

Lions tamed

Benfica came to Anfield confident of progressing to the semi-finals of the Europa League. Ninety minutes later, the eventual Portuguese champions were put in their place.

3

Goal of the season

Fernando Torres showed glimpses of what might have been in an injury-hit season. This magnificent top-corner effort was far too good for Sunderland goalkeeper Craig Gordon.

2

United woes

Against the odds after a run of poor form, the Reds produced arguably their best performance of the season in defeating Manchester United 2-0 at Anfield.

Derby double

A third home and away success in Merseyside derbies for five seasons at least gave Liverpool fans local bragging rights. A 2-0 win at Goodison was followed by a 1-0 victory at Anfield thanks to Dirk Kuyt's header – Liverpool winning despite being down to 10 men for an hour.

PLAYER STATISTICS 2009/2010

PLAYER	PLAYED	SUBBED	SUB UNUSED	MINS PLAYED	GOALS
Cavalieri	4	0	50	390	0
Johnson	33 + 2	4	0	2998	3
Aquilani	13 + 13	10	11	1213	2
Agger	36	3	4	3207	1
Gerrard	47 + 2	11	0	4128	12
Torres	29 + 3	15	2	2473	22
Voronin	3 + 9	1	3	377	0
Riera	12 + 4	9	9	899	0
Aurelio	13 + 10	6	4	1175	0
Benayoun	29 + 16	22	1	2829	9
Kyrgiakos	18 + 3	0	22	1669	1
Rodriguez	14 + 3	4	0	1208	1
Kuyt	51 + 2	17	2	4477	11
Babel	16 + 22	9	7	1708	6
Mascherano	44 + 4	4	1	3945	2
Lucas	46 + 4	7	3	4166	1
Insua	43 + 1	3	3	3905	1
Carragher	53	3	1	4724	0
Ngog	18 + 19	13	9	1750	8
Reina	52	0	3	4710	0
Spearing	3 + 2	1	17	256	0
Degen	6 + 5	5	14	589	0
Plessis	1	1	6	77	0
El Zhar	1 + 6	1	7	130	0
Darby	2 + 1	0	8	181	0
Kelly	1 + 2	1	11	123	0
Skrtel	23 + 6	3	8	2063	1
Dossena	3 + 2	1	10	235	0
Eccleston	0 + 2	0	0	14	0
Ayala	2 + 3	0	10	234	0
Gulacsi	0	0	3	0	0
Pacheco	0 + 7	0	9	78	0
Robinson	0 + 1	0	0	2	0

FINAL LEAGUE TABLE 2009/10

	Team	Pd	HOME					AWAY					Pts	GD
			W	D	L	F	A	W	D	L	F	A		
1	Chelsea	38	17	1	1	68	14	10	4	5	35	18	86	+71
2	Man Utd	38	16	1	2	52	12	11	3	5	34	16	85	+58
3	Arsenal	38	15	2	2	48	15	8	4	7	35	26	75	+42
4	Tottenham	38	14	2	3	40	12	7	5	7	27	29	70	+26
5	Man City	38	12	4	3	41	20	6	9	4	32	25	67	+28
6	Aston Villa	38	8	8	3	29	16	9	5	5	23	23	64	+13
7	**Liverpool**	**38**	**13**	**3**	**3**	**43**	**15**	**5**	**6**	**8**	**18**	**20**	**63**	**+26**
8	Everton	38	11	6	2	35	21	5	7	7	25	28	61	+11
9	Birmingham	38	8	9	2	19	13	5	2	12	19	34	50	-9
10	Blackburn	38	10	6	3	28	18	3	5	11	13	37	50	-14
11	Stoke City	38	7	6	6	24	21	4	8	7	10	27	47	-14
12	Fulham	38	11	3	5	27	15	1	7	11	12	31	46	-7
13	Sunderland	38	9	7	3	32	19	2	4	13	16	37	44	-8
14	Bolton	38	6	6	7	26	31	4	3	12	16	36	39	-25
15	Wolves	38	5	6	8	13	22	4	5	10	19	34	38	-24
16	Wigan	38	6	7	6	19	24	3	2	14	18	55	36	-42
17	West Ham	38	7	5	7	30	29	1	6	12	17	37	35	-19
18	Burnley	38	7	5	7	25	30	1	1	17	17	52	30	-40
19	Hull City	38	6	6	7	22	29	0	6	13	12	46	30	-41
20	Portsmouth	38	5	3	11	24	32	2	4	13	10	34	19	-32

* Portsmouth deducted 9 points for going into administration

Steven Gerrard and Jamie Carragher salute the fans

APPEARANCES & GOALS FOR LIVERPOOL

L'POOL	LGE GMS	LGE GLS	FA GMS	FA GLS	L. CUP GMS	L. CUP GLS	EURO GMS (inc Spr Cup)	EURO GLS	OTHER GMS (inc C. Shield & C. World)	OTHER GLS	L'POOL GMS	GLS
Cavalieri	0	0	2	0	4	0	2	0	0	0	8	0
Johnson	25	3	0	0	1	0	9	0	0	0	35	3
Aquilani	18	1	2	0	1	0	5	1	0	0	26	2
Agger	77	3	3	0	4	2	30	2	1	0	115	7
Gerrard	366	80	28	10	20	7	114	34	4	1	532	132
Torres	79	56	6	1	3	3	28	12	0	0	116	72
Aurelio	71	3	4	0	5	0	29	1	1	0	110	4
Kyrgiakos	14	1	0	0	2	0	5	0	0	0	21	1
Rodriguez	17	1	0	0	0	0	0	0	0	0	17	1
Kuyt	141	36	9	2	3	0	47	13	0	0	200	51
Babel	82	11	8	1	6	0	33	8	0	0	129	20
Mascherano	93	2	5	0	2	0	38	1	0	0	138	3
Lucas	78	1	8	1	5	1	30	2	0	0	121	5
Insua	46	0	3	0	3	1	10	0	0	0	62	1
Carragher	435	4	34	0	28	0	129	1	4	0	630	5
Ngog	38	7	2	0	4	1	12	3	0	0	56	11
Reina	182	0	8	0	1	0	65	0	3	0	259	0
Spearing	3	0	0	0	2	0	2	0	0	0	7	0
Degen	7	0	1	0	4	0	1	0	0	0	13	0
Plessis	3	0	0	0	3	1	2	0	0	0	8	1
Itandje	0	0	4	0	3	0	0	0	0	0	7	0
El Zhar	21	0	1	0	4	1	6	0	0	0	32	1
Darby	1	0	1	0	1	0	2	0	0	0	5	0
Kelly	1	0	0	0	0	0	3	0	0	0	4	0
Skrtel	54	1	5	0	2	0	18	0	0	0	79	1
Eccleston	1	0	0	0	1	0	0	0	0	0	2	0
Ayala	5	0	0	0	0	0	0	0	0	0	5	0
Pacheco	4	0	0	0	0	0	3	0	0	0	7	0
Robinson	1	0	0	0	0	0	0	0	0	0	1	0

Table heading: AT END OF 2009/10 - SORTED BY SQUAD NUMBER ORDER (AT START OF 2010/11)

LFC MAGAZINE AWARDS 2009/10

Player of the season: Pepe Reina
The World Cup winner played every minute in the Premier League, his consistency and 17 clean sheets earning him runners-up spot for the Golden Glove award.

Young player of the season: Lucas Leiva
Consistent performer in the Liverpool midfield.

Goal of the season: Fernando Torres v Sunderland
Mention too for the striker's goals v Benfica in the Europa League and in the league at West Ham.

Pepe Reina – Reds winner

RESERVES 2009/10

SEASON REVIEW

The reserve league campaign proved a season of two halves as new boss John McMahon enjoyed a mixed first season in charge. An 11-match unbeaten run – including 7 successive wins – saw the Reds challenging for the title, before a sequence of 5 straight defeats ended those ambitions.
The side featured a handful of first-team hopefuls as well as Academy players, with David Amoo, Daniel Ayala, Stephen Darby, Nathan Eccleston, Martin Kelly, Daniel Pacheco and Jay Spearing having all made the step up to first-team level. Unusually, the side also used 6 goalkeepers. Note that player stats include the Liverpool and Lancashire Senior Cup finals played in July 2010.

2009/10 STATISTICS

RES. LGE & CUP APPS. & GOALS 2009/10

	Appearances	Goals
Daniel Agger	1	0
David Amoo	21	5
Alberto Aquilani	1	0
Daniel Ayala	16	0
Dean Bouzanis	2	0
Jordy Brouwer	13	3
Gerardo Bruna	12	4
Chris Buchtmann	1	0
Conor Coady	3	1
Alex Cooper	11	2
Lauri Dalla Valle	11	3
Stephen Darby	10	0
Philipp Degen	2	0
Francisco Duran	6	0
Nathan Eccleston	10	5
Nabil El Zhar	2	0
John Flanagan	7	0
Vitor Flora	1	0
Peter Gulacsi	10	0
Martin Hansen	7	0
Steven Irwin	22	1
Liam Jacob	1	0
Alex Kacaniklic	20	2
Martin Kelly	3	1
Nicolaj Kohlert	12	1
Sotirios Kyrgiakos	1	0
David Martin	4	0
Chris Mavinga	17	0
Emmanuel Mendy	13	1
David Ngog	4	3
Michael Ngoo	2	0
Chris Oldfield	1	0
Daniel Pacheco	9	4
Victor Palsson	20	0
Damien Plessis	12	1
Zsolt Poloskei	3	0
Michael Roberts	2	0
Nikola Saric	20	3

RES. LGE & CUP APPS. & GOALS 2009/10

	Appearances	Goals
Toni Silva	3	1
Jakub Sokolik	2	0
Jay Spearing	8	2
Robbie Threlfall	8	1
Vincent Weijl	5	0
Andre Wisdom	2	0

RESERVES LEAGUE RESULTS 2009/10

			Result
27.08.09	Blackburn Rovers	A	2-3
02.09.09	**Bolton Wanderers**	**H**	**3-1**
17.09.09	**Manchester United**	**H**	**1-0**
29.09.09	Manchester City	A	2-0
07.10.09	**Burnley**	**H**	**1-0**
21.10.09	**Sunderland**	**H**	**2-0**
03.11.09	Everton	A	1-0
10.11.09	**Hull City**	**H**	**4-1**
19.01.10	**Manchester City**	**H**	**3-3**
23.03.10	Hull City	A	1-0
25.03.10	**Wigan Athletic**	**H**	**1-1**
29.03.10	Bolton Wanderers	A	2-1
07.04.10	Wigan Athletic	A	2-3
13.04.10	Manchester United	A	0-1
16.04.10	Burnley	A	1-3
20.04.10	**Everton**	**H**	**0-1**
27.04.10	**Blackburn Rovers**	**H**	**1-2**
04.05.10	Sunderland	A	1-0

RESERVES LEAGUE NORTH TABLE 2009/10

		Pld	W	D	L	F	A	Pts
1	Man Utd	18	13	2	3	35	10	41
2	Man City	18	10	5	3	34	20	35
3	**Liverpool**	**18**	**10**	**2**	**6**	**28**	**20**	**32**
4	Blackburn	18	8	5	5	35	24	29
5	Sunderland	18	7	1	10	25	32	22
6	Wigan Ath.	18	6	3	9	28	35	21
7	Burnley	18	6	3	9	22	36	21
8	Hull City	18	6	2	10	22	26	20
9	Everton	18	5	3	10	17	30	18
10	Bolton Wan.	18	5	2	11	24	37	17

RESERVES/ACADEMY CUP RESULTS 2009/10

LIVERPOOL IN THE LIVERPOOL SENIOR CUP 2009/10

Quarter-final

27th January 2010
Ashton Town 0-4 Liverpool (Edge Green Street Stadium)

Liverpool goalscorers: Kacaniklic (14), Brouwer (47), Spearing (58), Mendy (83)

Semi-final

10th March 2010
Liverpool 3-0 Tranmere Rovers (Liverpool Academy)

Liverpool goalscorers: Dalla Valle (42), Amoo (70), own goal

Final

31st July 2010
Skelmersdale United 2-3 Liverpool (Ashley Travel Stadium)

Liverpool goalscorers: Bruna (24), Coady (46), Cooper (85)
Team: Hansen, Flanagan, Mendy, Roberts (Kohlert 65), Wisdom, Coady, Silva (Weijl 85), Palsson, Saric, Bruna (Ngoo 76), Cooper.

LIVERPOOL IN THE LANCASHIRE SENIOR CUP 2009/10

Round 1

29th October 2009
Manchester Utd 1-1 Liverpool (Moss Lane, Altrincham)
Liverpool win 4-3 on penalties

Liverpool goalscorer: Eccleston (30)

Quarter-final

1st February 2010
Bolton Wanderers 0-2 Liverpool (County Ground, Leyland)

Liverpool goalscorers: Amoo (41), Plessis (84)

Semi-final

17th March 2010
Wigan Athletic 0-2 Liverpool (Robin Sports Park Arena,

Liverpool goalscorers: Dalla Valle (62), Pacheco (88) Wigan)

Final

27th July 2010
Oldham Athletic 0-3 Liverpool (County Ground, Leyland)

Liverpool goalscorers: Bruna (32), Cooper (43), Silva (71)
Team: Bouzanis, Flanagan, Mendy, Cooper, Wisdom, Coady, Silva, Kohlert (Roberts 65), Saric, Bruna, Weijl (Ngoo 75).

LIVERPOOL IN THE FA YOUTH CUP 2009/10

Round 3

30th November 2009
Liverpool 2-0 Wolves (Anfield)

Liverpool goalscorers: Ince (35), Adorjan (56)

Round 4

12th January 2010
Leicester City 1-5 Liverpool (Walkers Stadium)

Liverpool goalscorers: Dalla Valle (6, 8, 33), Ince (31), Ngoo (85)

Round 5

8th February 2010
Liverpool 0-1 Watford (Anfield)

THE ACADEMY 2009/10

SEASON REVIEW

John Owens' Academy side ended the season with a 10-match unbeaten run to finish fourth for a second consecutive season – although there was disappointment in the FA Youth Cup, with Watford inflicting defeat in round five at Anfield.

There has been progress to the first team in the form of Jack Robinson, who became the club's youngest post-war first-team player when he came on on the final day of the 2009/10 season at Hull City. Conor Coady and Andre Wisdom both helped England Under-17s to glory in the European Championships in the summer of 2010, while the defensive duo plus regulars John Flanagan, Michael Ngoo and Chris Oldfield have all made the step up to reserve level.

U18s APPEARANCES & GOALS 2009/10

	Appearances	Goals
Krisztian Adorjan	26	3
David Amoo	1	1
Christopher Buchtmann	9	1
Deale Chamberlain	8	0
Karl Clair	1	0
Conor Coady	28	2
Alex Cooper	6	0
Lauri Dalla Valle	10	6
Adam Dawson	4	1
James Ellison	11	3
Kristjan Gauti Emilsson	8	2
John Flanagan	27	0
Marcus Giglio	2	0
Michael Ihiekwe	6	0
Liam Jacob	1	0

U18s APPEARANCES & GOALS 2009/10

	Appearances	Goals
Thomas Ince	27	10
Nicolaj Beier Kohlert	2	1
Matty McGiveron	21	0
Michael Ngoo	25	7
Chris Oldfield	21	0
Adam Pepper	4	0
Patrick Poor	1	0
Michael Roberts	21	1
Chris Roddan	16	1
Jack Robinson	26	0
Stephen Sama	22	1
Nikola Saric	2	1
Tony Silva	9	3
Raheem Sterling	6	2
Andre Wisdom	28	0

U18s LEAGUE & YOUTH CUP RESULTS 09/10

			Result
22.08.09	Fulham	A	3-1
29.08.09	Leicester City	H	0-3
05.09.09	Nottingham Forest	A	0-2
12.09.09	Barnsley	H	2-0
19.09.09	Sunderland	A	0-3
26.09.09	Manchester City	H	2-6
03.10.09	West Bromwich Albion	A	4-1
10.10.09	Bolton Wanderers	H	0-1
17.10.09	Blackburn Rovers	A	3-0
31.10.09	Everton	H	0-2
07.11.09	Crewe Alexandra	H	1-0
14.11.09	Wolves	A	1-2
21.11.09	Manchester United	H	1-3
30.11.09	Wolves (FAYC3)	H	2-0
12.12.09	Blackburn Rovers	H	1-1
12.01.10	Leicester City (FAYC4)	A	5-1
16.01.10	Crewe Alexandra	A	0-3
23.01.10	Wolves	H	1-2
30.01.10	Manchester United	A	1-0
06.02.10	Stoke City	H	0-4
08.02.10	Watford (FAYC5)	H	0-1
20.02.10	Manchester City	A	2-1
27.02.10	West Bromwich Albion	H	0-0
06.03.10	Bolton Wanderers	A	2-1
09.03.10	Everton	A	4-3

U18s LEAGUE & YOUTH CUP RESULTS 09/10

			Result
20.03.10	Derby County	H	2-1
12.04.10	Stoke City	A	3-0
17.04.10	Sheffield United	A	1-1
24.04.10	Middlesbrough	H	3-0
29.04.10	Leeds United	H	4-0
08.05.10	Huddersfield Town	A	4-0

FA PREMIER ACADEMY 2009/10 GROUP C

	P	W	D	L	F	A	Pts
1 Man Utd	28	16	7	5	58	31	55
2 Everton	28	15	5	8	55	34	50
3 West Brom	28	12	9	7	55	34	45
4 Liverpool	28	14	3	11	45	41	45
5 Wolves	28	13	5	10	47	46	44
6 Man City	28	12	6	10	64	45	42
7 Blackburn	28	11	9	8	42	44	42
8 Stoke City	28	9	10	9	32	38	37
9 Crewe Alex.	28	10	6	12	45	54	36
10 Bolton W.	28	5	8	15	28	49	23

LIVERPOOL LADIES 2009/10

SEASON REVIEW

Liverpool Ladies will be one of eight teams in the Super League, which will begin in March 2011. The other teams will be Premier League champions Arsenal, runners-up and FA Cup winners Everton, Chelsea, Birmingham City, Doncaster Rovers Belles, Bristol Academy and Lincoln. The league is due to operate on a closed basis for a two-year period before it is ingratiated into the pyramid system.

Champions of the Northern Division, Cheryl Foster won the Players' Player of the Year prize after scoring 16 league goals, the best in the division, while the team also won an FA Fair Play Award after going through the campaign without picking up a single yellow or red card.

Led by Robbie Johnson, who scooped the Manager of the Year prize last season, and his assistant Graeme Hurst, they are again due to play their home fixtures at Skelmersdale United FC. For more on the team, log on to **www.liverpoolladiesfc.co.uk**

2009/10 STATISTICS

LADIES LEAGUE & CUP RESULTS 2009/10

Date	Opponent	H/A	Result
16.08.09	Lincoln	H	4-1
30.08.09	Luton Town	H	2-0
02.09.09	Preston North End	A	3-2
06.09.09	Leeds City Vixens	A	5-1
13.09.09	Sunderland (LC1)	A	1-5
27.09.09	Derby County	H	7-2
30.09.09	Preston North End	H	4-0
04.10.09	Newcastle United	A	2-1
11.10.09	Sheffield Wednesday	H	1-0
01.11.09	Manchester City	A	2-1
08.11.09	Lincoln	A	2-1
22.11.09	Luton Town	A	2-0
29.11.09	Leeds City Vixens	H	5-3
24.01.10	Preston NE (FAC3)	H	4-1
07.02.10	Chelsea (FAC4)	H	1-2 aet
14.02.10	Leicester City	A	2-0
14.03.10	Manchester City	H	1-2
24.03.10	Everton (CC)	H	0-1
28.03.10	Newcastle United	H	0-0
04.04.10	Aston Villa	A	2-1
11.04.10	Derby County	A	4-0
14.04.10	Curzon Ashton	A	1-1
18.04.10	Sheffield Wednesday	A	3-2
21.04.10	Curzon Ashton	H	3-1
25.04.10	Leicester City	H	2-0
16.05.10	Aston Villa	H	2-0

FA WOMEN'S NORTHERN DIVISION 2009/10

	P	W	D	L	F	A	Pts
1 Liverpool	**22**	**19**	**2**	**1**	**59**	**19**	**59**
2 Lincoln	22	15	4	3	52	22	49
3 Leicester C.	22	11	6	5	53	35	39
4 Man City	22	10	6	6	39	25	36
5 Curzon Ash.	22	9	4	9	40	39	31
6 Aston Villa	22	7	8	7	37	35	29
7 Leeds CV	22	9	2	11	41	48	29
8 Newcastle U.	22	7	6	9	38	48	27
9 Preston NE	22	6	6	10	56	54	24
10 Derby C.	22	5	5	12	30	51	20
11 Sheff. Wed.	22	4	6	12	29	50	18
12 Luton Town	22	1	3	18	12	60	6

2010 FIRST-TEAM SQUAD LIST

Anisha Bateman
Carmel Bennett
Emily Brown
Katie Brusell
Sam Chappell
Caroline Charlton
Louise Fillingham
Amie Flemming
Cheryl Foster
Danielle Gibson
Alicia Hardacre
Aly Hastie

Madeline Hills
Kelly Jones
Sophie Jones
Vicky Jones (captain)
Hannah Keryakoplis
Natalie Sage
Amber Simms
Jenny Toole
Jo Traynor
Fable Widdop
Hannah Williams
Katie Williams

Skipper Vicky Jones with the league trophy

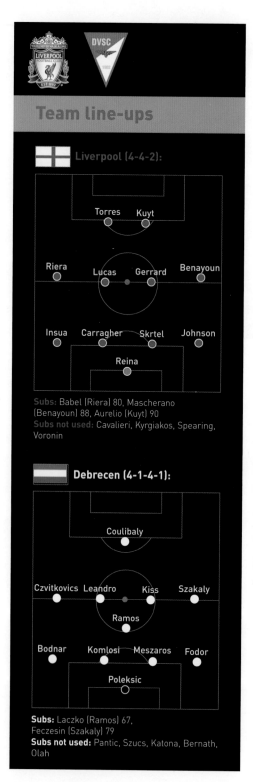

Team line-ups

Liverpool (4-4-2):

Torres Kuyt

Riera Lucas Gerrard Benayoun

Insua Carragher Skrtel Johnson

Reina

Subs: Babel (Riera) 80, Mascherano (Benayoun) 88, Aurelio (Kuyt) 90
Subs not used: Cavalieri, Kyrgiakos, Spearing, Voronin

Debrecen (4-1-4-1):

Coulibaly

Czvitkovics Leandro Kiss Szakaly

Ramos

Bodnar Komlosi Meszaros Fodor

Poleksic

Subs: Laczko (Ramos) 67, Feczesin (Szakaly) 79
Subs not used: Pantic, Szucs, Katona, Bernath, Olah

LIVERPOOL FC 1
DEBRECEN 0

**UEFA Champions League
Group E game 1
Anfield, Liverpool**
Wednesday September 16, 2009.
Attendance: 41,591

Goal: Kuyt (45)
Bookings: Gerrard (Liverpool), Fodor (Debrecen)
Referee: Pedro Proenca (Portugal)
Possession: Liverpool 58%, Debrecen 42%
Shots on (off) target: Liverpool 9 (15), Debrecen 5 (6)

Team line-ups

Debrecen (4-5-1):

Rudolf

Czvitkovics Laczko Kiss Szelesi Szakaly

Bodnar Mijadinoski Meszaros Fodor

Poleksic

Subs: Coulibaly (Szakaly) 62, Dombi (Fodor) 78
Subs not used: Pantic, Komlosi, Ramos, Bernath, Varga

Liverpool (4-4-1-1):

Ngog Kuyt

Aurelio Lucas Mascherano Gerrard

Insua Agger Carragher Johnson

Reina

Subs: Benayoun (Ngog) 77, Dossena (Aurelio) 89, Aquilani (Gerrard) 90
Subs not used: Cavalieri, Kyrgiakos, Skrtel, Spearing

DEBRECEN 0
LIVERPOOL FC 1

UEFA Champions League
Group E game 5
Ferenc Puskas Stadium, Budapest
Tuesday November 24, 2009.
Attendance: 41,500

Goal: Ngog (4)
Booking: Szelesi (Debrecen)
Referee: Bjorn Kuipers (Holland)
Possession: Debrecen 36%, Liverpool 64%
Shots on (off) target: Debrecen 2 (3), Liverpool 7 (8)

Team line-ups

Fiorentina (4-4-1-1):

Mutu

Jovetic

Vargas Zanetti Montolivo Marchionni

Gobbi Dainelli Gamberini Comotto

Frey

Subs: Jorgensen (Vargas) 74, Donadel (Mutu) 82, De Silvestri (Marchionni) 89
Subs not used: Avramov, Kroldrup, Pasqual, Castillo

Liverpool (4-4-1-1):

Torres

Gerrard

Benayoun Aurelio Lucas Kuyt

Insua Carragher Skrtel Johnson

Reina

Subs: Babel (Insua) 72, Voronin (Kuyt) 80
Subs not used: Cavalieri, Kyrgiakos, Riera, Spearing, Plessis

FIORENTINA   2
LIVERPOOL FC   0

UEFA Champions League
Group E game 2
Stadio Artemio Franchi, Florence
Tuesday September 29, 2009.
Attendance: 33,426

Goals: Jovetic (28, 37)
Bookings: None
Referee: Felix Brych (Germany)
Possession: Fiorentina 50%, Liverpool 50%
Shots on (off) target: Fiorentina 5 (3), Liverpool 5 (7)

Team line-ups

Liverpool (4-4-1-1):

Kuyt
Gerrard
Dossena   Benayoun
Mascherano   Aquilani
Insua   Darby
Agger   Skrtel
Cavalieri

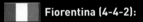

Subs: Torres (Kuyt) 65, Pacheco (Aquilani) 76, Aurelio (Mascherano) 86
Subs not used: Reina, Kyrgiakos, Carragher, Spearing

Fiorentina (4-4-2):

Gilardino   Santana
Jorgensen   Montolivo   Donadel   De Silvestri
Pasqual   Natali   Kroldrup   Comotto
Frey

Subs: Vargas (Jorgensen) 71, Marchionni (Santana) 71, Castillo (De Silvestri) 83
Subs not used: Avramov, Seculin, Aya, Federico Carrara

LIVERPOOL FC   1
FIORENTINA   2

**UEFA Champions League
Group E game 6
Anfield, Liverpool**
Wednesday December 9, 2009.
Attendance: 40,863

Goals: Benayoun (43), Jorgensen (63), Gilardino (90)
Bookings: Montolivo, Gilardino (Fiorentina)
Referee: Damir Skomina (Slovenia)
Possession: Liverpool 54%, Fiorentina 46%
Shots on (off) target: Liverpool 3 (2), Fiorentina 6 (3)

Team line-ups

Liverpool (4-4-2)

Ngog
Kuyt

Benayoun Mascherano Lucas Gerrard

Insua
Agger Carragher Kelly

Reina

Subs: Aurelio (Gerrard) 25, Skrtel (Kelly) 74, Voronin (Benayoun) 85
Subs not used: Cavalieri, Babel, Spearing, Plessis

Lyon (4-1-4-1)

Lopez
Ederson

Kallstrom Pjanic Govou
Makoun

Cissokho Reveillere
Cris Toulalan

Lloris

Subs: Gonalons (Cris) 43, Gomis (Ederson) 61, Delgado (Lisandro) 86
Subs not used: Vercoutre, Clerc, Bastos, Belfodil

LIVERPOOL FC 1
LYON 2

**UEFA Champions League
Group E game 3
Anfield, Liverpool**
Tuesday October 20, 2009.
Attendance: 41,562

Goals: Benayoun (41), Gonalons (72), Delgado (90)
Bookings: Ngog (Liverpool), Cris, Govou, Reveillere (Lyon)
Referee: Alberto Undiano Mallenco (Spain)
Possession: Liverpool 50%, Lyon 50%
Shots on (off) target: Liverpool 6 (6), Lyon 6 (6)

LYON   1
LIVERPOOL FC   1

Team line-ups

Lyon (4-1-4-1):

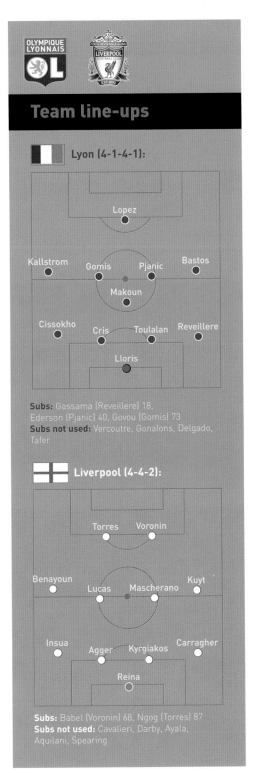

Lopez

Kallstrom   Gomis   Pjanic   Bastos

Makoun

Cissokho   Cris   Toulalan   Reveillere

Lloris

Subs: Gassama (Reveillere) 18, Ederson (Pjanic) 40, Govou (Gomis) 73
Subs not used: Vercoutre, Gonalons, Delgado, Tafer

Liverpool (4-4-2):

Torres   Voronin

Benayoun   Lucas   Mascherano   Kuyt

Insua   Agger   Kyrgiakos   Carragher

Reina

Subs: Babel (Voronin) 68, Ngog (Torres) 87
Subs not used: Cavalieri, Darby, Ayala, Aquilani, Spearing

UEFA Champions League
Group E game 4
Stade de Gerland, Lyon
Wednesday November 4, 2009.
Attendance: 39,180

Goals: Babel (83), Lopez (90)
Bookings: Lopez (Lyon), Agger (Liverpool)
Referee: Frank De Bleeckere (Belgium)
Possession: Lyon 58%, Liverpool 42%
Shots on (off) target: Lyon 6 (7), Liverpool 8 (2)

Team line-ups

Liverpool (4-2-3-1)

Ngog

Gerrard

Riera
Kuyt

Aquilani
Mascherano

Aurelio
Carragher

Agger
Skrtel

Reina

Subs: Babel (Riera) 63, Pacheco (Aquilani) 75, Lucas (Ngog) 89
Subs not used: Cavalieri, Kyrgiakos, Insua, Degen

Unirea Urziceni (4-5-1)

Bilasco

Frunza
Apostol
Paduretu
Onofras

Paraschiv

Brandan
Fernandes
Galamaz
Maftei

Arlauskis

Subs: Marinescu (Onofras) 75, Vilana (Paraschiv) 86, Rusescu (Paduretu) 90
Subs not used: Tudor, Mehmedovic, Nicu, Bordeanu

LIVERPOOL FC 1
UNIREA URZICENI 0

**UEFA Europa League
Round of 32, 1st Leg
Anfield, Liverpool**
Thursday February 18, 2010.
Attendance: 40,450

Goal: Ngog (81)
Bookings: Mascherano (Liverpool), Fernandes, Brandan (Unirea Urziceni)
Referee: Eric Braamhaar (Holland)
Possession: Liverpool 59%, Unirea 41%
Shots on (off) target: Liverpool 11 (10), Unirea 1 (3)

Team line-ups

Unirea Urziceni (4-5-1):

Bilasco

Frunza Apostol Paraschiv Paduretu Onofras

Bordeanu Fernandes Galamaz Maftei

Arlauskis

Subs: Mehmedovic (Galamaz) 27, Vilana (Paraschiv) 56, Semedo (Onofras) 62
Subs not used: Tudor, Nicu, Marinescu, Rusescu

Liverpool (4-2-3-1):

Ngog

Gerrard

Babel Benayoun

Lucas Mascherano

Insua Agger Skrtel Carragher

Reina

Subs: Kelly (Carragher) 61, Kyrgiakos (Skrtel) 66, Aurelio (Benayoun) 77
Subs not used: Cavalieri, Aquilani, Torres, Kuyt

UNIREA URZICENI 1
LIVERPOOL FC 3

UEFA Europa League
Round of 32, 2nd Leg
Steaua Stadium, Bucharest
Thursday February 25, 2010.
Attendance: 25,000

Goals: Fernandes (18), Mascherano (29), Babel (40), Gerrard (57)
Bookings: Arlauskis, Fernandes, Onofras (Unirea Urziceni), Mascherano, Babel (Liverpool)
Referee: Stefan Johannesson (Sweden)
Possession: Unirea 36%, Liverpool 64%
Shots on (off) target: Unirea 3 (5), Liverpool 8 (1),

Team line-ups

Lille (4-3-3)

Frau

Obraniak
Hazard

Cabaye

Mavuba
Balmont

Emerson
Beria
Rami   Chedjou

Landreau

Subs: Dumont (Cabaye) 73, Aubameyang (Frau) 77, Toure (Obraniak) 83
Subs not used: Butelle, Vandam, Souare, Souquet

Liverpool (4-2-3-1)

Torres

Babel
Gerrard
Kuyt

Lucas   Mascherano

Insua
Agger   Carragher   Johnson

Reina

Subs: Riera (Babel) 73, El Zhar (Kuyt) 88
Subs not used: Cavalieri, Kyrgiakos, Kelly, Aquilani, Ngog

LILLE   1
LIVERPOOL FC   0

UEFA Europa League
Last 16, 1st Leg
Stadium Lille-Metropole, Villeneuve d'Ascq
Thursday March 11, 2010.
Attendance: 18,000

Goal: Hazard (84)
Bookings: Toure, Aubameyang (Lille), Insua, Torres (Liverpool)
Referee: Claus Bo Larsen (Denmark)
Possession: Lille 57%, Liverpool 43%
Shots on (off) target: Lille 5 (4), Liverpool 6 (1)

LIVERPOOL FC 3
LILLE 0

UEFA Europa League
Last 16, 2nd Leg
Anfield, Liverpool
Thursday March 18, 2010.
Attendance: 38,139

Goals: Gerrard (9 pen), Torres (49, 89)
Bookings: Insua, Torres (Liverpool),
Cabaye (Lille)
Referee: Nicola Rizzoli (Italy)
Possession: Liverpool 48%, Lille 52%
Shots on (off) target: Liverpool 10 (8),
Lille 2 (5)

Team line-ups

Liverpool (4-2-3-1)

Torres

Babel Gerrard Kuyt

Lucas Mascherano

Insua Agger Carragher Johnson

Reina

Subs: Benayoun (Babel) 80, Kyrgiakos (Agger)
90, Ngog (Torres) 90
Subs not used: Cavalieri, Degen, El Zhar, Kelly

Lille (4-1-4-1)

Frau

Obraniak Cabaye Hazard Balmont

Mavuba

Emerson Rami Chedjou Beria

Landreau

Subs: Toure (Frau) 59, Aubameyang (Balmont)
71, Vandam (Hazard) 86
Subs not used: Butelle, Dumont, Souare,
Souquet

Team line-ups

Benfica (4-2-3-1)

Cardoza

Aimar

Di Maria   Ramires

Martins Javi Garcia

Coentrao   Pereira
       Luiz   Luisao

Julio Cesar

Subs: Nuno Gomes (Pereira) 66, Ruben Amorim (Martins) 72, Airton (Aimar) 86
Subs not used: Moreira, Luis Filipe, Sidnei, Kardec

Liverpool (4-2-3-1)

Torres

Babel   Gerrard   Kuyt

Lucas   Mascherano

Insua   Agger Carragher Johnson

Reina

Subs: Ngog (Torres) 82, Benayoun (Gerrard) 90
Subs not used: Cavalieri, Kyrgiakos, Plessis, El Zhar, Pacheco

BENFICA 2
LIVERPOOL FC 1

UEFA Europa League
Quarter-final, 1st Leg
Stadium of Light, Lisbon
Thursday April 1, 2010.
Attendance: 62,629

Goals: Agger (9), Cardoza (59, 79 – 2 pens)
Bookings: Luisao, Luiz (Benfica), Reina, Insua, Carragher (Liverpool)
Sent off: Babel (Liverpool)
Referee: Jonas Eriksson (Sweden)
Possession: Benfica 52%, Liverpool 48%
Shots on (off) target: Benfica 5 (10), Liverpool 3 (2)

LIVERPOOL FC   4
BENFICA   1

Team line-ups

Liverpool (4-2-3-1)

Torres

Benayoun   Gerrard   Kuyt

Lucas   Mascherano

Agger   Kyrgiakos   Carragher   Johnson

Reina

Subs: Ngog (Torres) 86, Aquilani (Gerrard) 88, El Zhar (Benayoun) 90
Subs not used: Cavalieri, Degen, Ayala, Pacheco

Benfica (4-1-3-1-1)

Cardozo

Aimar

Di Maria   Martins   Ramires

Garcia

Luiz   Sidnei   Luisao   Amorim

Julio Cesar

Subs: Kardec (Martins) 66, Moreira (Julio Cesar) 79, Fabio Coentrao (Aimar) 86
Subs not used: Pereira, Airton, Menezes, Luis

**UEFA Europa League
Quarter-final, 2nd Leg
Anfield, Liverpool**
Thursday April 8, 2010.
Attendance: 42,377

Goals: Kuyt (28), Lucas (34), Torres (59, 82), Cardozo (70)
Bookings: Benayoun (Liverpool), Aimar (Benfica)
Referee: Bjorn Kuipers (Holland)
Possession: Liverpool **51%**, Benfica **49%**
Shots on (off) target: Liverpool **6 (2)**, Benfica **5 (5)**

Team line-ups

Atletico Madrid (4-2-3-1)

Forlan

Reyes

Jurado   Simao

Assuncao   Garcia

Lopez   Dominguez   Perez   Ujfalusi

de Gea

Subs: Valera (Simao) 77, Salvio (Forlan) 85, Camacho (Reyes) 90
Subs not used: Asenjo, Juanito, Cabrera, Borja

Liverpool (4-2-3-1)

Ngog

Benayoun   Gerrard   Kuyt

Lucas   Mascherano

Agger   Kyrgiakos   Carragher   Johnson

Reina

Subs: Babel (Ngog) 64, El Zhar (Benayoun) 83
Subs not used: Cavalieri, Degen, Ayala, Aquilani, Pacheco

ATLETICO MADRID   1
LIVERPOOL FC   0

UEFA Europa League
Semi-final, 1st Leg
Vicente Calderon Stadium, Madrid
Thursday April 22, 2010.
Attendance: 50,000

Goal: Forlan (9)
Bookings: Valera (Atletico Madrid), Kyrgiakos (Liverpool)
Referee: Laurent Duhamel (France)
Possession: Atletico 60%, Liverpool 40%
Shots on (off) target: Atletico 4 (3), Liverpool 0 (3)

Team line-ups

Liverpool (4-2-3-1)

Kuyt

Benayoun — Aquilani — Babel

Lucas — Gerrard

Johnson — Agger — Carragher — Mascherano

Reina

Subs: El Zhar (Aquilani) 89, Degen (Mascherano) 110, Pacheco (Benayoun) 113
Subs not used: Cavalieri, Kyrgiakos, Ayala, Ngog

Atletico Madrid (4-4-2)

Forlan — Aguero

Simao — Garcia — Assuncao — Reyes

Lopez — Dominguez — Perea — Valera

de Gea

Subs: Jurado (Assuncao) 99, Camacho (Forlan) 117, Salvio (Aguero) 120
Subs not used: Asenjo, Juanito, Ujfalusi, Cabrera

LIVERPOOL FC 2
ATLETICO MADRID 1
(AET)

**UEFA Europa League
Semi-final, 2nd Leg
Anfield, Liverpool**
Thursday April 29, 2010.
Attendance: 42,040

Goals: Aquilani (44), Benayoun (95), Forlan (102)
Bookings: Gerrard, Aquilani, Carragher (Liverpool), Assuncao, Valera, Forlan, Dominguez (Atletico Madrid)
Referee: Terje Hauge (Norway)
Possession: Liverpool 52%, Atletico 48%
Shots on (off) target: Liverpool 7 (3), Atletico 5 (6)

95

EUROPEAN/WORLD ROLL OF HONOUR

EUROPEAN CHAMPIONS CUP/UEFA CHAMPIONS LEAGUE

WINNERS
1976/1977, 1977/1978, 1980/1981, 1983/1984, 2004/2005

RUNNERS-UP
1984/1985, 2006/2007

SEMI-FINALISTS
1964/1965, 2007/2008

INTER-CITIES FAIRS CUP/UEFA CUP/EUROPA LEAGUE

WINNERS
1972/1973, 1975/1976, 2000/2001

SEMI-FINALISTS
1970/1971, 2009/2010

EUROPEAN CUP-WINNERS' CUP

RUNNERS-UP
1965/1966

SEMI-FINALISTS
1996/1997

UEFA SUPER CUP

WINNERS
1977, 2001, 2005

RUNNERS-UP
1978, 1985

INTERCONTINENTAL CUP/FIFA CLUB WORLD CUP

RUNNERS-UP
1981, 1984, 2005

LIVERPOOL FC RESULTS IN EUROPEAN COMPETITION

Season	Round	Venue	Opponents	Opponent Country	Score	Scorers	Att
1964/65	**EUROPEAN CUP**		**(WINNERS – INTER MILAN)**				
17th Aug	1 Leg 1	(a)	Reykjavik	Ice	5-0	Wallace 2, Hunt 2, Chisnall	10,000
14th Sept	1 Leg 2	(h)	Reykjavik	"	6-1	Byrne, St John 2, Hunt, Graham, Stevenson	32,957
25th Nov	2 Leg 1	(h)	Anderlecht	Bel	3-0	St John, Hunt, Yeats	44,516
16th Dec	2 Leg 2	(a)	Anderlecht	"	1-0	Hunt	60,000
10th Feb	3 Leg 1	(a)	FC Cologne	W.Ger	0-0		40,000
17th Mar	3 Leg 2	(h)	FC Cologne	"	0-0		48,432
24th Mar	Replay	Rotterdam	FC Cologne	"	2-2	St John, Hunt	45,000
			(Liverpool won on toss of a coin)				
4th May	SF Leg 1	(h)	Inter Milan	Ita	3-1	Hunt, Callaghan, St John	54,082
12th May	SF Leg 1	(a)	Inter Milan	"	0-3		90,000
1965/66	**CUP WINNERS' CUP**		**(WINNERS – BORUSSIA DORTMUND)**				
29th Sept	Pr Leg 1	(a)	Juventus	Ita	0-1		12,000
13th Oct	Pr Leg 2	(h)	Juventus	"	2-0	Lawler, Strong	51,055
1st Dec	1 Leg 1	(h)	Standard Liege	Bel	3-1	Lawler 2, Thompson	46,112
15th Dec	1 Leg 2	(a)	Standard Liege	"	2-1	Hunt, St John	35,000
1st Mar	2 Leg 1	(a)	Honved	Hun	0-0		20,000
8th Mar	2 Leg 2	(h)	Honved	"	2-0	Lawler, St John	54,631
14th Apr	SF Leg 1	(a)	Celtic	Sco	0-1		80,000
19th Apr	SF Leg 2	(h)	Celtic	"	2-0	Smith, Strong	54,208
5th May	Final	Glasgow	B. Dortmund	W.Ger	1-2 aet	Hunt	41,657
1966/67	**EUROPEAN CUP**		**(WINNERS – CELTIC)**				
28th Sept	Pr Leg 1	(h)	Petrolul Ploesti	Rom	2-0	St John, Callaghan	44,463
12th Oct	Pr Leg 2	(a)	Petrolul Ploesti	"	1-3	Hunt	20,000
19th Oct	Replay	Brussels	Petrolul Ploesti	"	2-0	St John, Thompson	15,000
7th Dec	1 Leg 1	(a)	Ajax Amsterdam	Hol	1-5	Lawler	65,000
14th Dec	1 Leg 2	(h)	Ajax Amsterdam	"	2-2	Hunt 2	53,846
1967/68	**I-C FAIRS CUP**		**(WINNERS – LEEDS UNITED)**				
19th Sept	1 Leg 1	(a)	Malmo	Swe	2-0	Hateley 2	14,314
4th Oct	1 Leg 2	(h)	Malmo	"	2-1	Yeats, Hunt	39,795
7th Nov	2 Leg 1	(h)	TSV Munich 1860	W.Ger	8-0	St John, Hateley, Smith (pen) Hunt 2, Thompson, Callaghan 2	44,812
14th Nov	2 Leg 2	(a)	TSV Munich 1860	"	1-2	Callaghan	10,000
28th Nov	3 Leg 1	(a)	Ferencvaros	Hun	0-1		30,000
9th Jan	3 Leg 2	(h)	Ferencvaros	"	0-1		46,892
1968/69	**I-C FAIRS CUP**		**(WINNERS – NEWCASTLE UNITED)**				
18th Sept	1 Leg 1	(a)	Athletic Bilbao	Spa	1-2	Hunt	35,000
2nd Oct	1 Leg 2	(h)	Athletic Bilbao	"	2-1 aet	Lawler, Hughes	49,567
			(Liverpool lost on toss of coin)				
1969/70	**I-C FAIRS CUP**		**(WINNERS – ARSENAL)**				
16th Sept	1 Leg 1	(h)	Dundalk	Rep. Ire	10-0	Evans 2, Lawler, Smith 2, Graham 2, Lindsay, Thompson, Callaghan	32,562
30th Sept	1 Leg 2	(a)	Dundalk	"	4-0	Thompson 2, Graham, Callaghan	6,000
12th Nov	2 Leg 1	(a)	Vitoria Setubal	Por	0-1		16,000
26th Nov	2 Leg 2	(h)	Vitoria Setubal	"	3-2	Smith (pen), Evans, Hunt	41,633

LIVERPOOL'S RESULTS IN EUROPEAN COMPETITION

Season	Round	Venue	Opponents	Opponent Country	Score	Scorers	Att
1970/71	**I-C FAIRS CUP**		**(WINNERS – LEEDS UNITED)**				
15th Sept	1 Leg 1	(h)	Ferencvaros	Hun	1-0	Graham	37,531
29th Sept	1 Leg 2	(a)	Ferencvaros	"	1-1	Hughes	25,000
21st Oct	2 Leg 1	(h)	D. Bucharest	Rom	3-0	Lindsay, Lawler, Hughes	36,525
4th Nov	2 Leg 2	(a)	D. Bucharest	"	1-1	Boersma	45,000
9th Dec	3 Leg 1	(a)	Hibernian	Sco	1-0	Toshack	30,296
22nd Dec	3 Leg 2	(h)	Hibernian	"	2-0	Heighway, Boersma	37,815
10th Mar	4 Leg 1	(h)	Bayern Munich	W.Ger	3-0	Evans 3	45,616
24th Mar	4 Leg 2	(a)	Bayern Munich	"	1-1	Ross	23,000
14th Apr	SF Leg 1	(h)	Leeds United	Eng	0-1		52,577
28th Apr	SF Leg 2	(a)	Leeds United	"	0-0		40,462
1971/72	**CUP WINNERS' CUP**		**(WINNERS – RANGERS)**				
15th Sept	1 Leg 1	(a)	Servette Geneva	Swi	1-2	Lawler	16,000
29th Sept	1 Leg 2	(h)	Servette Geneva	"	2-0	Hughes, Heighway	38,591
20th Oct	2 Leg 1	(h)	Bayern Munich	W.Ger	0-0		42,949
3rd Nov	2 Leg 2	(a)	Bayern Munich	"	1-3	Evans	40,000
1972/73	**UEFA CUP**		**(WINNERS – LIVERPOOL)**				
12th Sept	1 Leg 1	(h)	E. Frankfurt	W.Ger	2-0	Keegan, Hughes	33,380
26th Sept	1 Leg 2	(a)	E. Frankfurt	"	0-0		20,000
24th Oct	2 Leg 1	(h)	AEK Athens	Gre	3-0	Boersma, Cormack, Smith (pen)	31,906
7th Nov	2 Leg 2	(a)	AEK Athens	"	3-1	Hughes 2, Boersma	25,000
29th Nov	3 Leg 1	(a)	Dynamo Berlin	E.Ger	0-0		19,000
13th Dec	3 Leg 2	(h)	Dynamo Berlin	"	3-1	Boersma, Heighway, Toshack	34,140
7th Mar	4 Leg 1	(h)	Dynamo Dresden	E.Ger	2-0	Hall, Boersma	33,270
21st Mar	4 Leg 2	(a)	Dynamo Dresden	"	1-0	Keegan	35,000
10th Apr	SF Leg 1	(h)	Tottenham H.	Eng	1-0	Lindsay	42,174
25th Apr	SF Leg 2	(a)	Tottenham H.	"	1-2	Heighway	46,919
10th May	F Leg 1	(h)	B. Moench'bach	W.Ger	3-0	Keegan 2, Lloyd	41,169
23rd May	F Leg 2	(a)	B. Moench'bach	"	0-2		35,000
1973/74	**EUROPEAN CUP**		**(WINNERS – BAYERN MUNICH)**				
19th Sept	1 Leg 1	(a)	Jeunesse D'Esch	Lux	1-1	Hall	5,000
3rd Oct	1 Leg 2	(h)	Jeunesse D'Esch	"	2-0	Mond o.g., Toshack	28,714
24th Oct	2 Leg 1	(a)	R.S. Belgrade	Yug	1-2	Lawler	40,000
6th Nov	2 Leg 2	(h)	R.S. Belgrade"		1-2	Lawler	41,774
1974/75	**CUP WINNERS' CUP**		**(WINNERS – DYNAMO KIEV)**				
17th Sept	1 Leg 1	(h)	Stromsgodset	Nor	11-0	Lindsay (pen), Boersma 2, Thompson 2, Heighway, Cormack, Hughes, Smith Callaghan, Kennedy	24,743
1st Oct	1 Leg 2	(a)	Stromsgodset	"	1-0	Kennedy	17,000
23rd Oct	2 Leg 1	(h)	Ferencvaros	Hun	1-1	Keegan	35,027
5th Nov	2 Leg 2	(a)	Ferencvaros	"	0-0		30,000
1975/76	**UEFA CUP**		**(WINNERS – LIVERPOOL)**				
17th Sept	1 Leg 1	(a)	Hibernian	Sco	0-1		19,219
30th Sept	1 Leg 2	(h)	Hibernian	"	3-1	Toshack 3	29,963
22nd Oct	2 Leg 1	(a)	Real Sociedad	Spa	3-1	Heighway, Callaghan, Thompson	20,000
4th Nov	2 Leg 2	(h)	Real Sociedad	"	6-0	Toshack, Kennedy 2, Fairclough Heighway, Neal	23,796

LIVERPOOL'S RESULTS IN EUROPEAN COMPETITION

Season	Round	Venue	Opponents	Opponent Country	Score	Scorers	Att
1975/76	UEFA CUP (cont)		(WINNERS – LIVERPOOL)				
26th Nov	3 Leg 1	(a)	Slask Wroclaw	Pol	2-1	Kennedy, Toshack	46,000
10th Dec	3 Leg 2	(h)	Slask Wroclaw	"	3-0	Case 3	17,886
3rd Mar	4 Leg 1	(a)	Dynamo Dresden	E.Ger	0-0		33,000
17th Mar	4 Leg 2	(h)	Dynamo Dresden	"	2-1	Case, Keegan	39,300
30th Mar	SF Leg 1	(a)	Barcelona	Spa	1-0	Toshack	70,000
14th Apr	SF Leg 2	(h)	Barcelona	"	1-1	Thompson	55,104
28th Apr	F Leg 1	(h)	FC Bruges	Bel	3-2	Kennedy, Case, Keegan (pen)	49,981
19th May	F Leg 2	(a)	FC Bruges	"	1-1	Keegan	33,000
1976/77	EUROPEAN CUP		(WINNERS – LIVERPOOL)				
14th Sept	1 Leg 1	(h)	Crusaders	N.Ire	2-0	Neal (pen), Toshack	22,442
28th Sept	1 Leg 2	(a)	Crusaders	"	5-0	Keegan, Johnson 2, McDermott Heighway	10,500
20th Oct	2 Leg 1	(a)	Trabzonspor	Tur	0-1		25,000
3rd Nov	2 Leg 2	(h)	Trabzonspor	"	3-0	Heighway, Johnson, Keegan	42,275
2nd Mar	3 Leg 1	(a)	St Etienne	Fra	0-1		38,000
16th Mar	3 Leg 2	(h)	St Etienne	"	3-1	Keegan, Kennedy, Fairclough	55,043
6th Apr	SF Leg 1	(a)	FC Zurich	Swi	3-1	Neal 2 (1 pen), Heighway	30,500
20th Apr	SF Leg 2	(h)	FC Zurich	"	3-0	Case 2, Keegan	50,611
25th May	Final	Rome	B. Moench'bach	W.Ger	3-1	McDermott, Smith, Neal (pen)	52,078
1977/78	EUROPEAN CUP		(WINNERS – LIVERPOOL)				
19th Oct	2 Leg 1	(h)	Dynamo Dresden	E.Ger	5-1	Hansen, Case 2, Neal (pen) Kennedy	39,835
2nd Nov	2 Leg 2	(a)	Dynamo Dresden	"	1-2	Heighway	33,000
1st Mar	3 Leg 1	(a)	Benfica	Por	2-1	Case, Hughes	70,000
15th Mar	3 Leg 2	(h)	Benfica	"	4-1	Callaghan, Dalglish, McDermott, Neal	48,364
29th Mar	SF Leg 1	(a)	B. Moench'bach	W.Ger	1-2	Johnson	66,000
12th Apr	SF Leg 2	(h)	B. Moench'bach	"	3-0	Kennedy, Dalglish, Case	51,500
10th May	Final	Wembley	FC Bruges	Bel	1-0	Dalglish	92,000
1977/78	EURO. SUPER CUP		(WINNERS – LIVERPOOL)				
22nd Nov	Leg 1	(a)	SV Hamburg	W.Ger	1-1	Fairclough	16,000
6th Dec	Leg 2	(h)	SV Hamburg	"	6-0	Thompson, McDermott 3 Fairclough, Dalglish	34,931
1978/79	EUROPEAN CUP		(WINNERS – NOTTINGHAM FOREST)				
13th Sept	1 Leg 1	(a)	Nottingham Forest	Eng	0-2		38,316
27th Sept	1 Leg 2	(h)	Nottingham Forest	"	0-0		51,679
1978/79	EURO. SUPER CUP		(WINNERS – ANDERLECHT)				
4th Dec	1 Leg 1	(a)	Anderlecht	Bel	1-3	Case	35,000
19th Dec	1 Leg 2	(h)	Anderlecht	"	2-1	Hughes, Fairclough	23,598

LIVERPOOL'S RESULTS IN EUROPEAN COMPETITION

Season	Round	Venue	Opponents	Opponent Country	Score	Scorers	Att
1979/80	**EUROPEAN CUP**		**(WINNERS – NOTTINGHAM FOREST)**				
19th Sept	1 Leg 1	(h)	Dynamo Tblisi	Rus	2-1	Johnson, Case	35,270
3rd Oct	1 Leg 2	(a)	Dynamo Tblisi	"	0-3		80,000
1980/81	**EUROPEAN CUP**		**(WINNERS – LIVERPOOL)**				
17th Sept	1 Leg 1	(a)	Oulu Palloseura	Fin	1-1	McDermott	14,000
1st Oct	1 Leg 2	(h)	Oulu Palloseura	"	10-1	Souness 3 (1pen), McDermott 3, Lee, R.Kennedy, Fairclough 2	21,013
22nd Oct	2 Leg 1	(a)	Aberdeen	Sco	1-0	McDermott	24,000
5th Nov	2 Leg 2	(h)	Aberdeen	"	4-0	Miller o.g., Neal, Dalglish, Hansen	36,182
4th Mar	3 Leg 1	(h)	CSKA Sofia	Bul	5-1	Souness 3, Lee, McDermott	37,255
18th Mar	3 Leg 2	(a)	CSKA Sofia	"	1-0	Johnson	65,000
8th Apr	SF Leg 1	(h)	Bayern Munich	W.Ger	0-0		44,543
22nd Apr	SF Leg 2	(a)	Bayern Munich	"	1-1	R.Kennedy	77,600
27th May	Final	Paris	Real Madrid	Spa	1-0	A.Kennedy	48,360
1981/82	**EUROPEAN CUP**		**(WINNERS – ASTON VILLA)**				
16th Sept	1 Leg 1	(a)	Oulu Palloseura	Fin	1-0	Dalglish	8,400
30th Sept	1 Leg 2	(h)	Oulu Palloseura	"	7-0	Dalglish, McDermott 2, R.Kennedy, Johnson, Rush, Lawrenson	20,789
21st Oct	2 Leg 1	(a)	AZ '67 Alkmaar	Hol	2-2	Johnson, Lee	15,000
4th Nov	2 Leg 2	(h)	AZ '67 Alkmaar	"	3-2	McDermott (pen), Rush, Hansen	29,703
3rd Mar	3 Leg 1	(h)	CSKA Sofia	Bul	1-0	Whelan	27,388
17th Mar	3 Leg 2	(a)	CSKA Sofia	"	0-2 aet		60,000
1982/83	**EUROPEAN CUP**		**(WINNERS – HAMBURG)**				
14th Sept	1 Leg 1	(a)	Dundalk	Rep. Ire	4-1	Whelan 2, Rush, Hodgson	16,500
28th Sept	1 Leg 2	(h)	Dundalk	"	1-0	Whelan	12,021
19th Oct	2 Leg 1	(a)	HJK Helsinki	Fin	0-1		5,722
2nd Nov	2 Leg 2	(h)	HJK Helsinki	"	5-0	Dalglish, Johnson, Neal, A.Kennedy 2	16,434
2nd Mar	3 Leg 1	(a)	Widzew Lodz	Pol	0-2		45,531
16th Mar	3 Leg 2	(h)	Widzew Lodz	"	3-2	Neal (pen), Rush, Hodgson	44,494
1983/84	**EUROPEAN CUP**		**(WINNERS – LIVERPOOL)**				
14th Sept	1 Leg 1	(a)	BK Odense	Den	1-0	Dalglish	30,000
28th Sept	1 Leg 2	(h)	BK Odense	"	5-0	Robinson 2, Dalglish 2, Clausen o.g.	14,985
19th Oct	2 Leg 1	(h)	Athletic Bilbao	Spa	0-0		33,063
2nd Nov	2 Leg 2	(a)	Athletic Bilbao	"	1-0	Rush	47,500
7th Mar	3 Leg 1	(h)	Benfica	Por	1-0	Rush	39,096
21st Mar	3 Leg 2	(a)	Benfica	"	4-1	Whelan 2, Johnston, Rush	70,000
11th Apr	SF Leg 1	(h)	D. Bucharest	Rom	1-0	Lee	36,941
25th Apr	SF Leg 2	(a)	D. Bucharest	"	2-1	Rush 2	60,000
30th May	Final	Rome	AS Roma	Ita	1-1 aet	Neal	69,693
			(Liverpool won 4-2 on penalties)				

LIVERPOOL'S RESULTS IN EUROPEAN COMPETITION

Season	Round	Venue	Opponents	Opponent Country	Score	Scorers	Att
1984/85	**EUROPEAN CUP**		**(WINNERS – JUVENTUS)**				
19th Sept	1 Leg 1	(a)	Lech Poznan	Pol	1-0	Wark	35,000
3rd Oct	1 Leg 2	(h)	Lech Poznan	"	4-0	Wark 3, Walsh	22,143
24th Oct	2 Leg 1	(h)	Benfica	Por	3-1	Rush 3	27,733
7th Nov	2 Leg 2	(a)	Benfica	"	0-1		50,000
6th Mar	3 Leg 1	(a)	Austria Vienna	Aut	1-1	Nicol	21,000
20th Mar	3 Leg 2	(h)	Austria Vienna	"	4-1	Walsh 2, Nicol, Obermayer o.g.	32,761
10th Apr	SF Leg 1	(h)	Panathinaikos	Gre	4-0	Wark, Rush 2, Beglin	39,488
24th Apr	SF Leg 2	(a)	Panathinaikos	"	1-0	Lawrenson	60,000
29th May	Final	Brussels	Juventus	Ita	0-1		60,000
1984/85	**EURO. SUPER CUP**		**(WINNERS – JUVENTUS)**				
16th Jan		(a)	Juventus	Ita	0-2		60,000
1991/92	**UEFA CUP**		**(WINNERS – AJAX)**				
18th Sept	1 Leg 1	(h)	Kuusysi Lahti	Fin	6-1	Saunders 4, Houghton 2	17,131
2nd Oct	1 Leg 2	(a)	Kuusysi Lahti	"	0-1		8,435
23rd Oct	2 Leg 1	(a)	Auxerre	Fra	0-2		16,500
6th Nov	2 Leg 2	(h)	Auxerre	"	3-0	Molby (pen), Marsh, Walters	23,094
27th Nov	3 Leg 1	(a)	Swarovski Tirol	Aut	2-0	Saunders 2	12,500
11th Dec	3 Leg 2	(h)	Swarovski Tirol	"	4-0	Saunders 3, Venison	16,007
4th Mar	4 Leg 1	(a)	Genoa	Ita	0-2		40,000
18th Mar	4 Leg 2	(h)	Genoa	"	1-2	Rush	38,840
1992/93	**CUP WINNERS' CUP**		**(WINNERS – PARMA)**				
16th Sept	1 Leg 1	(h)	Apollon Limassol	Cyp	6-1	Stewart 2, Rush 4	12,769
29th Sept	1 Leg 2	(a)	Apollon Limassol	"	2-1	Rush, Hutchison	8,000
22nd Oct	2 Leg 1	(a)	Spartak Moscow	Rus	2-4	Wright, McManaman	60,000
4th Nov	2 Leg 2	(h)	Spartak Moscow	"	0-2		37,993
1995/96	**UEFA CUP**		**(WINNERS – BAYERN MUNICH)**				
12th Sept	1 Leg 1	(a)	S. Vladikavkaz	Rus	2-1	McManaman, Redknapp	43,000
26th Sept	1 Leg 2	(h)	S. Vladikavkaz	"	0-0		35,042
17th Oct	2 Leg 1	(a)	Brondby	Den	0-0		37,648
31st Oct	2 Leg 2	(h)	Brondby	"	0-1		35,878
1996/97	**CUP WINNERS' CUP**		**(WINNERS – FC BARCELONA)**				
12th Sept	1 Leg 1	(a)	MyPa 47	Fin	1-0	Bjornebye	5,500
26th Sept	1 Leg 2	(h)	MyPa 47	"	3-1	Berger, Collymore, Barnes	39,013
17th Oct	2 Leg 1	(a)	Sion	Swi	2-1	Fowler, Barnes	16,500
31st Oct	2 Leg 2	(h)	Sion	"	6-3	McManaman, Bjornebye Barnes, Fowler 2, Berger	38,514
6th Mar	3 Leg 1	(a)	Brann Bergen	Nor	1-1	Fowler	12,700
20th Mar	3 Leg 2	(h)	Brann Bergen	"	3-0	Fowler 2 (1 pen), Collymore	40,326
10th Apr	SF Leg 1	(a)	Paris St Germain	Fra	0-3		35,142
24th Apr	SF Leg 2	(h)	Paris St Germain	"	2-0	Fowler, Wright	38,984

LIVERPOOL'S RESULTS IN EUROPEAN COMPETITION

Season	Round	Venue	Opponents	Opponent Country	Score	Scorers	Att
1997/98	**UEFA CUP**		**(WINNERS – INTER MILAN)**				
16th Sept	1 Leg 1	(a)	Celtic	Sco	2-2	Owen, McManaman	48,526
30th Sept	1 Leg 2	(h)	Celtic	"	0-0		38,205
21st Oct	2 Leg 1	(a)	RC Strasbourg	Fra	0-3		18,813
4th Nov	2 Leg 2	(h)	RC Strasbourg	"	2-0	Fowler (pen), Riedle	32,426
1998/99	**UEFA CUP**		**(WINNERS – PARMA)**				
15th Sept	1 Leg 1	(a)	FC Kosice	Slovakia	3-0	Berger, Riedle, Owen	4,500
29th Sept	1 Leg 2	(h)	FC Kosice	"	5-0	Redknapp 2, Ince, Fowler 2	23,792
20th Oct	2 Leg 1	(h)	Valencia	Spa	0-0		36,004
3rd Nov	2 Leg 2	(a)	Valencia	"	2-2	McManaman, Berger	49,000
24th Nov	3 Leg 1	(a)	Celta Vigo	Spa	1-3	Owen	32,000
8th Dec	3 Leg 2	(h)	Celta Vigo	"	0-1		30,289
2000/01	**UEFA CUP**		**(WINNERS – LIVERPOOL)**				
14th Sept	1 Leg 1	(a)	Rapid Bucharest	Rom	1-0	Barmby	12,000
28th Sept	1 Leg 2	(h)	Rapid Bucharest	"	0-0		37,954
26th Oct	2 Leg 1	(h)	Slovan Liberec	Cz Rep	1-0	Heskey	29,662
9th Nov	2 Leg 2	(a)	Slovan Liberec	"	3-2	Barmby, Heskey, Owen	6,808
23rd Nov	3 Leg 1	(a)	Olympiakos	Gre	2-2	Barmby, Gerrard	43,855
7th Dec	3 Leg 2	(h)	Olympiakos	"	2-0	Heskey, Barmby	35,484
15th Feb	4 Leg 1	(a)	AS Roma	Ita	2-0	Owen 2	59,718
22nd Feb	4 Leg 2	(h)	AS Roma	"	0-1		43,688
8th Mar	5 Leg 1	(a)	FC Porto	Por	0-0		21,150
15th Mar	5 Leg 2	(h)	FC Porto	"	2-0	Murphy, Owen	40,502
5th Apr	SF Leg 1	(a)	Barcelona	Spa	0-0		90,000
19th Apr	SF Leg 2	(h)	Barcelona	"	1-0	McAllister	44,203
16th May	Final	Dortmund	Alaves	Spa	5-4 aet	Babbel, Gerrard, McAllister (pen), Fowler, Geli o.g.	65,000

(Liverpool won on golden goal)

Season	Round	Venue	Opponents	Opponent Country	Score	Scorers	Att
2001/02	**EUROPEAN CUP**		**(WINNERS – REAL MADRID)**				
8th Aug	Q. Leg 1	(a)	FC Haka	Fin	5-0	Heskey, Owen 3, Hyypia	33,217
21st Aug	Q. Leg 2	(h)	FC Haka	"	4-1	Fowler, Redknapp, Heskey, Wilson o.g.	31,602
	First Group Stage						
11th Sept	Group B	(h)	Boavista	Por	1-1	Owen	30,015
19th Sept	Group B	(a)	B. Dortmund	Ger	0-0		50,000
26th Sept	Group B	(h)	Dynamo Kiev	Ukr	1-0	Litmanen	33,513
16th Oct	Group B	(a)	Dynamo Kiev	"	2-1	Murphy, Gerrard	55,000
24th Oct	Group B	(a)	Boavista	Por	1-1	Murphy	6,000
30th Oct	Group B	(h)	B. Dortmund	Ger	2-0	Smicer, Wright	41,507
	Second Group Stage						
20th Nov	Group B	(h)	Barcelona	Spa	1-3	Owen	41,521
5th Dec	Group B	(a)	AS Roma	Ita	0-0		57,819
20th Feb	Group B	(h)	Galatasaray	Tur	0-0		41,605
26th Feb	Group B	(a)	Galatasaray	"	1-1	Heskey	22,100
13th Mar	Group B	(a)	Barcelona	Spa	0-0		75,362
19th Mar	Group B	(h)	AS Roma	Ita	2-0	Litmanen (pen), Heskey	41,794
3rd Apr	QF Leg 1	(h)	B. Leverkusen	Ger	1-0	Hyypia	42,454
9th Apr	QF Leg 2	(a)	B. Leverkusen	"	2-4	Xavier, Litmanen	22,500

LIVERPOOL'S RESULTS IN EUROPEAN COMPETITION

Season	Round	Venue	Opponents	Opponent Country	Score	Scorers	Att
2001/02	**EURO. SUPER CUP**	**(WINNERS – LIVERPOOL)**					
24th Aug		Monaco	Bayern Munich	Ger	3-2	Riise, Heskey, Owen	15,000
2002/03	**EUROPEAN CUP**	**(WINNERS – AC MILAN)**					
			First Group Stage				
17th Sept	Group B (a)		Valencia	Spa	0-2		43,000
25th Sept	Group B (h)		FC Basel	Swi	1-1	Baros	37,634
2nd Oct	Group B (h)		Spartak Moscow	Rus	5-0	Heskey 2, Cheyrou, Hyypia, Diao	40,812
22nd Oct	Group B (a)		Spartak Moscow	"	3-1	Owen 3	15,000
30th Oct	Group B (h)		Valencia	Spa	0-1		41,831
12th Nov	Group B (a)		FC Basel	Swi	3-3	Murphy, Smicer, Owen	35,000
2002/03	**UEFA CUP**	**(WINNERS – FC PORTO)**					
28th Nov	3 Leg 1 (a)		Vitesse Arnhem	Hol	1-0	Owen	28,000
12th Dec	3 Leg 2 (h)		Vitesse Arnhem	"	1-0	Owen	23,576
20th Feb	4 Leg 1 (a)		Auxerre	Fra	1-0	Hyypia	20,452
27th Feb	4 Leg 2 (h)		Auxerre	"	2-0	Owen, Murphy	34,252
13th Mar	5 Leg 1 (a)		Celtic	Sco	1-1	Heskey	59,759
20th Mar	5 Leg 2 (h)		Celtic	"	0-2		44,238
2003/04	**UEFA CUP**	**(WINNERS – VALENCIA)**					
24th Sept	1 Leg 1 (a)		Olimpija Ljubljana	Slovenia	1-1	Owen	10,000
15th Oct	1 Leg 2 (h)		Olimpija Ljubljana	"	3-0	LeTallec, Heskey, Kewell	42,880
6th Nov	2 Leg 1 (a)		Steaua Bucharest	Rom	1-1	Traore	25,000
27th Nov	2 Leg 2 (h)		Steaua Bucharest	"	1-0	Kewell	42,837
26th Feb	3 Leg 1 (h)		Levski Sofia	Bul	2-0	Gerrard, Kewell	39,149
3rd Mar	3 Leg 2 (a)		Levski Sofia	"	4-2	Gerrard, Owen, Hamann, Hyypia	40,281
11th Mar	4 Leg 1 (h)		O. Marseille	Fra	1-1	Baros	41,270
25th Mar	4 Leg 2 (a)		O. Marseille	"	1-2	Heskey	50,000
2004/05	**EUROPEAN CUP**	**(WINNERS – LIVERPOOL)**					
10th Aug	Q. Leg 1 (a)		AK Graz	Aut	2-0	Gerrard 2	15,000
24th Aug	Q. Leg 2 (h)		AK Graz	"	0-1		42,950
			Group Stage				
15th Sept	Group A (h)		AS Monaco	Fra	2-0	Cisse, Baros	33,517
28th Sept	Group A (a)		Olympiakos	Gre	0-1		33,000
19th Oct	Group A (h)		D. La Coruna	Spa	0-0		40,236
3rd Nov	Group A (a)		D. La Coruna	"	1-0	Andrade o.g.	32,000
23rd Nov	Group A (a)		AS Monaco	Fra	0-1		15,000
8th Dec	Group A (h)		Olympiakos	Gre	3-1	Sinama-Pongolle, Mellor, Gerrard	42,045
22nd Feb	L. 16 L1 (h)		B. Leverkusen	Ger	3-1	Garcia, Riise, Hamann	40,942
9th Mar	L. 16 L2 (a)		B. Leverkusen	"	3-1	Garcia 2, Baros	23,000
5th Apr	QF Leg 1 (h)		Juventus	Ita	2-1	Hyypia, Garcia	41,216
13th Apr	QF Leg 2 (a)		Juventus	"	0-0		55,464
27th Apr	SF Leg 1 (a)		Chelsea	Eng	0-0		40,497
3rd May	SF Leg 2 (h)		Chelsea	"	1-0	Garcia	42,529
25th May	Final	Istanbul	AC Milan	Ita	3-3 aet	Gerrard, Smicer, Alonso	65,000
			(Liverpool won 3-2 on penalties)				

LIVERPOOL'S RESULTS IN EUROPEAN COMPETITION

Season	Round	Venue	Opponents	Opponent Country	Score	Scorers	Att
2005/06	**EUROPEAN CUP**		**(WINNERS – BARCELONA)**				
13th July	Q.1 Leg 1	(h)	TNS	Wal	3-0	Gerrard 3	44,760
19th July	Q.1 Leg 2	(a)	TNS	"	3-0	Cisse, Gerrard 2	8,009
26th July	Q.2 Leg 1	(a)	FBK Kaunas	Lith	3-1	Cisse, Carragher, Gerrard (pen)	8,300
2nd Aug	Q.2 Leg 2	(h)	FBK Kaunas	"	2-0	Gerrard, Cisse	43,717
10th Aug	Q.3 Leg 1	(a)	CSKA Sofia	Bul	3-1	Cisse, Morientes 2	16,512
23rd Aug	Q.3 Leg 2	(h)	CSKA Sofia	"	0-1		42,175
	Group Stage						
13th Sept	Group G	(a)	Real Betis	Spa	2-1	Sinama-Pongolle, Garcia	45,000
28th Sept	Group G	(h)	Chelsea	Eng	0-0		42,743
19th Oct	Group G	(a)	Anderlecht	Bel	1-0	Cisse	25,000
1st Nov	Group G	(h)	Anderlecht	Bel	3-0	Morientes, Garcia, Cisse	42,607
23rd Nov	Group G	(h)	Real Betis	Spa	0-0		42,077
6th Dec	Group G	(a)	Chelsea	Eng	0-0		41,598
21st Feb	L. 16 L1	(a)	Benfica	Por	0-1		65,000
8th Mar	L. 16 L2	(h)	Benfica	Por	0-2		42,745
2005/06	**EURO. SUPER CUP**		**(WINNERS – LIVERPOOL)**				
26th Aug		Monaco	CSKA Moscow	Rus	3-1 aet	Cisse 2, Garcia	18,000
2006/07	**EUROPEAN CUP**		**(WINNERS – AC MILAN)**				
9th Aug	Q.3 Leg 1	(h)	Maccabi Haifa	Isr	2-1	Bellamy, Gonzalez	40,058
22nd Aug	Q.3 Leg 2	(a)	Maccabi Haifa	"	1-1	Crouch	12,500
	Group Stage						
12th Sept	Group C	(a)	PSV Eindhoven	Hol	0-0		35,000
27th Sept	Group C	(h)	Galatasaray	Tur	3-2	Crouch 2, Garcia	41,976
18th Oct	Group C	(a)	Bordeaux	Fra	1-0	Crouch	33,000
31st Oct	Group C	(h)	Bordeaux	Fra	3-0	Garcia 2, Gerrard	41,978
22nd Nov	Group C	(h)	PSV Eindhoven	Hol	2-0	Gerrard, Crouch	41,948
5th Dec	Group C	(a)	Galatasaray	Tur	2-3	Fowler 2	23,000
21st Feb	L. 16 L1	(a)	Barcelona	Spa	2-1	Bellamy, Riise	88,000
6th Mar	L. 16 L2	(h)	Barcelona	Spa	0-1		42,579
3rd Apr	QF L1	(a)	PSV Eindhoven	Hol	3-0	Gerrard, Riise, Crouch	36,500
11th Apr	QF L2	(h)	PSV Eindhoven	Hol	1-0	Crouch	41,447
25th Apr	SF L1	(a)	Chelsea	Eng	0-1		39,483
1st May	SF L2	(h)	Chelsea	Eng aet	1-0	Agger	42,554
			(Liverpool won 4-1 on penalties)				
23rd May	Final	Athens	AC Milan	Ita	1-2	Kuyt	74,000
2007/08	**EUROPEAN CUP**		**(WINNERS – MANCHESTER UNITED)**				
15th Aug	Q. Leg 1	(a)	Toulouse	Fra	1-0	Voronin	30,380
28th Aug	Q. Leg 2	(h)	Toulouse	"	4-0	Crouch, Hyypia, Kuyt 2	43,118
	Group Stage						
18th Sept	Group A	(a)	FC Porto	Por	1-1	Kuyt	41,208
3rd Oct	Group A	(h)	Marseille	Fra	0-1		41,355
24th Oct	Group A	(a)	Besiktas	Tur	1-2	Gerrard	32,500
6th Nov	Group A	(h)	Besiktas	"	8-0	Crouch 2, Benayoun 3, Gerrard, Babel 2	41,143

LIVERPOOL'S RESULTS IN EUROPEAN COMPETITION

Season	Round	Venue	Opponents	Opponent Country	Score	Scorers	Att
2007/08	**EURO. CUP (cont)**		**(WINNERS – MANCHESTER UNITED)**				
28th Nov	Group A	(h)	FC Porto	Por	4-1	Torres 2, Gerrard (pen), Crouch	41,095
11th Dec	Group A	(a)	Marseille	Fra	4-0	Gerrard, Torres, Kuyt, Babel	53,000
19th Feb	L. 16 L1	(h)	Inter Milan	Ita	2-0	Kuyt, Gerrard	41,999
11th Mar	L. 16 L2	(a)	Inter Milan	"	1-0	Torres	80,000
2nd Apr	QF Leg 1	(a)	Arsenal	Eng	1-1	Kuyt	60,041
8th Apr	QF Leg 2	(h)	Arsenal	"	4-2	Hyypia, Torres, Gerrard (pen), Babel	41,985
22nd Apr	SF Leg 1	(h)	Chelsea	Eng	1-1	Kuyt	42,180
30th Apr	SF Leg 2	(a)	Chelsea	"	2-3 aet	Torres, Babel	38,900
2008/09	**EUROPEAN CUP**		**(WINNERS – BARCELONA)**				
13th Aug	Q.3 Leg 1	(a)	Standard Liege	Bel	0-0		25,000
27th Aug	Q.3 Leg 2	(h)	Standard Liege	"	1-0 aet	Kuyt	43,889
42,175			**Group Stage**				
16th Sept	Group D	(a)	Marseille	Fra	2-1	Gerrard 2 (1 pen)	45,000
1st Oct	Group D	(h)	PSV Eindhoven	Hol	3-1	Kuyt, Keane, Gerrard	41,097
22nd Oct	Group D	(a)	Atletico Madrid	Spa	1-1	Keane	48,769
4th Nov	Group D	(h)	Atletico Madrid	Spa	1-1	Gerrard (pen)	42,010
26th Nov	Group D	(h)	Marseille	Fra	1-0	Gerrard	40,024
9th Dec	Group D	(a)	PSV Eindhoven	Hol	3-1	Babel, Riera, Ngog	35,000
25th Feb	L. 16 L1	(a)	Real Madrid	Spa	1-0	Benayoun	85,000
10th Mar	L. 16 L2	(h)	Real Madrid	"	4-0	Torres, Gerrard 2 (1 pen) Dossena	42,550
8th Apr	QF Leg 1	(h)	Chelsea	Eng	1-3	Torres	42,543
14th Apr	QF Leg 2	(a)	Chelsea	"	4-4	Aurelio, Alonso (pen), Lucas, Kuyt	38,286
2009/10	**EUROPEAN CUP**		**(WINNERS – INTER MILAN)**				
			Group Stage				
16th Sept	Group E	(h)	Debreceni VSC	Hun	1-0	Kuyt	41,591
29th Sept	Group E	(a)	Fiorentina	Ita	0-2		33,426
20th Oct	Group E	(h)	Lyon	Fra	1-2	Benayoun	41,562
4th Nov	Group E	(a)	Lyon	Fra	1-1	Babel	39,180
24th Nov	Group E	(a)	Debreceni VSC	Hun	1-0	Ngog	41,500
9th Dec	Group E	(h)	Fiorentina	Ita	1-2	Benayoun	40,863
2009/10	**EUROPA LEAGUE**		**(WINNERS – ATLETICO MADRID)**				
18th Feb	R. 32 L1	(h)	Unirea Urziceni	Rom	1-0	Ngog	40,450
25th Feb	R. 32 L2	(a)	Unirea Urziceni	"	3-1	Mascherano, Babel, Gerrard	25,000
11th Mar	R. 16 L1	(a)	Lille	Fra	0-1		18,000
18th Mar	R. 16 L2	(h)	Lille	"	3-0	Gerrard (pen), Torres 2	38,139
1st Apr	QF Leg 1	(a)	Benfica	Por	1-2	Agger	62,629
8th Apr	QF Leg 2	(h)	Benfica	"	4-1	Kuyt, Lucas, Torres 2	42,377
22nd Apr	SF Leg 1	(a)	Atletico Madrid	Spa	0-1		50,000
29th Apr	SF Leg 2	(h)	Atletico Madrid	"	2-1 aet	Aquilani, Benayoun	42,040

CLASSIC EUROPEAN SEASON – 1977/78

Liverpool began the defence of their European crown with a 6-3 aggregate success over East German champions Dynamo Dresden. Handed a first-round bye as holders, the Reds eased to a 5-1 first-leg success at Anfield, a game in which a youthful Alan Hansen headed his first goal for the club. The second leg saw a 2-1 defeat, enough to secure a quarter-final spot.

Before then, there was the small matter of a two-legged European Super Cup showdown with Hamburg – for whom Reds legend Kevin Keegan had signed only months earlier. A 1-1 draw in West Germany was followed by a stunning 6-0 Liverpool victory, a game which saw Terry McDermott come of age in a red shirt. His hat-trick came in 16 minutes either side of half-time, with Phil Thompson – who hit the first – David Fairclough and Kenny Dalglish also on target.

Portugal was next up on the European trail, and a meeting with Benfica at the Stadium of Light. Goals from Jimmy Case and Emlyn Hughes earned an impressive 2-1 win in front of 80,000 fans. The second leg saw a 4-1 victory with veteran Ian Callaghan setting the Reds on the way to a 6-2 aggregate victory.

The semi-final saw the Reds again paired with Borussia Moenchengladbach, the West German champions whom they had defeated 10 months earlier to secure their first European Cup crown. Liverpool went down to a 2-1 away defeat in the first leg. Sub David Johnson's 88th-minute strike, which levelled the tie, was a useful away goal despite the disappointment of Rainer Bonhof's last minute free-kick giving the West Germans an advantage. The game at the Rheinstadion in Dusseldorf – the tie had been switched from Borussia's smaller Bokelberg Stadium – is also notable for the fact it was Ian Callaghan's 857th and final appearance for the Reds.

The second leg saw first-half goals from Ray Kennedy and Kenny Dalglish leave the Reds in control, before Jimmy Case's 56th-minute strike put the tie out of reach to secure a 4-2 aggregate victory for the English champions.

The final was against Belgian champions FC Bruges, who Liverpool had beaten two years earlier in the UEFA Cup final. The game proved a drab affair, with Liverpool being constantly stifled by the defensive tactics of their opponents. It took a moment of magic from Kenny Dalglish to delight the vast majority of the Wembley crowd, his 65th-minute 'dink' over on-rushing goalkeeper Birger Jensen a moment that would pass into Anfield folklore. It was the Scotland star's 31st goal of a memorable first season with the club.

EUROPEAN CUP STATISTICS 1977/78

PLAYER	AGE (START OF 77/78)	GAMES	GOALS
Ian Callaghan	35	5	1
Jimmy Case	23	7	4
Ray Clemence	29	7	0
Kenny Dalglish	26	7	3
David Fairclough	20	1 + 1	0
Alan Hansen	22	3 + 1	1
Steve Heighway	29	6 + 1	1
Emlyn Hughes	29	7	1
David Johnson	25	0 + 1	1
Joey Jones	22	2	0
Ray Kennedy	26	7	2
Terry McDermott	25	6	1
Phil Neal	26	7	2
Tommy Smith	32	4	0
Graeme Souness	24	2 + 1	0
John Toshack	28	1	0
Phil Thompson	23	5	0

Team line-ups

Liverpool (4-4-1-1):

Fairclough

Dalglish

Kennedy Souness McDermott Case

Hughes Thompson Hansen Neal

Clemence

Sub: Heighway (Case) 63
Subs not used: Ogrizovic, Jones, Callaghan, Irwin

FC Bruges (4-4-2):

Sorensen Simoen

Ku de Cubber Vandereycken Cools

Maes Leekens Krieger Bastijns

Jensen

Subs: Sanders (Ku) 60, Volders (Maes) 70
Subs not used: N/A

LIVERPOOL FC   1
FC BRUGES   0

European Cup
Final
Wembley Stadium, London, England
Wednesday May 10, 1978.
Attendance: 92,000

Goal: Dalglish (65)
Bookings: Case (Liverpool),
Vandereycken (FC Bruges)
Referee: Charles Corver (Holland)

EUROPEAN PLAYER RECORDS

CORRECT AT END OF 2009/10 SEASON – Games played includes substitute appearances

EUROPEAN APPEARANCES – ALL COMPETITIONS (46+ GAMES)

		FIRST-TEAM CAREER	GAMES
1	Jamie Carragher	1997–	129
2	Steven Gerrard	1998–	114
3	Sami Hyypia	1999-2009	94
4	Ian Callaghan	1960-1978	89
5	Tommy Smith	1963-1978	85
6	Ray Clemence	1968-1981	80
7	Emlyn Hughes	1967-1979	79
=	John Arne Riise	2001-2008	79
9	Phil Neal	1974-1985	74
10	Steve Heighway	1970-1981	67
11	Chris Lawler	1963-1975	66
12	Pepe Reina	2005–	65
13	Dietmar Hamann	1999-2006	61
14	Kenny Dalglish	1977-1990	51
=	Steve Finnan	2003-2008	51
16	Ray Kennedy	1974-1981	50
=	Michael Owen	1997-2004	50
=	Phil Thompson	1972-1983	50
19	Xabi Alonso	2004-2009	48
20	Dirk Kuyt	2006–	47
21	Alan Hansen	1977-1990	46
=	Danny Murphy	1997-2004	46

EUROPEAN CUP/UEFA CHAMPIONS LEAGUE APPEARANCES (30+ GAMES)

		FIRST-TEAM CAREER	GAMES
1	Jamie Carragher	1997–	91
2	Steven Gerrard	1998–	81
2	John Arne Riise	2001-2008	68
3	Sami Hyypia	1999-2009	67
5	Phil Neal	1974-1985	57
6	Pepe Reina	2005–	56
7	Xabi Alonso	2004-2009	47
=	Kenny Dalglish	1977-1990	47
9	Steve Finnan	2003-2008	44
10	Alan Hansen	1977-1990	43
11	Dirk Kuyt	2006–	40
12	Dietmar Hamann	1999-2006	37
13	Graeme Souness	1978-1984	36
14	Alan Kennedy	1978-1985	34
15	Ray Clemence	1968-1981	33
=	Sammy Lee	1978-1986	33
17	Ray Kennedy	1974-1981	32
=	Phil Thompson	1972-1983	32
19	Luis Garcia	2004-2007	31
=	Terry McDermott	1974-1982	31
21	Ian Callaghan	1960-1978	30
=	Peter Crouch	2005-2008	30
=	Bruce Grobbelaar	1981-1994	30

First-team career noted as the year a player made his first appearance for the first team, and the year they made their last appearance

EUROPEAN PLAYER RECORDS

INTER-CITIES FAIRS CUP/UEFA CUP/EUROPA LEAGUE APPEARANCES (19+ GAMES)

		FIRST-TEAM CAREER	GAMES
1	Emlyn Hughes	1967-1979	45
2	Ian Callaghan	1960-1978	41
=	Tommy Smith	1963-1978	41
4	Ray Clemence	1968-1981	36
=	Jamie Carragher	1997-	36
6	Chris Lawler	1963-1975	35
7	Michael Owen	1997-2004	33
8	Steven Gerrard	1998-	32
9	Steve Heighway	1970-1981	30
10	Brian Hall	1969-1976	25
=	Sami Hyypia	1999-2009	25
12	Robbie Fowler	1993-2001 & 2006-2007	24
=	Danny Murphy	1997-2004	24
=	John Toshack	1970-1977	24
15	Larry Lloyd	1969-1974	23
16	Dietmar Hamann	1999-2006	22
=	Emile Heskey	2000-2004	22
=	Kevin Keegan	1971-1977	22
=	Alec Lindsay	1969-1977	22
20	Peter Thompson	1963-1972	20
21	Steve McManaman	1990-1999	19

EUROPEAN CUP WINNERS' CUP APPEARANCES (8+ GAMES)

		FIRST-TEAM CAREER	GAMES
1	Ian Callaghan	1960-1978	17
2	Tommy Smith	1963-1978	16
3	Chris Lawler	1963-1975	15
4	Steve McManaman	1990-1999	11
=	Jamie Redknapp	1991-2001	11
=	Peter Thompson	1963-1972	11
7	Gerry Byrne	1957-1969	9
=	David James	1992-1999	9
=	Tommy Lawrence	1962-1971	9
=	Willie Stevenson	1962-1967	9
=	Ian St John	1961-1971	9
=	Ron Yeats	1961-1971	9
13	Stig Inge Bjornebye	1992-1999	8
=	Ray Clemence	1968-1981	8
=	Steve Heighway	1970-1981	8
=	Emlyn Hughes	1967-1979	8
=	Jason McAteer	1995-1999	8
=	Michael Thomas	1991-1998	8
=	Mark Wright	1991-1998	8

First-team career noted as the year a player made his first appearance for the first team,
and the year they made their last appearance

EUROPEAN PLAYER RECORDS

CORRECT AT END OF 2009/10 SEASON – Games played includes substitute appearances

EUROPEAN GOALS

		FIRST-TEAM CAREER	GAMES	GOALS
1	Steven Gerrard	1998-	114	34
2	Michael Owen	1997-2004	50	22
3	Ian Rush	1980-87 & 1988-96	38	20
4	Roger Hunt	1959-1969	31	17
5	Terry McDermott	1974-1982	34	15
6	Robbie Fowler	1993-2001 & 2006-07	44	14
7	Jimmy Case	1975-1981	35	13
=	Emile Heskey	2000-2004	45	13
=	Dirk Kuyt	2006-	47	13
10	Fernando Torres	2007-	28	12
=	Kevin Keegan	1971-1977	40	12
=	Ray Kennedy	1974-1981	50	12
13	Peter Crouch	2005-2008	30	11
=	Luis Garcia	2004-2007	32	11
=	Kenny Dalglish	1977-1990	51	11
=	Chris Lawler	1963-1975	66	11
=	Steve Heighway	1970-1981	67	11
=	Phil Neal	1974-1985	74	11

(There are 110 different Liverpool goalscorers in European competition)

EUROPEAN CUP/UEFA CHAMPIONS LEAGUE GOALS

		FIRST-TEAM CAREER	GAMES	GOALS
1	Steven Gerrard	1998-	81	28
2	Ian Rush	1980-87 & 1988-96	25	14
3	Terry McDermott	1974-1982	31	12
=	Dirk Kuyt	2006-	40	12
5	Peter Crouch	2005-2008	30	11
6	Roger Hunt	1959-1969	14	10
=	Luis Garcia	2004-2007	31	10
=	Kenny Dalglish	1977-1990	47	10
=	Phil Neal	1974-1985	57	10
10	Michael Owen	1997-2004	16	9
11	David Johnson	1976-1982	20	8
=	Fernando Torres	2007-	24	8
13	Ian St John	1961-1971	13	7
=	Jimmy Case	1975-1981	22	7
=	Djibril Cisse	2004-2006	22	7
=	Ryan Babel	2007-	26	7
=	Emile Heskey	2000-2004	22	6
=	Ronnie Whelan	1981-1994	23	6
=	Yossi Benayoun	2007-2010	26	6
=	Ray Kennedy	1974-1981	32	6
=	Graeme Souness	1978-1984	36	6
=	Sami Hyypia	1999-2009	67	6
23	John Wark	1984-1987	9	5

First-team career noted as the year a player made his first appearance for the first team, and the year they made their last appearance

EUROPEAN PLAYER RECORDS

CORRECT AT END OF 2009/10 SEASON – Games played includes substitute appearances

INTER-CITIES FAIRS CUP/UEFA CUP/EUROPA LEAGUE GOALS

		FIRST-TEAM CAREER	GAMES	GOALS
1	Michael Owen	1997-2004	33	12
2	Dean Saunders	1991-1992	5	9
3	John Toshack	1970-1977	24	8
4	Kevin Keegan	1971-1977	22	7
5	Phil Boersma	1969-1975	13	6
=	Steven Gerrard	1998-	32	6
=	Ian Callaghan	1960-1978	41	6
=	Alun Evans	1968-1972	10	6
=	Emile Heskey	2000-2004	22	6
=	Emlyn Hughes	1967-1979	45	6
11	Jimmy Case	1975-1981	9	5
=	Steve Heighway	1970-1981	30	5
=	Roger Hunt	1959-1969	10	5
=	Tommy Smith	1963-1978	41	5

EUROPEAN CUP WINNERS' CUP GOALS

		FIRST-TEAM CAREER	GAMES	GOALS
1	Robbie Fowler	1993-2001 & 2006-2007	7	7
2	Chris Lawler	1963-1975	15	5
=	Ian Rush	1980-1987 & 1988-1996	4	5
4	John Barnes	1987-1997	7	3

EUROPEAN RANKINGS 2010

Based on UEFA co-efficient points taken from a club's performances in European competition over the last five seasons, the following table is the ranking of the continent's top sides, as noted at the end of the 2009/2010 season.

	CLUB	RANKING POINTS
1	FC Barcelona	136.951
2	Manchester United	125.371
3	Chelsea	118.371
4	Arsenal	115.371
=	**Liverpool**	**115.371**
6	Bayern Munich	110.841
7	Sevilla	108.951
8	Inter Milan	100.867
9	AC Milan	99.867
10	Olympique Lyon	96.748
11	Werder Bremen	94.841
12	Hamburg	86.841
13	Real Madrid	84.951
14	AS Roma	83.867
15	FC Porto	76.659
16	Shakhtar Donetsk	73.910
17	Benfica	72.659
18	Villarreal	70.951
19	Bordeaux	67.748
20	Valencia	66.951

BIGGEST EUROPEAN VICTORIES

DATE	OPPONENTS	VENUE	COMPETITION	SCORE
17th Sept 1974	Stromsgodset	Home	European Cup Winners' Cup	11-0
16th Sept 1969	Dundalk	Home	Inter Cities Fairs Cup	10-0
1st Oct 1980	Oulu Palloseura	Home	European Cup	10-1
7th Nov 1967	TSV Munich 1860	Home	Inter-Cities Fairs Cup	8-0
6th Nov 2007	Besiktas	Home	Champions League	8-0
30th Sept 1981	Oulu Palloseura	Home	European Cup	7-0
4th Nov 1975	Real Sociedad	Home	UEFA Cup	6-0
6th Dec 1977	SV Hamburg	Home	European Super Cup	6-0
14th Sept 1964	Reykjavik	Home	European Cup	6-1
18th Sept 1991	Kuusysi Lahti	Home	UEFA Cup	6-1
16th Sept 1992	Apollon Limassol	Home	European Cup Winners' Cup	6-1

21st century record – The scoreboard scene from the Champions League victory over Besiktas

MOST EUROPEAN SEMI-FINALS – BRITISH CLUBS

CLUB	EURO. CUP/ CHAMP. LGE	EURO. CUP WINNERS' CUP	FAIRS/UEFA CUP/ EUROPA LGE	TOTAL
Liverpool	9	2	5	16
Manchester United	11	2	1	14
Chelsea	5	4	1	10
Leeds United	3	1	5	9
Arsenal	2	3	2	7
Tottenham Hotspur	1	2	4	7
Celtic	3	2	1	6
Rangers	1	2	2	5
Birmingham City	0	0	3	3
Nottingham Forest	2	0	1	3
West Ham United	0	3	0	3
Aberdeen	0	2	0	2
Dundee	1	0	1	2
Dundee United	1	0	1	2
Hibernian	1	0	1	2
Manchester City	0	2	0	2
Newcastle United	0	0	2	2
Wolverhampton W.	0	1	1	2

EUROPEAN GOALS

Steven Gerrard set a new landmark record in British football during Liverpool's European campaign in 2009/10. His goal against Unirea Urziceni in the Europa League took him above Alan Shearer as the record British goalscorer in European competition (note Shearer's total includes 2 goals scored in the Intertoto Cup). He is also third in the European goals for one English club list, behind Ruud van Nistelrooy and Thierry Henry. Incidentally the list includes each of the three European tournaments past and present, plus the European/UEFA Super Cup and Intertoto Cup.

MOST GOALS BY A BRITISH PLAYER FOR AN ENGLISH CLUB IN EUROPE

PLAYER	CLUB (S)	GOALS	EUROPEAN CAREER
Steven Gerrard	Liverpool	34	1998-
Alan Shearer	Blackburn, Newcastle	32	1994-2006
Peter Lorimer	Leeds United	30	1962-1978
Ryan Giggs	Manchester United	28	1991-
Denis Law	Manchester United	28	1962-1972
Michael Owen	Liverpool, Man. Utd	26	1997-
Paul Scholes	Manchester United	26	1994-
Andy Cole	Newcastle, Man. Utd	23	1994-2001
John Wark	Ipswich T, Liverpool	23	1974-1985
Sir Bobby Charlton	Manchester United	22	1956-1972
Martin Chivers	Tottenham Hotspur	22	1967-1975
Frank Lampard	West Ham, Chelsea	22	1999-
Wayne Rooney	Manchester United	21	2004-
Ray Kennedy	Arsenal, Liverpool	20	1969-1981
Ian Rush	Liverpool	20	1981-1985 & 1991-1996

MOST GOALS IN EUROPE FOR ONE ENGLISH CLUB

PLAYER	CLUB	GOALS	EUROPEAN CAREER
Thierry Henry	Arsenal	42	1999-2007
Ruud van Nistelrooy	Manchester United	38	2001-2006
Steven Gerrard	Liverpool	34	1998-
Peter Lorimer	Leeds United	30	1962-1978
Alan Shearer	Newcastle United	30	1996-2006
Ryan Giggs	Manchester United	28	1991-
Denis Law	Manchester United	28	1962-1972
Didier Drogba	Chelsea	26	2004-
Paul Scholes	Manchester United	26	1994-
Sir Bobby Charlton	Manchester United	22	1956-1972
Martin Chivers	Tottenham Hotspur	22	1967-1975
Michael Owen	Liverpool	22	1997-2004
Frank Lampard	Chelsea	21	2001-
Wayne Rooney	Manchester United	21	2004-
Ian Rush	Liverpool	20	1981-1985 & 1991-1996
Ole Gunnar Solskjaer	Manchester United	20	1996-2007
Andy Cole	Manchester United	19	1994-2001
John Wark	Ipswich Town	18	1974-1983
Roger Hunt	Liverpool	17	1959-1969
Mick Jones	Leeds United	17	1967-1973

LIVERPOOL'S EUROPEAN OPPONENTS

Liverpool's early start to their Europa League campaign in 2010/11 saw the club visit Macedonia for the first time in the form of opponents FK Rabotnicki. The play-off round saw a return to Turkey and a clash with Trabzonspor, while the group phase sees two new opponents in the former of Italian side Napoli and FC Utrecht of Holland.

There are 18 countries that the club have yet to visit in European competition – namely Albania, Andorra, Armenia, Azerbaijan, Belarus, Bosnia-Herzegovina, Croatia, Estonia, Faroe Islands, Georgia, Kazakhstan, Latvia, Liechtenstein, Malta, Moldova, Montenegro, San Marino and Serbia.

The countries, and the clubs, that Liverpool have faced (up to August 31 2010) are listed below and opposite:

AUSTRIA (3)
AK Graz, Austria Vienna, Swarovski Tirol

BELGIUM (3)
Anderlecht, FC Bruges, Standard Liege

BULGARIA (2)
CSKA Sofia, Levski Sofia

CYPRUS (1)
Apollon Limassol

CZECH REPUBLIC (1)
Slovan Liberec

DENMARK (2)
Brondby, Odense

EAST GERMANY (2)
Dynamo Berlin, Dynamo Dresden

ENGLAND (5)
Arsenal, Chelsea, Leeds United, Nottingham Forest, Tottenham Hotspur

FINLAND (5)
FC Haka, HJK Helsinki, Kuusysi Lahti, MyPa 47, Oulu Palloseura

FRANCE (10)
Auxerre, Bordeaux, Lille, Lyon, Marseille, Monaco, Paris St Germain, RC Strasbourg, St Etienne, Toulouse

GERMANY (2)
Bayer Leverkusen, Borussia Dortmund

GREECE (3)
AEK Athens, Olympiakos, Panathinaikos

HOLLAND (4)
Ajax Amsterdam, AZ '67 Alkmaar, PSV Eindhoven, Vitesse Arnhem

HUNGARY (3)
Debreceni VSC, Ferencvaros, Honved

ICELAND (1)
Reykjavik

ISRAEL (1)
Maccabi Haifa

ITALY (6)
AC Milan, AS Roma, Fiorentina, Genoa, Inter Milan, Juventus

LIVERPOOL'S EUROPEAN OPPONENTS

 LITHUANIA (1)
FBK Kaunas

 LUXEMBOURG (1)
Jeunesse D'Esch

 MACEDONIA (1)
FK Rabotnicki

 NORTHERN IRELAND (1)
Crusaders

 NORWAY (2)
Brann Bergen, Stromsgodset

 POLAND (3)
Lech Poznan, Slask Wroclaw, Widzew Lodz

 PORTUGAL (4)
Benfica, Boavista, FC Porto, Vitoria Setubal

 REPUBLIC OF IRELAND (1)
Dundalk

 ROMANIA (5)
Dinamo Bucharest, Petrolul Ploesti, Rapid Bucharest, Steaua Bucharest, Unirea Urziceni

 RUSSIA (4)
CSKA Moscow, Dynamo Tblisi, Spartak Moscow, Spartak Vladikavkaz

 SCOTLAND (3)
Aberdeen, Celtic, Hibernian

 SLOVAKIA (1)
FC Kosice

 SLOVENIA (1)
Olimpija Ljubljana

 SPAIN (10)
Alaves, Athletic Bilbao, Atletico Madrid, Barcelona, Celta Vigo, Deportivo La Coruna, Real Betis, Real Madrid, Real Sociedad, Valencia

 SWEDEN (1)
Malmo

 SWITZERLAND (4)
FC Basel, FC Sion, FC Zurich, Servette Geneva

 TURKEY (3)
Besiktas, Galatasaray, Trabzonspor

 WALES (1)
Total Network Solutions

 WEST GERMANY (7)
Bayern Munich, Borussia Moenchengladbach, Borussia Dortmund, FC Cologne, Eintracht Frankfurt, Hamburg, 1860 Munich

 UKRAINE (1)
Dynamo Kiev

 YUGOSLAVIA (1)
Red Star Belgrade

LFC IN EUROPE: CLUB-BY-CLUB RECORD

OPPOSITION	PLAYED	WON	DRAWN	LOST	FOR	AGAINST
Aberdeen	2	2	0	0	5	0
AC Milan	2	1	0	1	4	5
AEK Athens	2	2	0	0	6	1
Ajax Amsterdam	2	0	1	1	3	7
Alaves	1	1	0	0	5	4
Anderlecht	6	5	0	1	11	4
Apollon Limassol	2	2	0	0	8	2
Arsenal	2	1	1	0	5	3
AS Monaco	2	1	0	1	2	1
AS Roma	5	3	1	1	5	2
Athletic Bilbao	4	2	1	1	4	3
Atletico Madrid	4	1	2	1	4	4
Austria Vienna	2	1	1	0	5	2
Auxerre	4	3	0	1	6	2
AZ '67 Alkmaar	2	1	1	0	5	4
Basel FC	2	0	2	0	4	4
Bayer Leverkusen	4	3	0	1	9	6
Bayern Munich	7	2	4	1	9	7
Benfica	10	6	0	4	19	11
Besiktas	2	1	0	1	9	2
Boavista	2	0	2	0	2	2
Bordeaux	2	2	0	0	4	0
Borussia Dortmund	3	1	1	1	3	2
Bor. Moenchengladbach	5	3	0	2	10	5
Brann Bergen	2	1	1	0	4	1
Brondby	2	0	1	1	0	1
Celta Vigo	2	0	0	2	1	4
Celtic	6	1	3	2	5	6
Chelsea	10	2	5	3	10	12
Club Brugge KV	3	2	1	0	5	3
Crusaders	2	2	0	0	7	0
CSKA Moscow	1	1	0	0	3	1
CSKA Sofia	6	4	0	2	10	5
Debreceni VSC	2	2	0	0	2	0
Deportivo La Coruna	2	1	1	0	1	0
Dinamo Bucharest	4	3	1	0	7	2
Dundalk	4	4	0	0	19	1
Dynamo Berlin	2	1	1	0	3	1
Dynamo Dresden	6	4	1	1	11	4
Dynamo Kiev	2	2	0	0	3	1
Dynamo Tblisi	2	1	0	1	2	4
Eintracht Frankfurt	2	1	1	0	2	0
FC Barcelona	8	3	3	2	6	6
FC Cologne	3	0	3	0	2	2
FC Porto	4	2	2	0	7	2
Ferencvaros	6	1	3	2	3	4
Fiorentina	2	0	0	2	1	4
Galatasaray	4	1	2	1	6	6
Genoa	2	0	0	2	1	4
Graz AK	2	1	0	1	2	1
Haka FC	2	2	0	0	9	1
Hamburg	2	1	1	0	7	1
Hibernian	4	3	0	1	6	2
HJK Helsinki	2	1	0	1	5	1
Honved	2	1	1	0	2	0
Inter Milan	4	3	0	1	6	4
Jeunesse D'Esch	2	1	1	0	3	1

LFC IN EUROPE: CLUB-BY-CLUB RECORD

OPPOSITION	PLAYED	WON	DRAWN	LOST	FOR	AGAINST
Juventus	6	2	1	3	4	5
Kaunas FBK	2	2	0	0	5	1
Kosice FC	2	2	0	0	8	0
Kuusysi Lahti	2	1	0	1	6	2
Lech Poznan	2	2	0	0	5	0
Leeds United	2	0	1	1	0	1
Levski Sofia	2	2	0	0	6	2
Lille	2	1	0	1	3	1
Maccabi Haifa	2	1	1	0	3	2
Malmo	2	2	0	0	4	1
Munich 1860	2	1	0	1	9	2
MyPa 47	2	2	0	0	4	1
Nottingham Forest	2	0	1	1	0	2
Odense	2	2	0	0	6	0
Olimpija Ljubljana	2	1	1	0	4	1
Olympiakos	4	2	1	1	7	4
Olympique Lyon	2	0	1	1	2	3
Olympique Marseille	6	3	1	2	9	5
Oulu Palloseura	4	3	1	0	19	2
Panathinaikos	2	2	0	0	5	0
Paris St Germain	2	1	0	1	2	3
Petrolul Ploesti	3	2	0	1	5	3
PSV Eindhoven	6	5	1	0	12	2
Rapid Bucharest	2	1	1	0	1	0
RC Strasbourg	2	1	0	1	2	3
Real Betis	2	1	1	0	2	1
Real Madrid	3	3	0	0	6	0
Real Sociedad	2	2	0	0	9	1
Red Star Belgrade	2	0	0	2	2	4
Reykjavik	2	2	0	0	11	1
St Etienne	2	1	0	1	3	2
Servette Geneva	2	1	0	1	3	2
Sion FC	2	2	0	0	8	4
Slask Wroclaw	2	2	0	0	5	1
Slovan Liberec	2	2	0	0	4	2
Spartak Moscow	4	2	0	2	10	7
Spartak Vladikavkaz	2	1	1	0	2	1
Standard Liege	4	3	1	0	6	2
Steaua Bucharest	2	1	1	0	2	1
Stromsgodset	2	2	0	0	12	0
Swarowski Tirol	2	2	0	0	6	0
Total Network Solutions	2	2	0	0	6	0
Tottenham Hotspur	2	1	0	1	2	2
Toulouse	2	2	0	0	5	0
Trabzonspor	2	1	0	1	3	1
Unirea Urziceni	2	2	0	0	4	1
Valencia	4	0	2	2	2	5
Vitesse Arnhem	2	2	0	0	2	0
Vitoria Setubal	2	1	0	1	3	3
Widzew Lodz	2	1	0	1	3	4
Zurich FC	2	2	0	0	6	1
OVERALL	**314**	**178**	**66**	**70**	**566**	**260**

Games decided on toss of coin (Petrolul) in a third game counted as a draw.
One-game ties decided on penalties count as wins or losses.
Statistics correct at end of 2009/10 season.

MOST POINTS WON IN TOP-FLIGHT FOOTBALL

The tables below highlight Liverpool's consistency in terms of First Division/Premier League points, and wins in league football. The top 15 'best' clubs in the top flight are noted here, and show the Reds almost 100 points better off than their nearest challengers Arsenal, with the average points per game record only being bettered by Manchester United.

MOST POINTS WON IN TOP-FLIGHT LEAGUE FOOTBALL – AT END OF 2009/10 SEASON

CLUB	TOTAL POINTS WON	GAMES PLAYED	AVERAGE POINTS PER GAME	SEASONS IN TOP LEAGUE
Liverpool	5060	3792	1.33	95
Arsenal	4962	3792	1.31	93
Everton	4890	4176	1.17	107
Manchester United	4726	3436	1.38	85
Aston Villa	4492	3842	1.17	99
Chelsea	3644	3056	1.19	75
Tottenham Hotspur	3638	3052	1.19	75
Newcastle United	3557	3160	1.13	60
Manchester City	3519	3278	1.07	81
Sunderland	3235	3074	1.05	79
Blackburn Rovers	2873	2644	1.09	70
West Bromwich Albion	2795	2804	1.00	72
Sheffield Wednesday	2781	2582	1.08	66
Bolton Wanderers	2742	2726	1.01	71
Derby County	2510	2468	1.02	65

ALL-TIME LEAGUE WINS

Second on the all-time league wins table, Liverpool's achievement is thus more impressive in the fact that all but 11 of those seasons were spent at the highest level of English football. Only 18 victories behind Manchester United ahead of the 2010/11 season, the Reds have also played 32 less games in league football. The 2000th was achieved early in the 2010/11 season.

ALL-TIME LEAGUE WINS – AT END OF 2009/10 SEASON

CLUB	TOTAL LEAGUE WINS	GAMES PLAYED	WIN %	SEASONS IN LEAGUE (TOP FLIGHT)
Manchester United	2017	4252	47.44	107 (85)
Liverpool	1999	4220	47.37	106 (95)
Arsenal	1912	4220	45.31	106 (93)
Wolverhampton Wanderers	1824	4502	40.52	111 (60)
Aston Villa	1821	4356	41.80	111 (99)
Everton	1781	4344	41.00	111 (107)
Sunderland	1779	4386	40.56	109 (79)
Preston North End	1773	4546	39.00	111 (46)
Sheffield United	1755	4400	39.89	107 (60)
Newcastle United	1749	4252	41.13	106 (79)

MOST POINTS WON BY TEAMS
IN PREMIER LEAGUE HISTORY

09/10 POS.	POS.	CLUB	POINTS	HIGHEST POS	SEASONS IN PREMIERSHIP
1	1	Manchester United	1494	1st (11 times)	18
2	2	Arsenal	1311	1st (3 times)	18
3	3	Chelsea	1267	1st (3 times)	18
4	4	Liverpool	1224	2nd (2 times)	18
5	5	Aston Villa	1003	2nd (1992/1993)	18
7	6	Tottenham Hotspur	955	4th (2009/2010)	18
8	7	Everton	924	4th (2004/2005)	18
6	8	Newcastle United	906	2nd (2 times)	16
9	9	Blackburn Rovers	896	1st (1994/1995)	16
10	10	West Ham United	731	5th (1998/1999)	15
11	11	Leeds United	692	3rd (1999/2000)	12
12	12	Middlesbrough	633	7th (2004/2005)	14
14	13	Manchester City	624	5th (2009/2010)	13
13	14	Southampton	587	8th (2002/2003)	13
15	15	Bolton Wanderers	493	6th (2004/2005)	11
19	16	Fulham	410	7th (2008/2009)	9
16	17	Coventry City	409	11th (2 times)	9
17	18	Sheffield Wednesday	392	7th (3 times)	8
18	19	Wimbledon (MK Dons)	391	6th (1993/1994)	8
20	20	Charlton Athletic	361	7th (2003/2004)	8
22	21	Sunderland	348	7th (2 times)	9
21	22	Leicester City	342	8th (1999/2000)	8
23	23	Portsmouth	293*	8th (2007/2008)	7
23	24	Derby County	274	8th (1998/1999)	7
28	25	Birmingham City	262	9th (2009/2010)	6
25	26	Nottingham Forest	239	3rd (1994/1995)	5
26	27	Ipswich Town	224	5th (2000/2001)	5
27	28	Queens Park Rangers	216	5th (1992/1993)	4
30	29	Wigan Athletic	210	10th (2005/2006)	5
29	30	Norwich City	201	3rd (1992/1993)	4
31	31	Crystal Palace	160	18th (2004/2005)	4
32	32	Sheffield United	132	14th (1992/1993)	3
33	33	West Bromwich Albion	122	17th (2004/2005)	4
38	34	Stoke City	92	11th (2009/2010)	2
34	35	Reading	91	8th (2006/2007)	2
35	36	Oldham Athletic	89	19th (1992/1993)	2
41	37	Wolverhampton Wanderers	71	15th (2009/2010)	2
39	38	Hull City	65	17th (2008/09)	2
36	39	Bradford City	62	17th (1999/2000)	2
37	40	Watford	52	20th (1999/2000)	2
39	41	Barnsley	35	19th (1997/1998)	1
-	42	Burnley	30	18th (2009/2010)	1
42	=	Swindon Town	30	22nd (1994/1995)	1

* Portsmouth docked 9 points after going into administration during 2009/10 season*

FULL PREMIER LEAGUE RECORD - CLUB-BY-CLUB

	PLD	HOME W	D	L	F	A	AWAY W	D	L	F	A	PTS
Arsenal	36	9	5	4	35	18	5	6	7	14	21	53
Aston Villa	36	11	3	4	37	19	8	5	5	22	16	65
Barnsley	2	0	0	1	0	1	1	0	0	3	2	3
Birmingham City	12	1	4	1	8	7	1	3	2	9	9	12
Blackburn Rovers	32	10	5	1	29	10	5	6	5	22	24	56
Bolton Wanderers	22	10	1	0	27	5	5	3	3	18	15	49
Bradford City	4	2	0	0	4	1	1	0	1	2	1	9
Burnley	2	1	0	0	4	0	1	0	0	4	0	6
Charlton Athletic	16	4	3	1	14	7	4	0	4	13	9	27
Chelsea	36	11	3	4	31	19	2	4	12	7	27	46
Coventry City	18	6	1	2	17	6	3	2	4	10	11	30
Crystal Palace	8	3	1	0	10	3	2	1	1	10	3	17
Derby County	14	5	1	1	18	4	5	0	2	12	5	31
Everton	36	8	8	2	21	13	8	4	6	23	20	60
Fulham	18	5	4	0	16	2	5	0	4	14	12	34
Hull City	4	1	1	0	8	3	1	1	0	3	1	8
Ipswich Town	10	2	1	2	6	2	3	2	0	14	5	18
Leeds United	24	8	1	3	28	11	6	3	3	20	12	46
Leicester City	16	4	1	3	8	7	3	3	2	11	7	25
Manchester City	26	9	3	1	25	11	3	8	2	15	12	47
Manchester United	36	6	3	9	25	25	4	4	10	15	27	37
Middlesbrough	28	10	4	0	28	8	3	5	6	12	16	48
Newcastle United	32	13	2	1	39	15	6	4	6	27	20	63
Norwich City	8	3	0	1	11	2	2	1	1	6	5	16
Nottingham Forest	10	4	1	0	14	5	0	3	2	4	6	16
Oldham Athletic	4	2	0	0	3	1	1	0	1	5	3	9
Portsmouth	14	5	2	0	16	3	3	1	3	9	9	27
Queens Park Rangers	8	3	1	0	6	3	3	0	1	7	4	19
Reading	4	2	0	0	4	1	1	0	1	3	4	9
Sheffield United	6	2	0	1	7	3	0	2	1	1	2	8
Sheffield Wednesday	16	7	0	1	16	4	2	4	2	11	12	31
Southampton	26	7	4	2	28	14	5	3	5	17	19	43
Stoke City	4	1	1	0	4	0	0	2	0	1	1	6
Sunderland	18	5	4	0	12	2	6	1	2	12	5	38
Swindon Town	2	0	1	0	2	2	1	0	0	5	0	4
Tottenham Hotspur	36	12	5	1	38	15	5	5	8	23	24	61
Watford	4	1	0	1	2	1	2	0	0	6	2	9
West Bromwich Alb.	8	4	0	0	9	0	4	0	0	15	0	24
West Ham United	30	11	4	0	30	4	7	3	5	21	17	61
Wigan Athletic	10	4	1	0	11	4	3	1	1	7	2	23
Wimbledon	16	4	3	1	17	8	1	3	4	5	9	21
Wolverhampton W.	4	2	0	0	3	0	0	2	0	1	1	8

FOOTBALL LEAGUE RECORD - CLUB-BY-CLUB

TEAM	PLAYED	WON	DRAWN	LOST	FOR	AGAINST
Arsenal	172	68	44	60	244	220
Aston Villa	170	80	38	52	300	247
Barnsley	12	7	2	3	23	15
Birmingham City	98	46	24	28	162	137
Blackburn Rovers	124	52	38	34	220	166
Blackpool	40	18	9	13	72	62
Bolton Wanderers	114	50	29	35	184	137
Bradford City	26	18	2	6	45	22
Bradford Park Avenue	6	3	1	2	10	8
Brentford	10	4	3	3	16	16
Brighton & Hove Albion	16	8	6	2	36	20
Bristol City	30	16	3	11	52	39
Bristol Rovers	16	10	1	5	32	21
Burnley	76	31	19	26	125	95
Burton Swifts	4	3	1	0	17	3
Burton United	2	1	0	1	3	2
Burton Wanderers	2	1	0	1	5	3
Bury	48	26	14	8	92	53
Cardiff City	26	8	2	16	35	51
Carlisle United	2	2	0	0	3	0
Charlton Athletic	56	29	8	19	93	70
Chelsea	134	60	28	46	206	187
Chesterfield	2	1	1	0	7	2
Coventry City	68	39	16	13	113	45
Crewe Alexandra	4	4	0	0	20	1
Crystal Palace	26	15	6	5	57	17
Darwen	2	1	1	0	4	0
Derby County	126	66	28	32	248	156
Doncaster Rovers	10	5	2	3	19	13
Everton	182	70	56	56	247	214
Fulham	46	25	13	8	84	44
Gainsborough Trinity	2	2	0	0	8	2
Glossop	4	3	1	0	11	5
Grimsby Town	36	18	10	8	87	47
Huddersfield Town	68	25	17	26	113	113
Hull City	10	7	3	0	26	11
Ipswich Town	60	28	19	13	110	59
Leeds United	100	51	25	24	164	101
Leicester City	88	36	19	33	143	121
Leyton Orient	14	9	2	3	37	15
Lincoln City	20	11	4	5	42	28
Loughborough Town	2	2	0	0	5	2
Luton Town	28	13	9	6	52	33
Manchester City	148	74	37	37	265	193
Manchester United	154	52	43	59	201	213
Middlesbrough	134	57	39	38	229	172
Middlesbrough Ironopolis	2	2	0	0	8	0
Millwall	4	3	1	0	6	3
Newcastle United	148	71	37	40	259	184
Northampton Town	2	1	1	0	5	0

FOOTBALL LEAGUE RECORD - CLUB-BY-CLUB

TEAM	PLAYED	WON	DRAWN	LOST	FOR	AGAINST
Northwich Victoria	2	2	0	0	7	2
Norwich City	46	24	11	11	84	47
Nottingham Forest	100	50	24	26	167	99
Notts County	60	34	12	14	110	63
Oldham Athletic	24	14	4	6	39	30
Oxford United	6	5	1	0	20	3
Plymouth Argyle	10	5	3	2	22	15
Portsmouth	60	25	15	20	106	90
Port Vale	12	7	3	2	38	20
Preston North End	64	26	17	21	114	99
Queens Park Rangers	40	28	6	6	68	34
Reading	4	3	0	1	7	5
Rotherham United	20	14	3	3	57	21
Scunthorpe United	8	6	2	0	17	8
Sheffield United	118	55	27	36	192	153
Sheffield Wednesday	116	54	26	36	197	165
Southampton	74	35	18	21	112	86
Stoke City	110	54	30	26	181	114
Sunderland	146	65	31	50	245	211
Swansea City	20	10	4	6	51	27
Swindon Town	2	1	1	0	7	2
Tottenham Hotspur	134	63	34	37	214	150
Walsall	4	2	2	0	11	3
Watford	16	12	1	3	37	16
West Bromwich Albion	116	55	33	28	181	127
West Ham United	106	56	29	21	175	95
Wigan Athletic	10	7	2	1	18	6
Wimbledon	28	11	10	7	41	31
Wolverhampton Wanderers	90	44	17	29	138	106

Peter Beardsley on target in one of Liverpool's 12 Football League wins over Watford

THE PREMIER/FOOTBALL LEAGUE FINISHES

PREMIER LEAGUE/DIVISION ONE – 95 SEASONS		
POSITION	**NUMBER OF FINISHES**	**MOST RECENT FINAL POSITION**
1st	18	1989/90
2nd	12	2008/09
3rd	7	2006/07
4th	8	2007/08
5th	9	2004/05
6th	2	1992/93
7th	5	2009/10
8th	4	1993/94
9th	4	1950/51
10th	2	1931/32
11th	5	1951/52
12th	4	1948/49
13th	2	1914/15
14th	1	1932/33
15th	1	1906/07
16th	4	1927/28
17th	3	1952/53
18th	2	1936/37
19th	1	1935/36
20th	0	–
21st	0	–
22nd	1	1953/54

DIVISION TWO – 11 SEASONS		
POSITION	**NUMBER OF FINISHES**	**MOST RECENT FINAL POSITION**
1st	4	1961/62
3rd	4	1960/61
4th	2	1958/59
11th	1	1954/55

THE PREMIER LEAGUE FINISHES

18 SEASONS		
POSITION	**NUMBER OF TIMES**	**MOST RECENT FINAL POSITION**
1st	0	–
2nd	2	2008/09
3rd	5	2006/07
4th	5	2007/08
5th	2	2004/05
6th	1	1992/93
7th	2	2009/10
8th	1	1993/94

BIGGEST-EVER FOOTBALL LEAGUE WINS

DATE	OPPONENTS	SCORE	LIVERPOOL SCORERS	ATT.
18th Feb 1896	Rotherham Town	10-1	Allan 4, Becton, McVean 3, Ross 2	2,000
12th Sept 1989	Crystal Palace	9-0	Nicol 2, McMahon, Rush, Gillespie, Beardsley, Aldridge (pen), Barnes, Hysen	35,779
26th Dec 1928	Burnley	8-0	Clark 2, Edmed 2, Hodgson 3, Salisbury	42,449
6th Dec 1902	Grimsby Town	9-2	Chadwick 2, Goddard 2, Raybould 4 (1 pen), Livingstone	5,000
8th Apr 1905	Burslem Port Vale	8-1	Cox 2, Parkinson 3, Raybould, Robinson 2	13,000
29th Feb 1896	Burton Swifts	7-0*	Becton 3, Ross 3, McCartney	1,500
28th Mar 1896	Crewe Alexandra	7-0*	Allan 3, McQue, McVean 2, Becton	3,000
4th Jan 1902	Stoke City	7-0	McGuigan 5, Raybould 2	10,000
26th Nov 1955	Fulham	7-0	Evans, Arnell, Liddell 2, Twentyman, A'Court, Payne	34,995
2nd Sept 1978	Tottenham Hotspur	7-0	Dalglish 2, R. Kennedy, Johnson 2, Neal (pen), McDermott	50,705

Matches played away from Anfield

BIGGEST-EVER FOOTBALL LEAGUE DEFEATS

DATE	OPPONENTS	SCORE	LIVERPOOL SCORERS	ATT.
11th Dec 1954	Birmingham City	1-9	Liddell	17,500
10th Nov 1934	Huddersfield Town	0-8		12,512
1st Jan 1934	Newcastle United	2-9	Taylor, Betton (o.g.)	17,242
7th May 1932	Bolton Wanderers	1-8	McRorie	9,209
1st Sept 1934	Arsenal	1-8	Hanson	54,062
7th Dec 1912	Sunderland	0-7		14,000
1st Sept 1930	West Ham United	0-7		11,682

All matches played away from Anfield

BIGGEST-EVER PREMIER LEAGUE WINS

DATE	OPPONENTS	SCORE	LIVERPOOL SCORERS	ATT.
16th Jan 1999	Southampton	7-1	Fowler 3, Matteo, Carragher, Owen, Thompson	44,011
1st Sept 2007	Derby County	6-0	Alonso 2, Babel, Torres 2, Voronin	44,076
26th Apr 2003	West Brom	6-0*	Owen 4, Baros 2	27,128
9th Feb 2002	Ipswich Town	6-0*	Abel Xavier, Heskey 2, Hyypia, Owen 2	25,608
28th Oct 1995	Manchester City	6-0	Rush 2, Redknapp, Fowler 2, Ruddock	39,267

Matches played away from Anfield

BIGGEST-EVER PREMIER LEAGUE DEFEATS

DATE	OPPONENTS	SCORE	LIVERPOOL SCORER	ATT.
19th Dec 1992	Coventry City	1-5	Redknapp	19,779
5th Apr 2003	Manchester Utd	0-4		67,639
2nd Oct 2005	Chelsea	1-4*	Gerrard	44,235
16th Dec 2001	Chelsea	0-4		41,174
25th Apr 1998	Chelsea	1-4	Riedle	34,639
3rd Apr 1992	Blackburn Rovers	1-4	Rush	15,032

Match played at Anfield

UNBEATEN HOME RUNS

Liverpool's best run in the Premier League era came to an end in the first home league game of the 2009/10 campaign, Aston Villa's 3-1 win ending a sequence of 31 fixtures stretching from December 2007. It beat the previous post-1992 best of 30 games, although still some way short of the 63-game club record which lasted nearly three calendar years.

LIVERPOOL'S LONGEST RUNS UNBEATEN AT HOME (LEAGUE)

NO. OF GAMES	FIRST GAME OF RUN	DAY BEFORE RUN ENDED	DATE OF DEFEAT	VISITING WINNERS
63	25/02/1978	30/01/1981	31/01/1981	Leicester City
34	24/03/1970	31/12/1971	01/01/1972	Leeds United
31	27/03/1976	04/11/1977	05/11/1977	Aston Villa
31	22/12/2007	23/08/2009	24/08/2009	Aston Villa
30	15/10/2005	02/03/2007	03/03/2007	Manchester United
29	21/01/1961	17/08/1962	18/08/1962	Blackpool
27	01/01/1966	21/04/1967	22/04/1967	West Bromwich Albion
27	24/02/1973	23/04/1974	24/04/1974	Arsenal
26	20/03/1982	22/04/1983	23/04/1983	Norwich City
26	26/11/1989	02/03/1991	03/03/1991	Arsenal
25	18/04/1987	30/09/1988	01/10/1988	Newcastle United
23	13/02/1904	08/09/1905	09/09/1905	Blackburn Rovers
22	29/01/1972	09/02/1973	10/02/1973	Arsenal
22	23/11/1974	28/11/1975	29/11/1975	Norwich City

Villa woe for the Reds as the 31-match unbeaten home league run comes to an end

PREMIER LEAGUE APPEARANCES

Liverpool's home-grown duo Jamie Carragher and Steven Gerrard were in the top five of Premier League regulars for one club going into the 2010/11 campaign. The top-16 list also includes Sami Hyypia, third in the list of overseas players behind goalkeepers Mark Schwarzer and Jussi Jaaskelainen.

Jamie Carragher is 8th on the all-time Premier League list, one of 16 players to make 400 or more Premier League appearances. He is well in sight of Alan Shearer's 441 mark.

MOST PREMIER LEAGUE APPEARANCES FOR ONE CLUB (AT END OF 2009/10 SEASON)

PLAYER	APPEARANCES	CLUB
Ryan Giggs	548*	Manchester United
Paul Scholes	444*	Manchester United
Jamie Carragher	**435***	**Liverpool**
Gary Neville	397*	Manchester United
Steven Gerrard	**366***	**Liverpool**
Gareth Barry	365	Aston Villa
Shay Given	354	Newcastle United
Ray Parlour	333	Arsenal
Mark Schwarzer	332	Middlesbrough
Jason Dodd	329	Southampton
Jussi Jaaskelainen	326*	Bolton Wanderers
Roy Keane	326	Manchester United
Gary Kelly	325	Leeds United
David Seaman	325	Arsenal
Frank Lampard	320*	Chelsea
Sami Hyypia	**318**	**Liverpool**

Steven Gerrard and Jamie Carragher, Premier regulars

* Still at club at end of 2009/10 season

MOST PREMIER LEAGUE APPEARANCES IN CAREER (AT END OF 2009/10 SEASON)

PLAYER	APPEARANCES	CLUB(S)
David James	572	Liverpool, Aston Villa, West Ham, Man. City, Portsmouth
Ryan Giggs	548*	Manchester United
Gary Speed	535	Leeds United, Everton, Newcastle United, Bolton Wanderers
Sol Campbell	496*	Tottenham, Arsenal, Portsmouth
Emile Heskey	469*	Leicester C., Liverpool, Birmingham C., Wigan A., Aston Villa
Frank Lampard	468*	West Ham, Chelsea
Paul Scholes	444*	Manchester United
Alan Shearer	441	Blackburn Rovers, Newcastle United
Jamie Carragher	**435***	**Liverpool**
Phil Neville	429*	Manchester United, Everton
Gareth Southgate	426	Crystal Palace, Aston Villa, Middlesbrough
Teddy Sheringham	418	Nottingham Forest, Tottenham Hotspur (x2), Manchester United, Portsmouth, West Ham
Andy Cole	414	Newcastle United, Manchester United, Blackburn Rovers, Fulham, Manchester City, Portsmouth, Sunderland
Nicky Butt	411	Manchester United, Newcastle United, Birmingham City
Mark Schwarzer	407*	Middlesbrough, Fulham
Shay Given	406*	Blackburn Rovers, Newcastle United, Manchester City
Rio Ferdinand	402*	West Ham, Leeds United, Manchester United

* Still playing in Premier League at start of 2010/11 season

MOST APPEARANCES IN PREMIER LEAGUE

POS.	PLAYER	GAMES	POS.	PLAYER	GAMES
1	Jamie Carragher	435	24	Phil Babb	128
2	Steven Gerrard	366	25	Jerzy Dudek	127
3	Sami Hyypia	318	=	Dominic Matteo	127
4	Robbie Fowler	266	27	Vladimir Smicer	121
5	Steve McManaman	240	28	Neil Ruddock	115
6	John Arne Riise	234	29	Michael Thomas	107
7	Jamie Redknapp	231	30	Jason McAteer	100
8	Michael Owen	216			
9	David James	214			
10	Dietmar Hamann	191			
11	Pepe Reina	182			
12	Danny Murphy	170			
13	John Barnes	162			
14	Rob Jones	155			
15	Emile Heskey	150			
16	Patrik Berger	148			
17	Steve Finnan	145			
18	Xabi Alonso	143			
19	Dirk Kuyt	141			
20	Stig Inge Bjornebye	139			
21	Mark Wright	137			
22	Stephane Henchoz	135			
23	Ian Rush	130			

Sami Hyypia – In third

MOST GOALS IN PREMIER LEAGUE

POS.	PLAYER	GOALS
1	Robbie Fowler	128
2	Michael Owen	118
3	Steven Gerrard	80
4	Fernando Torres	56
5	Ian Rush	45
6	Steve McManaman	41
7	Emile Heskey	39
8	Dirk Kuyt	36
9	Jamie Redknapp	29
10	Patrik Berger	28
=	Own Goals	28
12	Stan Collymore	26
13	Danny Murphy	25
14	John Barnes	22
=	Peter Crouch	22
=	Sami Hyypia	22
17	John Arne Riise	21
18	Milan Baros	19
19	Yossi Benayoun	18
=	Luis Garcia	18
21	Xabi Alonso	15
22	Paul Ince	14
23	Djibril Cisse	13
24	Harry Kewell	12

Patrik Berger – Joint tenth

MOST APPEARANCES IN FOOTBALL LEAGUE

	PLAYER	FIRST-TEAM CAREER	GAMES
	TOTAL APPEARANCES (300+ GAMES)		
1	Ian Callaghan	1960-1978	640
2	Billy Liddell	1946-1960	492
3	Emlyn Hughes	1967-1979	474
4	Ray Clemence	1968-1981	470
5	Tommy Smith	1963-1978	467
6	Phil Neal	1974-1985	455
7	Alan Hansen	1977-1990	434
8	Elisha Scott	1913-1934	430
9	Bruce Grobbelaar	1981-1994	406
=	Chris Lawler	1963-1975	406
11	Roger Hunt	1959-1969	404
12	Donald MacKinlay	1910-1928	393
13	Arthur Goddard	1902-1914	386
14	Gordon Hodgson	1926-1935	358
=	Ron Yeats	1961-1971	358
16	Kenny Dalglish	1977-1990	355
17	Alan A'Court	1953-1964	354
18	Ephraim Longworth	1910-1928	342
=	Ronnie Moran	1952-1965	342
20	Tom Bromilow	1919-1930	341
=	Tommy Lucas	1919-1932	341
22	Phil Thompson	1972-1983	340
23	Ian Rush	1980-1987 & 1988-1996	339
24	Jimmy McDougall	1928-1938	338
25	Ian St John	1961-1971	336
26	Fred Hopkin	1921-1931	335
27	Steve Heighway	1970-1981	331
28	Jack Cox	1898-1909	328
29	Billy Dunlop	1895-1909	325
30	Arthur Riley	1925-1939	322
=	Peter Thompson	1963-1972	322
=	Ronnie Whelan	1981-1994	322
33	Alex Raisbeck	1898-1909	312
=	Phil Taylor	1936-1954	312
35	Harry Chambers	1919-1928	310
36	Ray Lambert	1946-1955	308
37	Tommy Lawrence	1962-1971	306
38	Laurie Hughes	1946-1957	303

***FIRST-TEAM CAREER NOTED AS THE YEAR A PLAYER MADE HIS FIRST APPEARANCE FOR THE FIRST TEAM, AND THE YEAR THEY MADE THEIR LAST APPEARANCE.
PREMIER LEAGUE APPEARANCES WOULD GIVE THE FOLLOWING APPEARANCE FIGURES, AT END OF 2009/10 SEASON (300+ APPEARANCES ONLY):**

Ian Rush 469, Bruce Grobbelaar 440, Jamie Carragher 435, Steven Gerrard 366, Ronnie Whelan 362, Steve Nicol 343, Sami Hyypia 318, John Barnes 314.

MOST GOALS IN FOOTBALL LEAGUE

	PLAYER	FIRST-TEAM CAREER	GOALS
	TOTAL GOALS (60+ GOALS)		
1	Roger Hunt	1959-1969	245
2	Gordon Hodgson	1926-1935	233
3	Billy Liddell	1946-1960	215
4	Ian Rush	1980-1987 & 1988-1996	184
5	Harry Chambers	1919-1928	135
6	Jack Parkinson	1903-1914	124
7	Sam Raybould	1900-1907	119
8	Kenny Dalglish	1977-1990	118
9	Dick Forshaw	1919-1927	117
10	Jack Balmer	1935-1952	98
11	Ian St John	1961-1971	95
12	Jimmy Melia	1955-1964	77
13	Albert Stubbins	1946-1953	75
14	Berry Nieuwenhuys	1933-1947	74
=	John Toshack	1970-1977	74
16	Jack Cox	1898-1909	73
17	Arthur Goddard	1902-1914	72
18	Joe Hewitt	1904-1909	68
=	Kevin Keegan	1971-1977	68
20	Robert Robinson	1904-1912	63
21	John Barnes	1987-1997	62
22	Alan A'Court	1953-1964	61

*FIRST-TEAM CAREER NOTED AS THE YEAR A PLAYER MADE HIS FIRST APPEARANCE FOR THE FIRST TEAM, AND THE YEAR THEY MADE THEIR LAST APPEARANCE.
PREMIER LEAGUE GOALS WOULD GIVE THE FOLLOWING FIGURES, AT END OF 2009/10 SEASON (50+ GOALS ONLY):

Ian Rush 229, Robbie Fowler 128, Michael Owen 118, John Barnes 84, Steven Gerrard 80.

0 GOALS IN FOOTBALL LEAGUE

	PLAYER	FIRST-TEAM CAREER	GAMES
	TOTAL APPEARANCES WITHOUT A GOAL FOR LIVERPOOL - OUTFIELD PLAYERS ONLY		
1	Eph Longworth		371
2	Tom Cooper		160
3	Jim Harley		134
4	William Steel		128
5	Bob Pursell		113

*FIRST-TEAM CAREER NOTED AS THE YEAR A PLAYER MADE HIS FIRST APPEARANCE FOR THE FIRST TEAM, AND THE YEAR THEY MADE THEIR LAST APPEARANCE.
PREMIER LEAGUE APPEARANCES WOULD GIVE THE FOLLOWING APPEARANCE FIGURES, AT END OF 2009/10 SEASON (100+ APPEARANCES ONLY):

Rob Jones 243, Stephane Henchoz 205

PREMIER LEAGUE PLAYERS' RECORD (A-G)

The full records of players who have played for Liverpool since the inception of the Premier League in 1992. Note that the figures take into account their full record for the club, which includes the period prior to 1992 (all figures correct at end of 2009/10 season).

PLAYER	FIRST GAME-LAST GAME	LEAGUE		FA CUP		LEAGUE CUP		EUROPE		OTHER GAMES		LFC CAREER	
		A	G	A	G	A	G	A	G	A	G	A	G
Daniel Agger	2006-2010	77	3	3	0	4	2	30	2	1	0	115	7
Xabi Alonso	2004-2009	143	15	12	2	4	0	48	2	3	0	210	19
Nicolas Anelka	2001-2002	20	4	2	1	0	0	0	0	0	0	22	5
Alberto Aquilani	2009-2010	18	1	2	0	1	0	5	1	0	0	26	2
Alvaro Arbeloa	2007-2009	66	2	3	0	3	0	26	0	0	0	98	2
Pegguy Arphexad	2000-2002	2	0	0	0	2	0	2	0	0	0	6	0
Fabio Aurelio	2006-2010	71	3	4	0	5	0	29	1	1	0	110	4
Daniel Ayala	2009-2010	5	0	0	0	0	0	0	0	0	0	5	0
Phil Babb	1994-1999	128	1	12	0	16	0	14	0	0	0	170	1
Markus Babbel	2000-2002	42	3	5	1	7	1	17	1	2	0	73	6
Ryan Babel	2007-2010	82	11	8	1	6	0	33	8	0	0	129	20
Nick Barmby	2000-2002	32	2	5	1	7	1	13	4	1	0	58	8
John Barnes	1987-1997	314	84	51	16	26	3	12	3	4	2	407	108
Milan Baros	2002-2005	68	19	3	0	8	4	28	4	1	0	108	27
Antonio Barragan	2005-2005	0	0	0	0	0	0	1	0	0	0	1	0
Craig Bellamy	2006-2007	27	7	0	0	2	0	12	2	1	0	42	9
Yossi Benayoun	2007-2010	92	18	6	3	4	1	32	7	0	0	134	29
Patrik Berger	1996-2003	148	28	8	0	11	3	28	4	1	0	196	35
Igor Biscan	2000-2005	72	2	7	0	15	1	23	0	1	0	118	3
Stig I. Bjornebye	1992-1999	139	2	13	0	16	0	16	2	0	0	184	4
David Burrows	1988-1993	146	3	17	0	16	0	11	0	3	0	193	3
Titi Camara	1999-2000	33	9	2	1	2	0	0	0	0	0	37	10
Jamie Carragher	1997-2010	435	4	34	0	28	0	129	1	4	0	630	5
Scott Carson	2005-2006	4	0	1	0	1	0	3	0	0	0	9	0
Diego Cavalieri	2008-2010	0	0	2	0	4	0	2	0	0	0	8	0
Phil Charnock	1992-1992	0	0	0	0	1	0	1	0	0	0	2	0
Bruno Cheyrou	2002-2004	31	2	6	2	2	0	8	1	1	0	48	5
Djibril Cisse	2004-2006	49	13	6	2	0	0	23	9	1	0	79	24
Nigel Clough	1993-1995	39	7	2	0	3	2	0	0	0	0	44	9
Stan Collymore	1995-1997	61	26	9	7	4	0	7	2	0	0	81	35
Peter Crouch	2005-2008	85	22	11	5	5	1	30	11	3	3	134	42
Stephen Darby	2008-2010	1	0	1	0	1	0	2	0	0	0	5	0
Philipp Degen	2008-2010	7	0	1	0	4	0	1	0	0	0	13	0
Salif Diao	2002-2005	37	1	2	0	8	1	14	1	0	0	61	3
Julian Dicks	1993-1994	24	3	1	0	3	0	0	0	0	0	28	3
Bernard Diomede	2000-2001	2	0	0	0	0	0	3	0	0	0	5	0
El-Hadji Diouf	2002-2004	55	3	4	0	7	3	13	0	1	0	80	6
Andrea Dossena	2008-2009	18	1	2	0	2	0	9	1	0	0	31	2
Jerzy Dudek	2001-2007	127	0	9	0	11	0	38	0	1	0	186	0
Sean Dundee	1998-1999	3	0	0	0	1	0	1	0	0	0	5	0
Nathan Eccleston	2009-2009	1	0	0	0	1	0	0	0	0	0	2	0
Nabil El Zhar	2006-2009	21	0	1	0	4	1	6	0	0	0	32	1
Jean Michel Ferri	1999-1999	2	0	0	0	0	0	0	0	0	0	2	0
Steve Finnan	2003-2008	145	1	13	0	6	0	51	0	2	0	217	1
Robbie Fowler	1993-2007	266	128	24	12	35	29	44	14	0	0	369	183
Brad Friedel	1998-1999	25	0	0	0	4	0	2	0	0	0	31	0
Luis Garcia	2004-2007	77	18	4	1	5	0	32	11	3	0	121	30
Steven Gerrard	1998-2010	366	80	28	10	20	7	114	34	4	1	532	132
Mark Gonzalez	2006-2007	25	2	0	0	2	0	8	1	1	0	36	3
Bruce Grobbelaar	1981-1994	440	0	62	0	70	0	38	0	18	0	628	0
Danny Guthrie	2006-2007	3	0	0	0	3	0	1	0	0	0	7	0

PREMIER LEAGUE PLAYERS' RECORD (H-N)

PLAYER	FIRST GAME-LAST GAME	LEAGUE		FA CUP		LEAGUE CUP		EUROPE		OTHER GAMES		LFC CAREER	
		A	G	A	G	A	G	A	G	A	G	A	G
Dietmar Hamann	1999-2006	191	8	16	1	12	0	61	2	3	0	283	11
Steve Harkness	1991-1999	102	2	6	0	15	1	16	0	0	0	139	3
Vegard Heggem	1998-2000	54	3	1	0	4	0	6	0	0	0	65	3
Stephane Henchoz	1999-2004	135	0	15	0	16	0	37	0	2	0	205	0
Emile Heskey	2000-2004	150	39	14	6	12	2	45	13	2	0	223	60
Jack Hobbs	2007-2007	2	0	0	0	3	0	0	0	0	0	5	0
Mike Hooper	1986-1993	51	0	5	0	10	0	4	0	3	0	73	0
Don Hutchison	1992-1994	45	7	3	0	8	2	3	1	1	0	60	10
Sami Hyypia	1999-2009	318	22	29	2	19	3	94	8	4	0	464	35
Paul Ince	1997-1999	65	14	3	1	6	1	7	1	0	0	81	17
Emiliano Insua	2007-2010	46	0	3	0	3	1	10	0	0	0	62	1
Charles Itandje	2007-2008	0	0	4	0	3	0	0	0	0	0	7	0
David James	1992-1999	214	0	19	0	22	0	22	0	0	0	277	0
Glen Johnson	2009-2010	25	3	0	0	1	0	9	0	0	0	35	3
Lee Jones	1994-1996	3	0	0	0	1	0	0	0	0	0	4	0
Paul Jones	2004-2004	2	0	0	0	0	0	0	0	0	0	2	0
Rob Jones	1991-1998	183	0	27	0	22	0	11	0	0	0	243	0
Josemi	2004-2005	21	0	0	0	1	0	12	0	1	0	35	0
Robbie Keane	2008-2009	19	5	1	0	1	0	7	2	0	0	28	7
Martin Kelly	2008-2010	1	0	0	0	0	0	3	0	0	0	4	0
Mark Kennedy	1995-1998	16	0	1	0	2	0	2	0	0	0	21	0
Harry Kewell	2003-2008	93	12	10	0	5	1	30	3	1	0	139	16
Frode Kippe	1999-2001	0	0	0	0	2	0	0	0	0	0	2	0
Chris Kirkland	2001-2004	25	0	3	0	6	0	11	0	0	0	45	0
Istvan Kozma	1992-1992	6	0	2	0	1	0	0	0	1	0	10	0
Jan Kromkamp	2006-2006	14	0	4	0	0	0	0	0	0	0	18	0
Dirk Kuyt	2006-2010	141	36	9	2	3	0	47	13	0	0	200	51
Bjorn Tore Kvarme	1997-1999	45	0	2	0	2	0	5	0	0	0	54	0
Sotiros Kyrgiakos	2009-2010	14	1	0	0	2	0	5	0	0	0	21	1
Lucas Leiva	2007-2010	78	1	8	1	5	1	30	2	0	0	121	5
O. Leonhardsen	1997-1999	37	7	1	0	6	0	5	0	0	0	49	7
Anthony Le Tallec	2003-2005	17	0	4	0	2	0	9	1	0	0	32	1
Sebastian Leto	2007-2007	0	0	0	0	2	0	2	0	0	0	4	0
Jari Litmanen	2001-2002	26	5	3	1	3	0	11	3	0	0	43	9
Patrice Luzi	2004-2004	1	0	0	0	0	0	0	0	0	0	1	0
Gary McAllister	2000-2002	55	5	5	0	6	1	20	2	1	1	87	9
Jason McAteer	1995-1999	100	3	12	3	13	0	14	0	0	0	139	6
Steve McManaman	1990-1999	272	46	29	5	33	10	30	5	0	0	364	66
Mike Marsh	1989-1993	69	2	8	0	11	3	12	1	1	0	101	6
Javier Mascherano	2007-2010	93	1	5	0	2	0	38	1	0	0	138	1
Dominic Matteo	1993-2000	127	1	8	1	9	0	11	0	0	0	155	2
Layton Maxwell	1999-1999	0	0	0	0	1	1	0	0	0	0	1	1
Erik Meijer	1999-2000	24	0	0	0	3	2	0	0	0	0	27	2
Neil Mellor	2002-2005	12	2	2	0	6	3	2	1	0	0	22	6
Jan Molby	1984-1995	218	44	28	4	28	9	7	1	11	3	292	61
F. Morientes	2005-2006	41	8	5	1	3	0	11	3	1	0	61	12
Danny Murphy	1997-2004	170	25	15	3	16	11	46	5	2	0	249	44
Jon Newby	1999-2000	1	0	2	0	1	0	0	0	0	0	4	0
David Ngog	2008-2010	38	7	2	0	4	1	12	3	0	0	56	11
Steve Nicol	1982-1994	343	36	50	3	42	4	20	2	13	1	468	46
Antonio Nunez	2004-2005	18	0	1	0	3	1	5	0	0	0	27	1
Steve Nicol	1982-1994	343	36	50	3	42	4	20	2	13	1	468	46
Antonio Nunez	2004-2005	18	0	1	0	3	1	5	0	0	0	27	1

PREMIER LEAGUE PLAYERS' RECORD (O-Z)

PLAYER	FIRST GAME-LAST GAME	LEAGUE		FA CUP		LEAGUE CUP		EUROPE		OTHER GAMES		LFC CAREER	
		A	G	A	G	A	G	A	G	A	G	A	G
Jon Otsemobor	2002-2003	4	0	0	0	2	0	0	0	0	0	6	0
Michael Owen	1997-2004	216	118	15	8	14	9	50	22	2	1	297	158
Daniel Pacheco	2009-2010	4	0	0	0	0	0	3	0	0	0	7	0
Daniele Padelli	2007-2007	1	0	0	0	0	0	0	0	0	0	1	0
Gabriel Paletta	2006-2007	3	0	0	0	3	1	2	0	0	0	8	1
Richie Partridge	2000-2004	0	0	0	0	3	0	0	0	0	0	3	0
M. Pellegrino	2005-2005	12	0	0	0	1	0	0	0	0	0	13	0
Lee Peltier	2006-2007	0	0	0	0	3	0	1	0	0	0	4	0
Jermaine Pennant	2006-2008	55	3	3	0	3	0	19	0	1	0	81	3
Torben Piechnik	1992-1993	17	0	2	0	5	0	0	0	0	0	24	0
Damien Plessis	2008-2009	3	0	0	0	3	1	2	0	0	0	8	1
Darren Potter	2004-2005	2	0	1	0	5	0	9	0	0	0	17	0
David Raven	2004-2005	1	0	1	0	2	0	0	0	0	0	4	0
Jamie Redknapp	1991-2001	237	30	18	2	27	5	26	4	0	0	308	41
Pepe Reina	2005-2010	182	0	8	0	1	0	65	0	3	0	259	0
Karlheinz Riedle	1997-1999	60	11	2	0	7	2	7	2	0	0	76	15
Albert Riera	2008-2010	40	3	3	1	1	0	12	1	0	0	56	5
John Arne Riise	2001-2008	234	21	17	3	13	2	79	4	5	1	348	31
Jack Robinson	2010-2010	1	0	0	0	0	0	0	0	0	0	1	0
Maxi Rodriguez	2010-2010	17	1	0	0	0	0	0	0	0	0	17	1
Miki Roque	2006-2006	0	0	0	0	0	0	1	0	0	0	1	0
Ronny Rosenthal	1990-1993	74	21	8	0	9	1	4	0	2	0	97	22
Neil Ruddock	1993-1997	115	11	11	0	20	1	6	0	0	0	152	12
Ian Rush	1980-1996	469	229	61	39	78	48	38	20	14	10	660	346
Dean Saunders	1991-1992	42	11	8	2	5	2	5	9	1	1	61	25
John Scales	1994-1996	65	2	14	0	10	2	5	0	0	0	94	4
F. S-Pongolle	2003-2006	38	4	5	2	8	1	12	2	3	0	66	9
Mohamed Sissoko	2005-2007	51	1	6	0	4	0	23	0	3	0	87	1
Martin Skrtel	2008-2010	54	1	5	0	2	0	18	0	0	0	79	1
Vladimir Smicer	1999-2005	121	10	10	1	15	5	37	3	1	0	184	19
Jamie Smith	2006-2006	0	0	0	0	1	0	0	0	0	0	1	0
Mark Smyth	2004-2004	0	0	0	0	1	0	0	0	0	0	1	0
Rigobert Song	1999-2000	34	0	1	0	2	0	1	0	0	0	38	0
Jay Spearing	2008-2009	3	0	0	0	2	0	2	0	0	0	7	0
Steve Staunton	1988-2000	109	0	18	1	13	5	7	0	1	1	148	7
Paul Stewart	1992-1993	32	1	1	0	6	0	2	2	1	0	42	3
Nick Tanner	1989-1992	40	1	2	0	8	0	8	0	1	0	59	1
Michael Thomas	1991-1998	124	9	17	2	10	1	12	0	0	0	163	12
David Thompson	1996-2000	48	5	1	0	5	0	2	0	0	0	56	5
Fernando Torres	2007-2010	79	56	6	1	3	3	28	12	0	0	116	72
Djimi Traore	1999-2006	88	0	5	0	14	0	32	1	2	0	141	1
Gregory Vignal	2001-2003	11	0	1	0	3	0	5	0	0	0	20	0
Andriy Voronin	2007-2009	27	5	1	0	2	0	10	1	0	0	40	6
Mark Walters	1991-1995	94	14	9	0	12	4	8	1	1	0	124	19
Stephen Warnock	2004-2007	40	1	3	0	8	0	15	0	1	0	67	1
John Welsh	2002-2005	4	0	1	0	3	0	2	0	0	0	10	0
Sander Westerveld	1999-2001	75	0	8	0	5	0	14	0	1	0	103	0
Ronnie Whelan	1981-1994	362	46	41	7	50	14	24	6	16	0	493	73
Zak Whitbread	2004-2005	0	0	1	0	4	0	2	0	0	0	7	0
Mark Wright	1991-1997	158	5	18	0	16	2	17	2	1	0	210	9
Stephen Wright	2000-2002	14	0	2	0	2	0	3	1	0	0	21	1
Abel Xavier	2002-2002	14	1	0	0	1	0	5	1	1	0	21	2
Boudewijn Zenden	2005-2007	23	2	0	0	2	0	21	0	1	0	47	2
Christian Ziege	2000-2001	16	1	3	0	4	1	9	0	0	0	32	2

GOALS SCORED BY OVERSEAS PLAYERS

PREMIER LEAGUE ONLY – CORRECT AT END OF 2009/10

PLAYER	GOALS	PLAYER	GOALS
Fernando Torres	56	Florent Sinama-Pongolle	4
Dirk Kuyt	36	Daniel Agger	3
Patrik Berger	28	Fabio Aurelio	3
Sami Hyypia	22	Markus Babbel	3
John Arne Riise	21	El-Hadji Diouf	3
Milan Baros	19	Vegard Heggem	3
Yossi Benayoun	18	Albert Riera	3
Luis Garcia	18	Alvaro Arbeloa	2
Xabi Alonso	15	Igor Biscan	2
Djibril Cisse	13	Stig Inge Bjornebye	2
Harry Kewell	12	Bruno Cheyrou	2
Ryan Babel	11	Mark Gonzalez	2
Karlheinz Riedle	11	Javier Mascherano	2
Vladimir Smicer	10	Bolo Zenden	2
Titi Camara	9	Alberto Aquilani	1
Dietmar Hamann	8	Salif Diao	1
Fernando Morientes	8	Andrea Dossena	1
Oyvind Leonhardsen	7	Sotirios Kyrgiakos	1
Jan Molby	7	Lucas Leiva	1
David Ngog	7	Maxi Rodriguez	1
Ronny Rosenthal	6	Momo Sissoko	1
Jari Litmanen	5	Martin Skrtel	1
Andriy Voronin	5	Abel Xavier	1
Nicolas Anelka	4	Christian Ziege	1

QUICKEST TO 50 GOALS

LEAGUE GOALS FOR LIVERPOOL

PLAYER	GAMES	DATE OF 50TH GOAL	PLAYER	GAMES	DATE OF 50TH GOAL
Fernando Torres	72	29/12/2009	David Johnson	121	29/11/1980
Sam Raybould	80	01/11/1902	Dick Forshaw	125	24/03/1923
Albert Stubbins	80	22/01/1949	Tom Miller	125	01/09/1920
Roger Hunt	81	14/10/1961	Jimmy Melia	129	16/01/1960
Jack Parkinson	82	12/04/1909	Jack Balmer	139	30/11/1946
John Aldridge	83	12/09/1989	Berry Niewenhuys	158	04/12/1937
Ian Rush	84	29/10/1983	Alf Hanson	162	16/04/1938
Robbie Fowler	88	17/12/1995	Billy Liddell	167	16/12/1950
Gordon Hodgson	90	27/10/1928	Kevin Keegan	175	10/01/1976
Harry Chambers	98	25/03/1922	Jack Cox	208	08/04/1905
Kenny Dalglish	98	10/11/1979	Terry McDermott	221	30/01/1982
Michael Owen	98	26/08/2000	Ray Kennedy	269	17/10/1981
Joe Hewitt	104	29/02/1908	Arthur Goddard	271	19/02/1910
Ian St John	105	08/02/1964	Alan A'Court	278	14/01/1961
John Barnes	111	22/09/1990	Steven Gerrard	281	08/12/2007
Robert Robinson	114	07/12/1907	Steve Heighway	302	11/11/1978
John Toshack	116	20/09/1975			

PREMIER LEAGUE NUMBERS GAME

SQUAD NUMBERS

SHIRT	PLAYERS (PREMIER LEAGUE APPEARANCES IN BRACKETS)				
1	Grobbelaar (29),	James (171),	Westerveld (75),	Dudek (92)	
2	R.Jones (125), Johnson (25)	Henchoz (135),	Kromkamp (14),	Arbeloa (9),	Dossena (16),
3	Burrows (4), Xavier (14),	Dicks (24), Finnan (145)	Scales (3),	Kvarme (45),	Ziege (16),
4	Nicol (35),	McAteer (100),	Song (34),	Hyypia (245),	Aquilani (18)
5	M.Wright (104),	Staunton (44),	Baros (68),	Agger (77)	
6	Hutchison (11),	Babb (128),	Babbel (42),	Riise (131)	
7	Clough (39),	McManaman (101),	Smicer (91),	Kewell (93),	Keane (19)
8	Stewart (8),	Collymore (61),	Leonhardsen (37),	Heskey (150),	Gerrard (196)
9	Rush (98), Torres (79)	Fowler (144),	Anelka (20),	Diouf (55),	Cisse (49),
10	Barnes (135),	Owen (178),	Garcia (77),	Voronin (27)	
11	Walters (35), Benayoun (30),	Redknapp (103), Riera (40)	Smicer (30),	Fowler (14),	Gonzalez (25),
12	Whelan (23), P.Jones (2),	Scales (62), Pellegrino (12),	Harkness (38), Aurelio (71)	Hyypia (73),	Dudek (35),
13	James (14),	Riedle (60),	Murphy (130),	Le Tallec (4)	
14	Molby (25),	Ruddock (19),	Heggem (54),	Alonso (143)	
15	Redknapp (99),	Berger (148),	Diao (11),	Crouch (85),	Benayoun (62)
16	Thomas (99),	Dundee (3),	Hamann (191),	Pennant (55),	Kyrgiakos (14)
17	McManaman (108), Arbeloa (57),	Ince (65), Rodriguez (17)	Gerrard (129),	Josemi (21)	Bellamy (27),
18	Rosenthal (3), Nunez (18),	Owen (38), Kuyt (141)	Ferri (2),	Meijer (24),	Riise (103),
19	Piechnik (1), Babel (82)	Kennedy (16),	Friedel (14),	Arphexad (2),	Morientes (41),
20	Bjornebye (128),	Barmby (32),	Le Tallec (13),	Carson (4),	Mascherano (93)
21	Marsh (2), Lucas (78)	Matteo (127),	McAllister (55),	Diao (26),	Traore (48),
22	Harkness (43),	Camara (33),	Kirkland (25),	Sissoko (51),	Insua (41)
23	Fowler (108),	Carragher (435)			
24	L.Jones (3),	Murphy (40),	Diomede (2),	S-Pongolle (38),	Ngog (38)
25	Ruddock (96),	Thompson (48),	Biscan (72),	Reina (182)	
26	Spearing (3)				
27	Vignal (11),	Degen (7)			
28	Gerrard (41),	Cheyrou (31),	Warnock (40),	Plessis (1)	
29	Friedel (11),	S.Wright (14),	Luzi (1),	Paletta (3)	
30	Traore (40),	Zenden (7),	Padelli (1)		
31	Raven (1),	El Zhar (18)			
32	Newby (1),	Welsh (4),	Zenden (16),	Darby (1)	
33	Mellor (12)				
34	Potter (2),	Kelly (1)			
35	Guthrie (3)				
36	Otsemobor (4)				
37	Litmanen (26),	Skrtel (54)			
38	Dossena (2)				
39	Eccleston (1)				
40	Ayala (5)				
42	El Zhar (3)				
46	Hobbs (2)				
47	Plessis (2),	Pacheco (4)			
48	Insua (5)				
49	Robinson (1)				

NUMBERS GAME

With squad numbers introduced for the 1993/94 Premier League season, keeping tabs on Liverpool's spiralling number wearers has proved more problematic with increased squad sizes signalling a continual shift further away from the traditional 1-11 of yore. While the Premier League Numbers Game page (opposite) is updated with the 2009/10 players, the table below shows the players who are the most consistent performers in a particular shirt.

MOST CONSECUTIVE APPEARANCES IN A NUMBER SHIRT (LEAGUE ONLY)

SHIRT	PLAYER	APPEARANCES
1	Ray Clemence	232
2	Phil Neal	253
3	Alan Kennedy	131
4	Steve Nicol	87
5	Larry Lloyd	85
6	Alan Hansen	78
7	Kenny Dalglish	147
8	Roger Hunt	104
9	Ian Rush	73
10	Jimmy Melia	90
11	Ian Callaghan	162
12	Sami Hyypia	42
13	Danny Murphy	39
14	Neil Ruddock	42
15	Jamie Redknapp	48
16	Dietmar Hamann	42
17	Steve McManaman	61
18	John Arne Riise	41
19	Ryan Babel	15*
20	Stig Inge Bjornebye	55
21	Dominic Matteo	24
22	Steve Harkness	27
23	Robbie Fowler	91
24	Danny Murphy	14
25	Pepe Reina	114*
26	Jay Spearing	3
27	Gregory Vignal	4
28	Steven Gerrard	12
29	Brad Friedel	11
30	Djimi Traore	14
31	Nabil El Zhar	4
32	Bolo Zenden	5
33	Neil Mellor	3
34	Martin Kelly	1
35	Danny Guthrie	2
36	Jon Otsemobor	4
37	Martin Skrtel	12
38	Andrea Dossena	1
39	Nathan Eccleston	1
40	Daniel Ayala	2
42	Nabil El Zhar	2
46	Jack Hobbs	2
47	Damien Plessis	1
	Daniel Pacheco	1*
48	Emiliano Insua	3
49	Jack Robinson	1*

No. 6 – Alan Hansen

No. 7 – Kenny Dalglish

CONSISTENT REDS

Sixteen players have played 100 or more consecutive league games for Liverpool. Phil Neal's remarkable near 9-year run is unlikely to be beaten, considering the increasing demands on footballers and the use of squad rotation. Only goalkeepers David James and Pepe Reina, whose run was unbroken for 3 seasons prior to the 2010/11 season, have reached the landmark in the Premier League era.

	100 OR MORE CONSECUTIVE LEAGUE APPEARANCES FOR LIVERPOOL	
GAMES	**PLAYER**	**FIRST APPEARANCE-LAST APPEARANCE**
365	Phil Neal	14th December 1974-24th September 1983
241	Chris Lawler	2nd October 1965-24th April 1971
232	Ray Clemence	9th September 1972-4th March 1978
210	Bruce Grobbelaar	29th August 1981-3rd May 1986
162	Ian Callaghan	17th January 1971-29th March 1975
159	David James	19th February 1994-22nd February 1998
147	Kenny Dalglish	20th August 1977-6th December 1980
141	Alan Kennedy	26th December 1981-31st March 1985
124	Emlyn Hughes	4th November 1972-25th October 1975
119	William Goldie	23rd December 1899-27th April 1903
119	Elisha Scott	17th December 1921-25th October 1924
116	Tommy Lawrence	22nd April 1967-17th January 1970
114	Tommy Smith	21st August 1965-2nd March 1968
114	Pepe Reina	11th August 2007-
104	Roger Hunt	18th November 1961-4th April 1964
102	Chris Lawler	1st May 1971-24th November 1973

Phil Neal – Reds regular

PREMIER LEAGUE CAPTAINS

A total of 14 players have started as captain during Liverpool's 18 Premier League campaigns, ahead of the 2010/11 season. Dirk Kuyt shared captaincy duties with Steven Gerrard and Jamie Carragher in 2009/10 to become No.14 on the list. The success of each is noted below.

LIVERPOOL CAPTAINS IN PREMIER LEAGUE GAMES (MOST SUCCESSFUL FIRST)

CAPTAIN	PLD	W	D	L	PTS	WIN %	AVE PTS. PER GAME
Steve Nicol	9	6	2	1	20	66.67	2.22
Steve McManaman	8	5	1	2	16	62.50	2.00
Jamie Carragher	27	14	9	4	51	51.85	1.89
Steven Gerrard	217	118	54	45	408	54.37	1.88
Robbie Fowler	22	12	4	6	40	54.55	1.82
Sami Hyypia	131	69	32	30	239	52.67	1.82
John Barnes	87	43	25	19	154	49.43	1.77
Ian Rush	87	40	20	27	140	45.98	1.61
Jamie Redknapp	22	10	5	7	35	45.45	1.59
Paul Ince	65	28	18	19	102	43.08	1.57
Neil Ruddock	2	0	2	0	2	0.00	1.00
Dirk Kuyt	1	0	1	0	1	0.00	1.00
Mark Wright	17	4	4	9	16	23.53	0.94
Phil Babb	1	0	0	1	0	0.00	0.00
TOTAL	**696**	**349**	**177**	**170**	**1224**	**50.14**	**1.76**

Steve McManaman – Five wins in eight

FOOTBALL LEAGUE EVER-PRESENTS

The full list of Liverpool regulars during the club's Football League years, taking in the 1893/94 season until 1991/92, the final year of First Division football before the Premier League began.

PLAYERS WHO HAVE PLAYED EVERY LEAGUE GAME FOR LIVERPOOL DURING ONE SEASON

SEASON	GAMES	PLAYER
1894/95	30	Tom Bradshaw
1896/97	30	John McCartney
1897/98	30	Thomas Cleghorn, Harry Storer
1899/00	34	Billy Dunlop, Tom Robertson
1900/01	34	Bill Goldie, Bill Perkins, Tom Robertson
1901/02	34	Bill Goldie
1902/03	34	Bill Goldie
1904/05	34	Ned Doig
1905/06	38	Arthur Goddard
1909/10	38	Tom Chorlton
1910/11	38	Robbie Robinson
1912/13	38	Robert Ferguson
1913/14	38	Thomas Fairfoul
1914/15	38	Jimmy Nicholl
1920/21	42	Walter Wadsworth
1921/22	42	Dick Forshaw, Fred Hopkin
1922/23	42	Dick Forshaw, Donald McKinlay, Elisha Scott
1923/24	42	Elisha Scott
1924/25	42	Danny Shone
1925/26	42	Harry Chambers
1926/27	42	Harry Chambers
1927/28	42	Tom Bromilow, Dick Edmed
1928/29	42	James Jackson, Tom Morrison
1930/31	42	Tommy Lucas, Archie McPherson
1931/32	42	Tom Bradshaw, Gordon Gunson
1932/33	42	Willie Steel
1936/37	42	Alf Hanson
1938/39	42	Jack Balmer, Matt Busby
1948/49	42	Jack Balmer
1950/51	42	Eddie Spicer
1955/56	42	Geoff Twentyman
1956/57	42	Ronnie Moran
1958/59	42	Dick White
1959/60	42	Alan A'Court, Ronnie Moran
1960/61	42	Bert Slater, Dick White
1961/62	42	Alan A'Court, Gerry Byrne, Jimmy Melia, Gordon Milne
1962/63	42	Roger Hunt
1963/64	42	Ian Callaghan, Gordon Milne, Peter Thompson
1965/66	42	Gerry Byrne, Ian Callaghan, Tommy Lawrence, Tommy Smith, Ron Yeats
1966/67	42	Chris Lawler, Tommy Smith, Peter Thompson
1967/68	42	Chris Lawler, Tommy Lawrence
1968/69	42	Ian Callaghan, Chris Lawler, Tommy Lawrence, Tommy Smith, Peter Thompson

FOOTBALL LEAGUE EVER-PRESENTS

PLAYERS WHO HAVE PLAYED EVERY LEAGUE GAME FOR LIVERPOOL DURING ONE SEASON

SEASON	GAMES	PLAYER
1969/70	42	Bobby Graham, Chris Lawler
1971/72	42	Ray Clemence, Emlyn Hughes, Chris Lawler
1972/73	42	Ian Callaghan, Chris Lawler, Larry Lloyd
1973/74	42	Ian Callaghan, Ray Clemence, Peter Cormack,
1973/74	42	Emlyn Hughes, Kevin Keegan
1974/75	42	Ray Clemence, Emlyn Hughes
1975/76	42	Ray Clemence, Phil Neal
1976/77	42	Ray Clemence, Emlyn Hughes, Phil Neal
1977/78	42	Kenny Dalglish, Phil Neal
1978/79	42	Ray Clemence, Kenny Dalglish, Ray Kennedy, Phil Neal
1979/80	42	Kenny Dalglish, Phil Neal, Phil Thompson
1980/81	42	Phil Neal
1981/82	42	Kenny Dalglish, Bruce Grobbelaar, Phil Neal
1982/83	42	Kenny Dalglish, Bruce Grobbelaar, Alan Kennedy, Phil Neal
1983/84	42	Bruce Grobbelaar, Alan Hansen, Alan Kennedy, Mark Lawrenson, Sammy Lee
1984/85	42	Bruce Grobbelaar, Phil Neal
1985/86	42	Bruce Grobbelaar
1986/87	42	Ian Rush
1987/88	40	Steve McMahon, Steve Nicol
1988/89	38	Ray Houghton, Steve Nicol
1989/90	38	Bruce Grobbelaar, Steve McMahon

PREMIER LEAGUE EVER-PRESENTS

Pepe Reina levelled David James' record in the Premier League era, playing every league game for 3 consecutive seasons – Liverpool's No. 25 achieving the feat in the last three seasons, while James made his mark from 1994-97. Twelve different players have appeared in every game for at least one season. Incidentally Jamie Carragher has played every league game in two out of the last four Premier League seasons.

PLAYERS WHO HAVE PLAYED EVERY LEAGUE GAME FOR LIVERPOOL DURING ONE SEASON

SEASON	GAMES	PLAYER
1993/94	42	Ian Rush
1994/95	42	Robbie Fowler, David James
1995/96	38	Steve McManaman, Robbie Fowler, David James
1996/97	38	Stig Inge Bjornebye, David James
1999/00	38	Sami Hyypia
2000/01	38	Markus Babbel, Sander Westerveld
2001/02	38	John Arne Riise
2003/04	38	Sami Hyypia
2004/05	38	Jamie Carragher
2007/08	38	Pepe Reina
2008/09	38	Jamie Carragher, Dirk Kuyt, Pepe Reina
2009/10	38	Pepe Reina

WORLD CUP FINALISTS

Fernando Torres and Pepe Reina became the first Liverpool players since 1966 to win the World Cup last summer in South Africa, two years after enjoying success with Spain at the European Championships. Indeed, at the tournament only Barcelona had more players representing their countries – 13 – with Liverpool's tally of 12 only being matched by Chelsea. The table below and opposite showcases the players who have played or been included in final squads at the world's greatest international competition while on Liverpool's books.

LIVERPOOL PLAYERS AT THE WORLD CUP FINALS

YEAR	HOSTS	PLAYER	COUNTRY	APPS.	GLS.	HOW COUNTRY FARED
1950	Brazil	Laurie Hughes	England	3	0	Group Stage
1958	Sweden	Alan A'Court	England	3	0	Group Stage Play-Off
		Tommy Younger	Scotland	2	0	Group Stage
1962	Chile	Roger Hunt	England	0	0	Quarter-Finals
1966	England	Gerry Byrne	England	0	0	Winners
		Ian Callaghan	England	1	0	Winners
		Roger Hunt	England	6	3	Winners
1970	Mexico	Emlyn Hughes	England	0	0	Quarter-Finals
1974	W. Germany	Peter Cormack	Scotland	0	0	Group Stage
1978	Argentina	Kenny Dalglish	Scotland	3	1	Group Stage
		Graeme Souness	Scotland	1	0	Group Stage
1982	Spain	Kenny Dalglish	Scotland	2	1	1st Group Stage
		Alan Hansen	Scotland	3	0	1st Group Stage
		Terry McDermott	England	0	0	2nd Group Stage
		Phil Neal	England	2	0	2nd Group Stage
		Graeme Souness	Scotland	3	1	1st Group Stage
		Phil Thompson	England	5	0	2nd Group Stage
1986	Mexico	Jan Molby	Denmark	4	0	Last 16
		Steve Nicol	Scotland	3	0	Group Stage
1990	Italy	John Barnes	England	5	0	4th
		Peter Beardsley	England	5	0	4th
		Gary Gillespie	Scotland	1	0	Group Stage
		Ray Houghton	Rep. Ire.	5	0	Quarter-Finals
		Glenn Hysen	Sweden	2	0	Group Stage
		Steve McMahon	England	4	0	4th

WORLD CUP FINALISTS

YEAR	HOSTS	PLAYER	COUNTRY	APPS.	GLS.	HOW COUNTRY FARED
1990	Italy	Steve Staunton	Rep. Ire.	5	0	Quarter-Finals
		Ronnie Whelan	Rep. Ire.	1	0	Quarter-Finals
1994	USA	Stig Inge Bjornebye	Norway	3	0	Group Stage
		Ronnie Whelan	Rep. Ire.	1	0	Last 16
1998	France	Stig Inge Bjornebye	Norway	4	0	Last 16
		Brad Friedel	USA	1	0	Group Stage
		Paul Ince	England	4	0	Last 16
		Oyvind Leonhardsen	Norway	3	0	Last 16
		Steve McManaman	England	1	0	Last 16
		Michael Owen	England	4	2	Last 16
2002	Japan/	Jerzy Dudek	Poland	2	0	Group Stage
	S. Korea	Dietmar Hamann	Germany	6	0	Runners-Up
		Emile Heskey	England	5	1	Quarter-Finals
		Michael Owen	England	5	2	Quarter-Finals
		Abel Xavier	Portugal	1	0	Group Stage
2006	Germany	Xabi Alonso	Spain	3	1	Last 16
		Jamie Carragher	England	4	0	Quarter-Finals
		Scott Carson	England	0	0	Quarter-Finals
		Peter Crouch	England	4	1	Quarter-Finals
		Luis Garcia	Spain	3	0	Last 16
		Steven Gerrard	England	5	2	Quarter-Finals
		Harry Kewell	Australia	3	1	Last 16
		Jan Kromkamp	Holland	0	0	Last 16
		Pepe Reina	Spain	0	0	Last 16
2010	South Africa	Daniel Agger	Denmark	3	0	Group Stage
		Ryan Babel	Holland	0	0	Runners-Up
		Jamie Carragher	England	2	0	Last 16
		Steven Gerrard	England	4	1	Last 16
		Glen Johnson	England	4	0	Last 16
		Dirk Kuyt	Holland	7	1	Runners-Up
		Sotirios Kyrgiakos	Greece	2	0	Group Stage
		Javier Mascherano	Argentina	4	0	Quarter-Finals
		Pepe Reina	Spain	0	0	Winners
		Maxi Rodriguez	Argentina	5	0	Quarter-Finals
		Martin Skrtel	Slovakia	4	0	Last 16
		Fernando Torres	Spain	7	0	Winners

WORLD CUP FINALISTS

The following table gives the appearance details of every Liverpool player to have seen action at the finals. There are 44 players noted, with Steven Gerrard and Michael Owen the top appearance makers with 9 caps each, won playing at the World Cup for England.

LIVERPOOL PLAYERS' APPEARANCES AT WORLD CUP FINALS

PLAYER	COUNTRY	NO. APPS	FINALS ATTENDED	PLAYER	COUNTRY	NO. APPS	FINALS ATTENDED
Steven Gerrard	England	9	2	Martin Skrtel	Slovakia	4	1
Michael Owen	England	9	2	Graeme Souness	Scotland	4	2
Stig Inge Bjornebye	Norway	7	2	Alan A'Court	England	3	1
Dirk Kuyt	Holland	7	1	Daniel Agger	Denmark	3	1
Fernando Torres	Spain	7	1	Xabi Alonso	Spain	3	1
Jamie Carragher	England	6	2	Luis Garcia	Spain	3	1
Roger Hunt	England	6	2	Alan Hansen	Scotland	3	1
Dietmar Hamann	Germany	6	1	Laurie Hughes	England	3	1
John Barnes	England	5	1	Harry Kewell	Australia	3	1
Peter Beardsley	England	5	1	Oyvind Leonhardsen	Norway	3	1
Kenny Dalglish	Scotland	5	2	Steve Nicol	Scotland	3	1
Emile Heskey	England	5	1	Jerzy Dudek	Poland	2	1
Ray Houghton	Rep. Ireland	5	1	Glenn Hysen	Sweden	2	1
Maxi Rodriguez	Argentina	5	1	Sotirios Kyrgiakos	Greece	2	1
Steve Staunton	Rep. Ireland	5	1	Phil Neal	England	2	1
Phil Thompson	England	5	1	Ronnie Whelan	Rep. Ireland	2	2
Peter Crouch	England	4	1	Tommy Younger	Scotland	2	1
Paul Ince	England	4	1	Ian Callaghan	England	1	1
Glen Johnson	England	4	1	Brad Friedel	USA	1	1
Steve McMahon	England	4	1	Gary Gillespie	Scotland	1	1
Javier Mascherano	Argentina	4	1	Steve McManaman	England	1	1
Jan Molby	Denmark	4	1	Abel Xavier	Portugal	1	1

Michael Owen and Steven Gerrard (left), top LFC World Cup players, and (right) 2010 finalist Dirk Kuyt

ENGLAND

Joe Cole's move to the club in the summer of 2010 raised the possibility of a 59th Liverpool player being capped by England. Having represented his country at three World Cups plus the 2004 European Championships (where he did not play), he will hope to add to his 50+ caps during his time at Anfield. Incidentally, Steven Gerrard, who captained England in a friendly against Hungary in August 2010, could reach 100 caps should he remain a regular – and should England qualify – for the 2012 European Championships.

LIVERPOOL PLAYERS CAPPED BY ENGLAND (AT END OF AUGUST 2010)

PLAYER	CAPS WON AT LIVERPOOL	TOTAL CAPS	PLAYER	CAPS WON AT LIVERPOOL	TOTAL CAPS
Steven Gerrard	85	85	Laurie Hughes	3	3
Michael Owen	60	89	Larry Lloyd	3	4
Emlyn Hughes	59	62	Tommy Lucas	3	3
Ray Clemence	56	61	John Scales	3	3
Phil Neal	50	50	Phil Taylor	3	3
John Barnes	48	79	Gerry Byrne	2	2
Phil Thompson	42	42	Scott Carson	2	3
Jamie Carragher	38	38	Bill Jones	2	2
Emile Heskey	35	62	Alan Kennedy	2	2
Peter Beardsley	34	59	Jimmy Melia	2	2
Roger Hunt	34	34	Jack Parkinson	2	2
Peter Crouch	28	40	John Bamber	1	1
Kevin Keegan	28	63	Frank Becton	1	2
Terry McDermott	25	25	Thomas Bradshaw	1	1
Steve McManaman	24	37	Raby Howell	1	2
Robbie Fowler	22	26	David James	1	53
Ray Kennedy	17	17	Chris Kirkland	1	1
Steve McMahon	17	17	Neil Ruddock	1	1
Jamie Redknapp	17	17	Tommy Smith	1	1
Peter Thompson	16	16			
Sam Hardy	14	21			
Sammy Lee	14	14			
Gordon Milne	14	14			
Paul Ince	12	53			
Glen Johnson	12	27			
Danny Murphy	9	9			
Nick Barmby	8	23			
Harry Chambers	8	8			
Rob Jones	8	8			
Alan A'Court	5	5			
Tom Bromilow	5	5			
David Johnson	5	8			
Ephraim Longworth	5	5			
Mark Wright	5	45			
Ian Callaghan	4	4			
Chris Lawler	4	4			
Alec Lindsay	4	4			
Jack Cox	3	3			
Gordon Hodgson	3	3			

Emlyn Hughes, third most-capped England player at Liverpool

HOME NATIONS

Noted below are the international caps won by Liverpool's Scotland, Wales, Northern Ireland and Republic of Ireland players. With Robbie Keane being the last Liverpool player capped by one of the other 'Home Nations' in the autumn of 2008, new Scottish defender Danny Wilson will be hoping to change that statistic in the coming months and years.

The table opposite page is a complete run-down of all the international caps won by Home Nations-capped Liverpool players, while overleaf is a list of the goals scored.

LIVERPOOL PLAYERS CAPPED BY SCOTLAND (AT END OF AUGUST 2010)

PLAYER	CAPS WON AT LIVERPOOL	TOTAL CAPS	PLAYER	CAPS WON AT LIVERPOOL	TOTAL CAPS
Kenny Dalglish	55	102	John Wark	3	29
Graeme Souness	37	54	Jimmy McDougall	2	2
Billy Liddell	28	28	Frank McGarvey	2	7
Steve Nicol	27	27	Donald MacKinlay	2	2
Alan Hansen	26	26	Ron Yeats	2	2
Tommy Younger	16	24	George Allan	1	1
Ian St John	14	21	Billy Dunlop	1	1
Gary Gillespie	13	13	Jock McNab	1	1
Alex Raisbeck	8	8	Tom Miller	1	3
Ken Campbell	3	8	Hugh Morgan	1	2
Tommy Lawrence	3	3			

LIVERPOOL PLAYERS CAPPED BY WALES (AT END OF AUGUST 2010)

PLAYER	CAPS WON AT LIVERPOOL	TOTAL CAPS	PLAYER	CAPS WON AT LIVERPOOL	TOTAL CAPS
Ian Rush	67	73	Cyril Sidlow	7	7
John Toshack	26	40	Ray Lambert	5	5
Joey Jones	18	72	Richard Morris	5	11
Maurice Parry	16	16	Edward Parry	5	5
Craig Bellamy	11	58	John Hughes	3	3
Ernest Peake	10	11	Lee Jones	1	2
George Lathom	8	10	Robert Matthews	1	3
Dean Saunders	8	75			

LIVERPOOL PLAYERS CAPPED BY NORTHERN IRELAND & REPUBLIC OF IRELAND (AT END OF AUGUST 2010)

PLAYER	CAPS WON AT LIVERPOOL	TOTAL CAPS	PLAYER	CAPS WON AT LIVERPOOL	TOTAL CAPS
Ronnie Whelan	51	53	Mark Kennedy	17	34
Steve Staunton	38	102	Jim Beglin	15	15
Ray Houghton	34	73	Jason McAteer	14	52
Steve Heighway	33	34	Billy Lacey (NI)	12	23
Steve Finnan	28	53	Michael Robinson	5	24
Elisha Scott (NI)	27	31	Robbie Keane	4	99
Phil Babb	25	35	David McMullan (NI)	3	3
Mark Lawrenson	24	39	Ken De Mange	1	2
John Aldridge	19	69			

INTERNATIONAL CAPS

LFC PLAYERS CAPPED FOR THEIR COUNTRIES – HOME NATIONS (AT END OF AUGUST 2010)

PLAYER	COUNTRY	CAPS	PLAYER	COUNTRY	CAPS
Steven Gerrard	England	85	George Lathom	Wales	=
Ian Rush	Wales	67	Alex Raisbeck	Scotland	=
Michael Owen	England	60	Dean Saunders	Wales	=
Emlyn Hughes	England	59	Cyril Sidlow	Wales	7
Ray Clemence	England	56	Alan A'Court	England	5
Kenny Dalglish	Scotland	55	Tom Bromilow	England	=
Ronnie Whelan	Republic of Ireland	51	David Johnson	England	=
Phil Neal	England	50	Ray Lambert	Wales	=
John Barnes	England	48	Ephraim Longworth	England	=
Phil Thompson	England	42	Richard Morris	Wales	=
Jamie Carragher	England	38	Edward Parry	Wales	=
Steve Staunton	Republic of Ireland	=	Michael Robinson	Republic of Ireland	=
Graeme Souness	Scotland	37	Mark Wright	England	=
Emile Heskey	England	35	Ian Callaghan	England	4
Peter Beardsley	England	34	Robbie Keane	Republic of Ireland	=
Ray Houghton	Republic of Ireland	=	Chris Lawler	England	=
Roger Hunt	England	=	Alec Lindsay	England	=
Steve Heighway	Republic of Ireland	33	Ken Campbell	Scotland	3
Peter Crouch	England	28	Jack Cox	England	=
Steve Finnan	Republic of Ireland	=	Gordon Hodgson	England	=
Kevin Keegan	England	=	John Hughes	Wales	=
Billy Liddell	Scotland	=	Laurie Hughes	England	=
Steve Nicol	Scotland	27	Tommy Lawrence	Scotland	=
Elisha Scott	Northern Ireland	=	Larry Lloyd	England	=
Alan Hansen	Scotland	26	Tommy Lucas	England	=
John Toshack	Wales	=	David McMullan	Northern Ireland	=
Phil Babb	Republic of Ireland	25	John Scales	England	=
Terry McDermott	England	=	Phil Taylor	England	=
Mark Lawrenson	Republic of Ireland	24	John Wark	Scotland	=
Steve McManaman	England	=	Gerry Byrne	England	2
Robbie Fowler	England	22	Scott Carson	England	=
John Aldridge	Republic of Ireland	19	Bill Jones	England	=
Joey Jones	Wales	18	Alan Kennedy	England	=
Mark Kennedy	Republic of Ireland	17	Donald MacKinlay	Scotland	=
Ray Kennedy	England	=	Jimmy McDougall	Scotland	=
Steve McMahon	England	=	Frank McGarvey	Scotland	=
Jamie Redknapp	England	=	Jimmy Melia	England	=
Maurice Parry	Wales	16	Jack Parkinson	England	=
Peter Thompson	England	=	Ron Yeats	Scotland	=
Tommy Younger	Scotland	=	George Allan	Scotland	1
Jim Beglin	Republic of Ireland	15	John Bamber	England	=
Sam Hardy	England	14	Frank Becton	England	=
Sammy Lee	England	=	Thomas Bradshaw	England	=
Jason McAteer	Republic of Ireland	=	Ken De Mange	Republic of Ireland	=
Gordon Milne	England	=	Billy Dunlop	Scotland	=
Ian St John	Scotland	=	Raby Howell	England	=
Gary Gillespie	Scotland	13	David James	England	=
Paul Ince	England	12	Lee Jones	Wales	=
Glen Johnson	England	=	Chris Kirkland	England	=
Billy Lacey	Northern Ireland	=	Robert Matthews	Wales	=
Craig Bellamy	Wales	11	Jock McNab	Scotland	=
Ernest Peake	Wales	10	Tom Miller	Scotland	=
Danny Murphy	England	9	Hugh Morgan	Scotland	=
Nick Barmby	England	8	Neil Ruddock	England	=
Harry Chambers	England	=	Tommy Smith	England	=
Rob Jones	England	=			

INTERNATIONAL GOALS

LFC PLAYERS WHO'VE SCORED FOR THEIR COUNTRIES – HOME NATIONS (AT 31 AUGUST 2010)

PLAYER	COUNTRY	GOALS	PLAYER	COUNTRY	GOALS
Michael Owen	England	26	Ronnie Whelan	Republic of Ireland	3
Ian Rush	Wales	=	Frank Becton	England	2
Steven Gerrard	England	19	Robbie Keane	Republic of Ireland	=
Roger Hunt	England	18	Billy Lacey	Northern Ireland	=
Peter Crouch	England	14	Sammy Lee	England	=
Kenny Dalglish	Scotland	13	Tom Miller	Scotland	=
John Barnes	England	8	Dean Saunders	Wales	=
Ian St John	Scotland	=	Steve Staunton	Republic of Ireland	=
John Toshack	Wales	=	Alan A'Court	England	1
Kevin Keegan	England	7	John Aldridge	Republic of Ireland	=
Peter Beardsley	England	6	Nick Barmby	England	=
Billy Liddell	Scotland	=	Steve Finnan	Republic of Ireland	=
Harry Chambers	England	5	Gordon Hodgson	England	=
Robbie Fowler	England	=	Emlyn Hughes	England	=
Emile Heskey	England	=	Glen Johnson	England	=
Phil Neal	England	=	Chris Lawler	England	=
Craig Bellamy	Wales	4	Jason McAteer	Republic of Ireland	=
Graeme Souness	Scotland	=	Jimmy Melia	England	=
Ray Houghton	Republic of Ireland	3	Danny Murphy	England	=
David Johnson	England	=	Ernest Peake	Wales	=
Ray Kennedy	England	=	Jamie Redknapp	England	=
Mark Lawrenson	Republic of Ireland	=	Phil Thompson	England	=
Terry McDermott	England	=			

Ian Rush, joint-top Liverpool marksman for his country

NATIONALITIES

At the end of the 2009/10 season, 96 overseas players had represented the club in competitive first-team games. The below list is accurate up to the end of the 2009/10. Note that Gordon Hodgson, Craig Johnston (both South Africa) and John Barnes (Jamaica) have represented England at the minimum of Under-21 level.

OVERSEAS LIVERPOOL FIRST-TEAM PLAYERS

COUNTRY	NO. OF PLAYERS	PLAYERS
France	13	Jean-Michel Ferri, Pegguy Arphexad, Bernard Diomede, Gregory Vignal, Nicolas Anelka, Bruno Cheyrou, Patrice Luzi, Anthony Le Tallec, Florent Sinama-Pongolle, Djibril Cisse, Charles Itandje, Damien Plessis, David Ngog
Spain	=	Josemi, Luis Garcia, Xabi Alonso, Antonio Nunez, Fernando Morientes, Pepe Reina, Antonio Barragan, Miki Roque, Alvaro Arbeloa, Fernando Torres, Albert Riera, Daniel Ayala, Daniel Pacheco
South Africa	8	Lance Carr, Hugh Gerhadi, Dirk Kemp, Berry Nieuwenhuys, Robert Priday, Arthur Riley, Doug Rudham, Harman Van Den Berg
Holland	6	Erik Meijer, Sander Westerveld, Bolo Zenden, Jan Kromkamp, Dirk Kuyt, Ryan Babel
Norway	=	Stig Inge Bjornebye, Oyvind Leonhardsen, Bjorn Tore Kvarme, Vegard Heggem, Frode Kippe, John Arne Riise
Argentina	=	Mauricio Pellegrino, Gabriel Paletta, Javier Mascherano, Emiliano Insua, Sebastian Leto, Maxi Rodriguez
Germany	5	Karlheinz Riedle, Dietmar Hamann, Markus Babbel, Christian Ziege, Sean Dundee
Brazil	3	Fabio Aurelio, Lucas Leiva, Diego Cavalieri
Denmark	=	Jan Molby, Torben Piechnik, Daniel Agger
Czech Republic	=	Patrik Berger, Vladimir Smicer, Milan Baros
Israel	=	Avi Cohen, Ronny Rosenthal, Yossi Benayoun
Italy	=	Daniele Padelli, Andrea Dossena, Alberto Aquilani
Finland	2	Sami Hyypia, Jari Litmanen
Mali	=	Djimi Traore, Mohamed Sissoko
Senegal	=	El-Hadji Diouf, Salif Diao
Switzerland	=	Stephane Henchoz, Philipp Degen
USA	=	Brad Friedel, Zak Whitbread
Australia	1	Harry Kewell
Cameroon	=	Rigobert Song
Chile	=	Mark Gonzalez
Croatia	=	Igor Biscan
Greece	=	Sotirios Kyrgiakos
Guinea	=	Titi Camara
Hungary	=	Istvan Kozma
Morocco	=	Nabil El Zhar
Poland	=	Jerzy Dudek
Portugal	=	Abel Xavier
Slovakia	=	Martin Skrtel
Sweden	=	Glenn Hysen
Ukraine	=	Andriy Voronin
Zimbabwe	=	Bruce Grobbelaar

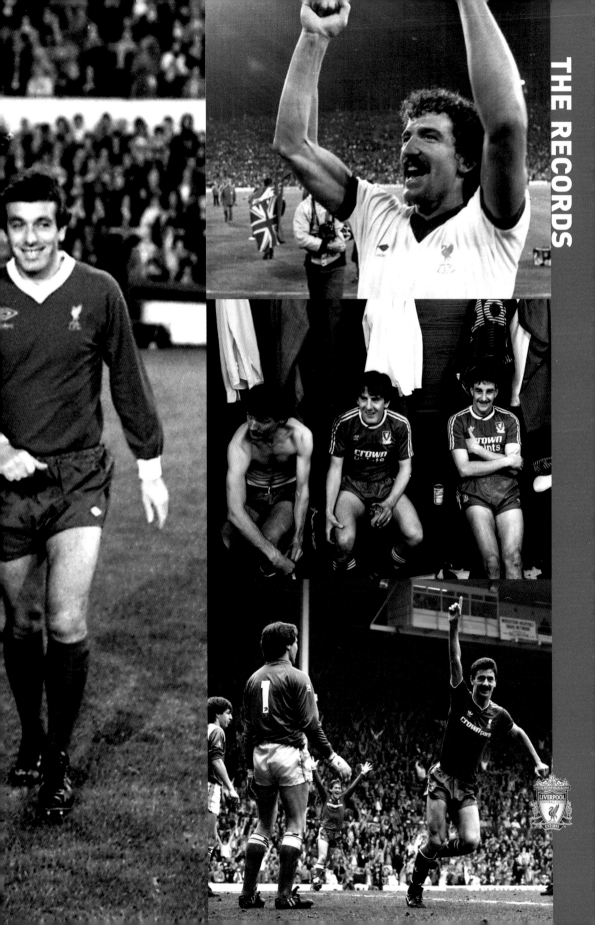

THE COMPLETE FIRST-TEAM RECORD

A statistical breakdown of every competitive first-team game the club have played, correct at the end of the 2009/10 season.

LIVERPOOL FOOTBALL CLUB 1892-2010						
COMPETITION	**P**	**W**	**D**	**L**	**F**	**A**
FA Premier League Home	348	218	82	48	671	269
FA Premier League Away	348	131	95	122	459	400
FA Premier League	696	349	177	170	1130	669
First Division Home	1548	924	354	270	3164	1570
First Division Away	1548	483	415	650	1930	2386
First Division	3096	1407	769	920	5094	3956
FA Premier League/First Division Home	1896	1142	436	318	3835	1839
FA Premier League/First Division Away	1896	614	510	772	2389	2786
FA Premier League/First Division	3792	1756	946	1090	6224	4625
Second Division Home	214	162	32	20	614	223
Second Division Away	214	81	50	83	363	348
Second Division	428	243	82	103	977	571
All League Games Home	2110	1304	468	338	4449	2062
All League Games Away	2110	695	560	855	2752	3134
All League Games	4220	1999	1028	1193	7201	5196
Test Matches Home	3	3	0	0	8	0
Test Matches Away	2	0	1	1	0	2
Test Matches Neutral	1	0	0	1	0	1
Test Matches	6	3	1	2	8	3
FA Cup Home	179	120	31	28	364	141
FA Cup Away	177	74	47	56	239	184
FA Cup Neutral	48	20	11	17	68	57
FA Cup	404	214	89	101	671	382
League Cup Home	99	71	20	8	246	84
League Cup Away	91	42	19	30	148	98
League Cup Neutral	14	8	3	3	19	13
League Cup	204	121	42	41	413	195
European Cup/Champions League Home	83	59	13	11	191	50
European Cup/Champions League Away	83	36	23	24	112	84
European Cup/Champions League Neutral	9	7	0	2	14	10
European Cup/Champions League	175	101	37	37	317	144
European Cup-Winners' Cup Home	14	11	2	1	43	9
European Cup-Winners' Cup Away	14	5	3	6	13	18
European Cup-Winners' Cup Neutral	1	0	0	1	1	2
European Cup-Winners' Cup	29	16	5	8	57	29
Fairs Cup/UEFA Cup/Europa Lge Home	51	38	6	7	113	23
Fairs Cup/UEFA Cup/Europa Lge Away	51	18	17	16	58	50
Fairs Cup/UEFA Cup/Europa Lge Neutral	1	1	0	0	5	4
Fairs Cup/UEFA Cup/Europa Lge	103	57	23	23	176	77
European/UEFA Super Cup Home	2	2	0	0	8	1
European/UEFA Super Cup Away	3	0	1	2	2	6
European/UEFA Super Cup Neutral	2	2	0	0	6	3
European/UEFA Super Cup	7	4	1	2	16	10
All European Competitions Home	150	110	21	19	355	83
All European Competitions Away	151	59	44	48	185	158
All European Competitions Neutral	13	10	0	3	26	19
All European Competitions	314	178	66	70	566	260
World Club Championships	4	1	0	3	3	5

THE COMPLETE FIRST-TEAM RECORD

LIVERPOOL FOOTBALL CLUB 1892-2010						
COMPETITION	P	W	D	L	F	A
FA Charity/Community Shield Home	1	0	1	0	2	2
FA Charity/Community Shield Away	3	1	1	1	3	3
FA Charity/Community Shield Neutral	17	9	3	5	19	16
FA Charity/Community Shield	**21**	**10**	**5**	**6**	**24**	**21**
Screen Sport Super Cup Home	4	4	0	0	10	3
Screen Sport Super Cup Away	4	2	2	0	9	3
Screen Sport Super Cup	**8**	**6**	**2**	**0**	**19**	**6**
F. League Centenary Tournament Home	1	1	0	0	4	1
F. League Centenary Tournament Away	1	0	0	1	1	2
Football League Centenary Tournament	**2**	**1**	**0**	**1**	**5**	**3**
Overall Home	2547	1613	541	393	5438	2376
Overall Away	2539	873	674	992	3337	3584
TOTAL	**5183**	**2533**	**1233**	**1417**	**8910**	**6071**

Istanbul glory in 2005 – a memorable 'win' at a neutral venue

PLAYER RECORDS – APPEARANCES

Jamie Carragher moved into the top seven of the Liverpool all-time appearance holder table at the tail end of the 2009/10 season. He began 2010/11 as a regular in the Reds' backline, and is likely to move into the top five should he enjoy another successful season.

Steven Gerrard became the 13th player to have played 500 games for the club against Blackburn Rovers in December 2009.

	PLAYER	FIRST-TEAM CAREER	GAMES
	TOTAL APPEARANCES – ALL COMPETITIONS		
1	Ian Callaghan	1960-1978	857
2	Ray Clemence	1968-1981	665
=	Emlyn Hughes	1967-1979	665
4	Ian Rush	1980-1987 & 1988-1996	660
5	Phil Neal	1974-1985	650
6	Tommy Smith	1963-1978	638
7	Jamie Carragher	1997-	630
8	Bruce Grobbelaar	1981-1994	628
9	Alan Hansen	1977-1990	620
10	Chris Lawler	1963-1975	549
11	Billy Liddell	1946-1960	534
12	Steven Gerrard	1998-	532
13	Kenny Dalglish	1977-1990	515
14	Ronnie Whelan	1981-1994	493
15	Roger Hunt	1959-1969	492
16	Phil Thompson	1972-1983	477
17	Steve Heighway	1970-1981	475
18	Steve Nicol	1982-1994	468
=	Elisha Scott	1913-1934	468
20	Sami Hyypia	1999-2009	464
21	Ron Yeats	1961-1971	454
22	Donald MacKinlay	1910-1928	434
23	Ian St John	1961-1971	425
24	Peter Thompson	1963-1972	416
25	Arthur Goddard	1902-1914	414

PLAYER RECORDS – CONSECUTIVE APPEARANCES

	PLAYER	TIME SPAN	GAMES
	MOST CONSECUTIVE APPEARANCES – ALL COMPETITIONS		
1	Phil Neal	Oct 1976-Sept 1983	417
2	Ray Clemence	Sept 1972-Mar 1978	336
3	Bruce Grobbelaar	Aug 1981-Aug 1986	317
4	Chris Lawler	Oct 1965-Apr 1971	316
5	David James	Feb 1994-Feb 1998	213
6	Alan Kennedy	Jan 1982-Mar 1985	205
7	Ian Callaghan	Aug 1971-Sept 1974	185
8	Kenny Dalglish	Aug 1977-Aug 1980	180
9	Emlyn Hughes	Oct 1972-Oct 1975	177
10	Peter Thompson	Sept 1965-Apr 1968	153

PLAYER RECORDS – CUP APPEARANCES

Long-serving Jamie Carragher and Steven Gerrard feature prominently in the list of record appearances in cup competitions. With Liverpool involved in three knockout competitions, Carragher should pass the 200 mark during 2010/11, while Gerrard should at least surpass Tommy Smith's 167. Note that the games played in the 'Others' column are in the World Club Cup/ Championship, Screen Sport Super Cup and the Football League Centenary tournament.

	PLAYERS WHO HAVE PLAYED MORE THAN 100 CUP TIES FOR LIVERPOOL					
	PLAYER	TOTAL	FA CUP	LGE CUP	EUROPE	OTHERS
1	Ian Callaghan	210	79	42	89	0
2	Jamie Carragher	193	34	28	129	2
3	Ray Clemence	189	54	55	80	0
4	Phil Neal	188	45	66	74	3
5	Emlyn Hughes	187	62	46	79	0
6	Ian Rush	184	61	78	38	7
7	Bruce Grobbelaar	180	62	70	38	10
8	Alan Hansen	179	58	68	46	7
9	Tommy Smith	167	52	30	85	0
10	Steven Gerrard	164	28	20	114	2
11	Kenny Dalglish	153	37	59	51	6
12	Sami Hyypia	144	29	19	94	2
13	Steve Heighway	141	36	38	67	0
14	Chris Lawler	140	47	27	66	0
15	Phil Thompson	130	36	43	50	1
16	Ronnie Whelan	124	41	50	24	9
17	Steve Nicol	123	50	42	20	11
18	Ray Kennedy	114	28	35	50	1
19	Mark Lawrenson	111	24	50	28	9
=	John Arne Riise	111	17	13	79	2
21	Graeme Souness	108	24	45	38	1
22	Robbie Fowler	103	24	35	44	0
=	Alan Kennedy	103	21	45	36	1

Ray Clemence – Cup specialist

PLAYER RECORDS – GOALS

Steven Gerrard and Fernando Torres remain the only members of Liverpool's squad in the top 30 for goals – note figures are correct at end of 2009/10 season.

	PLAYER	FIRST-TEAM CAREER	GOALS
\multicolumn{4}{c}{TOTAL GOALS – ALL COMPETITIONS}			
1	Ian Rush	1980-1987 & 1988-1996	346
2	Roger Hunt	1959-1969	286
3	Gordon Hodgson	1926-1935	241
4	Billy Liddell	1946-1960	228
5	Robbie Fowler	1993-2001 & 2006-2007	183
6	Kenny Dalglish	1977-1990	172
7	Michael Owen	1997-2004	158
8	Harry Chambers	1919-1928	151
9	Steven Gerrard	1998-	132
10	Jack Parkinson	1903-1914	129
11	Sam Raybould	1900-1907	128
12	Dick Forshaw	1919-1927	124
13	Ian St John	1961-1971	118
14	Jack Balmer	1935-1952	110
15	John Barnes	1987-1997	108
16	Kevin Keegan	1971-1977	100
17	John Toshack	1970-1977	96
18	Albert Stubbins	1946-1953	83
19	Terry McDermott	1974-1982	81
=	Jack Cox	1898-1909	81
21	Berry Nieuwenhuys	1933-1947	79
=	Jimmy Melia	1955-1964	79
23	David Johnson	1976-1982	78
24	Arthur Goddard	1902-1914	77
25	Steve Heighway	1970-1981	76
26	Ronnie Whelan	1981-1994	73
27	Ray Kennedy	1974-1981	72
=	Fernando Torres	2007-	72
29	Joe Hewitt	1904-1909	70
30	Ian Callaghan	1960-1978	68

Robbie Fowler – Fifth on the all-time list

GOALSCORERS

MOST GOALS IN A SEASON

MOST GOALS IN A SEASON – ALL COMPS

NAME	SEASON	GAMES	GOALS
Ian Rush	1983/84	65	47
Roger Hunt	1961/62	46	42
Ian Rush	1986/87	57	40
Roger Hunt	1964/65	58	37
Gordon Hodgson	1930/31	41	36
Robbie Fowler	1995/96	53	36
John Evans	1954/55	42	33
Billy Liddell	1955/56	44	33
Roger Hunt	1963/64	46	33
Roger Hunt	1965/66	46	33
Fernando Torres	2007/08	46	33
Ian Rush	1985/86	56	33
Sam Raybould	1902/03	34	32
Gordon Hodgson	1928/29	41	32
Billy Liddell	1954/55	44	31
Robbie Fowler	1996/97	44	31
John Aldridge	1988/89	47	31
Ian Rush	1982/83	51	31
Robbie Fowler	1994/95	57	31
Kenny Dalglish	1977/78	62	31
Jack Parkinson	1909/10	32	30
Ian Rush	1981/82	49	30
Roger Hunt	1967/68	57	30

MOST GOALS IN A LEAGUE SEASON

NAME	SEASON	DIV	GA	GLS
Roger Hunt	1961/62	2	41	41
Gordon Hodgson	1930/31	1	40	36
Ian Rush	1983/84	1	41	32
Sam Raybould	1902/03	1	33	31
Roger Hunt	1963/64	1	41	31
Jack Parkinson	1909/10	1	31	30
Gordon Hodgson	1928/29	1	38	30
Billy Liddell	1954/55	2	40	30
Ian Rush	1986/87	1	42	30
Roger Hunt	1965/66	1	37	29
John Evans	1954/55	2	38	29
Robbie Fowler	1995/96	Prem	38	28
Dick Forshaw	1925/26	1	32	27
Gordon Hodgson	1934/35	1	34	27
Billy Liddell	1955/56	2	39	27
John Aldridge	1987/88	1	36	26
Gordon Hodgson	1931/32	1	39	26
George Allan	1895/96	2	20	25
Roger Hunt	1964/65	1	40	25
Roger Hunt	1967/68	1	40	25
Robbie Fowler	1994/95	Prem	42	25

Gordon Hodgson

Roger Hunt

GOALSCORERS – HAT-TRICK MEN

Yossi Benayoun and Fernando Torres trebles have been added to the all-time list following their hat-tricks against Burnley and Hull City respectively during 2009/10.

FULL RECORD OF LIVERPOOL HAT-TRICKS

17	Gordon Hodgson
16	Ian Rush
12	Roger Hunt
10	Robbie Fowler, Michael Owen
8	Dick Forshaw, Jack Parkinson
6	Sam Raybould
5	Harry Chambers, Billy Liddell
4	George Allan, Joe Hewitt, Fernando Torres
3	John Aldridge, Jack Balmer, Yossi Benayoun, Kenny Dalglish, Steven Gerrard, Tony Hateley, Fred Howe, Albert Stubbins, John Toshack, John Wark
2	John Barnes, Harold Barton, Frank Becton, Jimmy Case, William Devlin, Cyril Done, John Evans, Dick Johnson, Terry McDermott, Steve McMahon, Malcolm McVean, Fred Pagnam, Henry Race, Robert Robinson, Jimmy Ross, Antonio Rowley, Ian St John, Dean Saunders, Graeme Souness, Paul Walsh
1	Alan Arnell, Alf Arrowsmith, Milan Baros, Peter Beardsley, Patrik Berger, Louis Bimpson, Phil Boersma, Ian Callaghan, Stan Collymore, Peter Crouch, Alun Evans, David Fairclough, Gary Gillespie, Bobby Graham, Jimmy Harrower, Emile Heskey, Dave Hickson, 'Sailor' Hunter, David Johnson, Kevin Keegan, Kevin Lewis, Andy McGuigan, William McPherson, Arthur Metcalfe, Jan Molby, Steve Nicol, Ronald Orr, Tom Reid, Michael Robinson, Ronny Rosenthal, Danny Shone, Jimmy Smith, Steve Staunton, James Stewart, James Stott, John Walker, Jimmy Walsh, Mark Walters, Johnny Wheeler, Ronnie Whelan, Jack Whitham, Dave Wright

85 players have scored a total of 221 hat-tricks

WHERE HAT-TRICKS HAVE BEEN SCORED

	AT ANFIELD	AWAY	TOTAL
League	130	43	173
FA Cup	12	5	17
League Cup	8	6	14
Europe	14	2	16
Other Games	0	1	1
TOTAL	**164**	**57**	**221**

GOALSCORERS – CONSECUTIVE GAMES

The 2009/10 campaign saw Fernando Torres set a new club record for scoring 2+ goals in 4 consecutive games at Anfield. His hot streak came in the spring of 2010 and included goals in the Premier League and Europa League.

SCORERS OF 2 OR MORE GOALS IN 3 OR MORE CONSECUTIVE HOME GAMES

PLAYER	NO. OF GAMES	SEASON	OPPONENTS (NO. OF GOALS IN EACH GAME)
Fernando Torres	4	2009/10	Portsmouth (2), Lille (2), Sunderland (2), Benfica (2)
Harry Bradshaw	3	1894/95	Wolves (2), Small Heath (2), West Brom (2)
Jimmy Ross	3	1895/96	Manchester City (2), Arsenal (2), Lincoln City (2)
George Allan	3	1895/96	Rotherham (4), Grimsby Town (2), Burton Swifts (2)
Harry Chambers	3	1926/27	Burnley (2), Bolton (2), Bournemouth (2)
Gordon Hodgson	3	1927/28	Sheffield Wednesday (2), Huddersfield Town (2), Birmingham City (2)
Gordon Hodgson	3	1934/35	Leicester City (3), Aston Villa (2), Tottenham Hotspur (2)
Gordon Hodgson	3	1935/36	Everton (2), Grimsby Town (2), Stoke City (2)
Roger Hunt	3	1961/62	Middlesbrough (3), Derby County (2), Preston North End (2)
Robbie Fowler	3	1995/96	Manchester United (2), Arsenal (3), Nottingham Forest (2)
Robbie Fowler	3	1996/97	Derby County (2), Sion (2), Charlton Athletic (2)
Michael Owen	3	2000/01– 2001/02	Newcastle United (3), Chelsea (2), West Ham United (2)

GOALSCORERS – RECORD IN 100

Fernando Torres is joint fourth in the most goals scored in the first 100 games for Liverpool – exactly matching John Aldridge in terms of goals and substitute appearances.

MOST GOALS IN FIRST 100 GAMES

POS.	PLAYER	GOALS	SUB APPS
1	Roger Hunt	68	0
=	Sam Raybould	68	0
3	Jack Parkinson	64	0
4	John Aldridge	61	13
=	Albert Stubbins	61	0
=	Fernando Torres	61	13
7	Ian Rush	56	1
8	Robbie Fowler	55	4
=	Gordon Hodgson	55	0
10	Harry Chambers	53	0
11	John Evans	51	0
=	Michael Owen	51	8
13	Kenny Dalglish	49	0

Jack Parkinson – Third man in the 100 list

GOALSCORERS – DOUBLES

Roger Hunt and Ian Rush are the main men when it comes to scoring two goals in a game for the Reds, both hitting the half century during their LFC careers.

LIVERPOOL DOUBLES

NAME	OCCASIONS
Roger Hunt	53
Ian Rush	50
Gordon Hodgson	39
Billy Liddell	32
Robbie Fowler	29
Kenny Dalglish	23
Sam Raybould	22
Jack Parkinson	20
Michael Owen	19
Harry Chambers	18
OTHERS	
Fernando Torres	13
Steven Gerrard	11

Ian Rush – Half-century double

GOALSCORERS – SUPER SUBS

LIVERPOOL'S MOST PROLIFIC GOALSCORING SUBSTITUTES

	LEAGUE	FA CUP	LGE CUP	EUROPE	OTHERS	TOTAL
David Fairclough	7	2	7	2	0	18
Ryan Babel	6	0	0	6	0	12
Djibril Cisse	2	1	0	4	0	7
Michael Owen	4	0	1	1	0	6
Ian Rush	2	3	0	1	0	6
Vladimir Smicer	4	0	1	1	0	6
Robbie Fowler	3	1	0	1	0	5
Emile Heskey	2	3	0	0	0	5
David Johnson	3	0	1	1	0	5

LIVERPOOL SUBSTITUTES SCORING MORE THAN ONCE IN A GAME

PLAYER	SEASON	OPPOSITION	COMPETITION	RESULT
Steve Staunton (3)	1989/90	Wigan Athletic	League Cup	3-0
Roger Hunt	1969/70	Southampton	League	4-1
Alun Evans	1969/70	Leicester City	FA Cup	2-0
Phil Boersma	1972/73	Carlisle United	League Cup	5-1
David Fairclough	1975/76	Burnley	League	2-0
David Fairclough	1977/78	Derby County	League Cup	2-0
David Johnson	1978/79	Tottenham Hotspur	League	7-0
David Fairclough	1979/80	Exeter City	League Cup	2-0
David Fairclough	1979/80	Bury	FA Cup	2-0
Kenny Dalglish	1986/87	West Ham United	League	5-2
Ian Rush	1988/89	Everton	FA Cup	3-2 aet
Mark Walters	1992/93	Blackburn Rovers	League	2-1
Patrik Berger	1996/97	Leicester City	League	3-0
Milan Baros	2004/05	Millwall	League Cup	3-0
Steven Gerrard	2005/06	TNS	European Cup	3-0
Djibril Cisse	2005/06	CSKA Moscow	Euro. Super Cup	3-1 aet
Florent Sinama-Pongolle	2005/06	Luton Town	FA Cup	5-3
Ryan Babel	2007/08	Besiktas	European Cup	8-0
Ryan Babel	2009/10	Hull City	League	6-1

PENALTY KINGS

Steven Gerrard converted 3 and Dirk Kuyt 1 during 2009/10, while the Livrpool skipper's spot-kick against FK Rabotnicki in the Europa League ahead of the 2010/11 Premier League season took him up to joint fourth alongside Tommy Smith.

COMPLETE RECORD – SCORERS IN SHOOT-OUTS NOT INCLUDED

PLAYER	LEAGUE	OTHER COMPS	TOTAL
Jan Molby	30	12	42
Phil Neal	28	10	38
Billy Liddell	34	0	34
Steven Gerrard	14	8	22
Tommy Smith	15	7	22
Robbie Fowler	14	6	20
John Aldridge	15	2	17
Terry McDermott	13	3	16
Gordon Hodgson	15	0	15
Michael Owen	11	2	13
Kevin Keegan	10	1	11
John Barnes	7	3	10
Willie Fagan	7	2	9
Arthur Goddard	7	1	8
Alec Lindsay	6	2	=
Ronnie Moran	6	2	=
Danny Murphy	5	3	=
Sam Raybould	8	0	=
Willie Stevenson	7	1	=
Jackie Sheldon	7	0	7
Robert Done	6	0	6
Jack Parkinson	6	0	=
Mark Walters	6	0	=
Gary McAllister	1	4	5
Jack Balmer	4	0	4
Peter Beardsley	2	2	=
Tom Chorlton	4	0	=
Donald MacKinlay	3	1	=
Alec Raisbeck	4	0	=
Alf West	4	0	=
Xabi Alonso	2	1	3
Frank Becton	2	1	=
Djibril Cisse	3	0	=
Dick Edmed	2	1	=
Dirk Kuyt	3	0	=
Kevin Lewis	3	0	=
Jari Litmanen	1	2	=
Tommy Lucas	3	0	=
Mike Marsh	0	3	=
Jamie Redknapp	3	0	=
Tommy Robertson	3	0	=
Jimmy Ross	3	0	=
Ian Rush	2	1	=
Graeme Souness	1	2	=
John Wark	3	0	=

Phil Neal – Lethal from 12 yards

PLAYER	LEAGUE	OTHER COMPS	TOTAL
Milan Baros	2	0	2
Patrik Berger	2	0	=
Harry Chambers	2	0	=
Julian Dicks	2	0	=
John Evans	2	0	=
Dick Forshaw	2	0	=
Alf Hanson	2	0	=
Ray Lambert	2	0	=
Andrew McCowie	2	0	=
Duncan McLean	2	0	=
Jimmy Melia	2	0	=
George Allan	1	0	1
Lance Carr	1	0	=
Robert Crawford	1	0	=
El-Hadji Diouf	0	1	=
George Fleming	1	0	=
Gary Gillespie	1	0	=
Gordon Gunson	1	0	=
Brian Hall	0	1	=
Jimmy Harrower	1	0	=
Roger Hunt	1	0	=
Harry Kewell	1	0	=
Fred Morris	1	0	=
Ronald Orr	1	0	=
Robert Robinson	1	0	=
Florent S-Pongolle	0	1	=
Vladimir Smicer	0	1	=
Geoff Strong	1	0	=
Albert Stubbins	1	0	=
Geoff Twentyman	0	1	=

CONSECUTIVE SCORING GAMES

Liverpool came up 3 short in a bid to create a new club record during the 2009/10 season. The 0-0 draw with Fulham ended a run of 37 consecuitive scoring games at Anfield, the Reds falling short of breaking a century-old record of 40 games.

CONSECUTIVE SCORING GAMES AT HOME – ALL COMPETITIONS

NO. OF GAMES	PERIOD	TEAM THAT ENDED THE RUN
40	22nd February 1904-24th February 1906	Manchester City
37	13th December 2008-8th April 2010	Fulham
34	25th September 1979-5th November 1980	Nottingham Forest
33	20th January 1968-1st February 1969	Nottingham Forest
31	29th September 1956-11th January 1958	Middlesbrough
30	19th November 1932-3rd February 1934	Bolton Wanderers
30	26th December 1989-9th February 1991	Everton
29	19th February 1972-20th January 1973	Manchester City
28	10th April 1985-22nd February 1986	Everton
27	16th March 1991-26th February 1992	Southampton

BIGGEST-EVER VICTORIES – ALL COMPETITIONS

DATE	OPPONENTS	VENUE	COMPETITION	SCORE
17th Sept 1974	Stromsgodset	Home	European Cup Winners' Cup	11-0
16th Sept 1969	Dundalk	Home	Inter Cities' Fairs Cup	10-0
23rd Sept 1986	Fulham	Home	League Cup	10-0
18th Feb 1896	Rotherham Town	Home	League	10-1
1st Oct 1980	Oulu Palloseura	Home	European Cup	10-1
29th Oct 1892	Newtown	Home	FA Cup	9-0
12th Sept 1989	Crystal Palace	Home	League	9-0
26th Dec 1928	Burnley	Home	League	8-0
7th Nov 1967	TSV Munich 1860	Home	Inter Cities' Fairs Cup	8-0
9th Jan 1990	Swansea City	Home	FA Cup	8-0
29th Nov 2000	Stoke City	Away	League Cup	8-0
6th Nov 2008	Besiktas	Home	Champions League	8-0
6th Dec 1902	Grimsby Town	Home	League	9-2
8th Apr 1905	Burslem Port Vale	Home	League	8-1
29th Feb 1896	Burton Swifts	Away	League	7-0
28th Mar 1896	Crewe Alexandra	Away	League	7-0
4th Jan 1902	Stoke City	Home	League	7-0
26th Nov 1955	Fulham	Home	League	7-0
2nd Sept 1978	Tottenham Hotspur	Home	League	7-0
30th Sept 1981	Oulu Palloseura	Home	European Cup	7-0
20th Feb 1985	York City	Home	FA Cup	7-0
6th Jan 1996	Rochdale	Home	FA Cup	7-0
21st Mar 2006	Birmingham City	Away	FA Cup	7-0
1st Oct 1927	Portsmouth	Home	League	8-2
12th Oct 1895	Newton Heath	Home	League	7-1
12th Sept 1936	Grimsby Town	Home	League	7-1
23rd Mar 1991	Derby County	Away	League	7-1
16th Jan 1999	Southampton	Home	League	7-1

DEBUT GOALSCORERS

(SINCE RETURNING TO TOP-FLIGHT IN 1962)

PLAYER	DATE	OPPONENTS	COMPETITION	GOALS	RESULT
Bobby Graham	14/09/1964	Reykjavik	European Cup	1	6-1
John Sealey	26/04/1965	Wolves	League	1	3-1
Alun Evans	21/09/1968	Leicester City	League	1	4-0
Alec Lindsay	16/09/1969	Dundalk	Fairs Cup	1	10-0
Kevin Keegan	14/08/1971	Nottingham Forest	League	1	3-1
Ray Kennedy	31/08/1974	Chelsea	League	1	3-0
Sammy Lee	08/04/1978	Leicester City	League	1	3-2
Ronnie Whelan	03/04/1981	Stoke City	League	1	3-0
John Wark	31/03/1984	Watford	League	1	2-0
David Speedie	03/02/1991	Manchester United	League	1	1-1
Nigel Clough	14/08/1993	Sheffield Wednesday	League	2	2-0
Robbie Fowler	22/09/1993	Fulham	League Cup	1	3-1
Stan Collymore	19/08/1995	Sheffield Wednesday	League	1	1-0
Michael Owen	06/05/1997	Wimbledon	League	1	1-2
Titi Camara	07/08/1999	Sheffield Wednesday	League	1	2-1
Leyton Maxwell	21/09/1999	Hull City	League Cup	1	4-2
Abel Xavier	09/02/2002	Ipswich Town	League	1	6-0
Craig Bellamy	09/08/2006	Maccabi Haifa	European Cup	1	2-1
Mark Gonzalez	09/08/2006	Maccabi Haifa	European Cup	1	2-1
Gabriel Paletta	25/10/2006	Reading	League Cup	1	4-3

SHORT CAREERS

The current shortest careers of LFC first-team players are listed below. Note that statistics are correct up to the start of the 2010/11 Premier League season – while it is assumed that players who appeared before the introduction of subs in 1965/66 played a full 90 minutes.

SHORTEST LIVERPOOL FIRST-TEAM CAREERS

PLAYER	MINUTES	APPS	APPEARANCES SPAN
Jack Robinson*	2	1	2010
Miki Roque	6	1	2006
Lauri Dalla Valle	7	1	2010
Dave Wilson	10	1	1967
Antonio Barragan	11	1	2005
Patrice Luzi	13	1	2004
James Smith	16	1	2006
Nathan Eccleston*	21	3	2009-2010
Brian Mooney	30	1	1986
Lee Jones	33	4	1994-1996
Colin Russell	33	1	1981
Jon Newby	34	4	1999-2000
Mark Smyth	50	1	2004
Jean-Michel Ferri	51	2	1999
Sean Dundee	56	5	1998-1999
Barry Jones	68	1	1991

* Player still at club

OLDEST/YOUNGEST LIVERPOOL PLAYERS

Jack Robinson set a new youngest-ever player mark when coming on in the final minutes of Liverpool's final Premier League game of the 2009/10 season at Hull City. The Academy graduate beat Max Thompson's previous youngest post-war record in what proved to be Rafael Benitez's final game in charge. His potential involvement in 2010/11 means he could set a new youngest goalscorers mark should he find the net before the New Year.

OLDEST PLAYER

PLAYER	FINAL GAME	AGE
Ted Doig	11th April 1908	41 years & 165 days

OLDEST PLAYER (POST-WAR)

PLAYER	FINAL GAME	AGE
Kenny Dalglish	1st May 1990	39 years & 58 days
Billy Liddell	31st August 1960	38 years & 234 days
Gary McAllister	11th May 2002	37 years & 137 days
Paul Jones	17th January 2004	36 years & 274 days
Bruce Grobbelaar	19th February 1994	36 years & 136 days
Phil Taylor	25th December 1953	36 years & 98 days
Jack Balmer	16th February 1952	36 years & 10 days
Ian Callaghan	4th February 1978	35 years & 300 days
Sami Hyypia	24th May 2009	35 years & 229 days
Berry Nieuwenhuys	1st February 1947	35 years & 88 days
Bob Paisley	13th March 1954	35 years & 49 days

YOUNGEST PLAYER (POST-WAR)

PLAYER	DEBUT	AGE
Jack Robinson	9th May 2010	16 years & 250 days
Max Thompson	8th May 1974	17 years & 128 days
Michael Owen	6th May 1997	17 years & 144 days
Johnny Morrissey	23rd September 1957	17 years & 158 days
Reginald Blore	17th October 1959	17 years & 213 days
Phil Charnock	16th September 1992	17 years & 215 days

YOUNGEST-EVER GOALSCORERS FOR LIVERPOOL

PLAYER	DEBUT	AGE	OPPONENTS
Michael Owen	6th May 1997	17 years & 143 days	Wimbledon
Jimmy Melia	17th December 1955	18 years & 46 days	Nottingham Forest
Jamie Redknapp	7th December 1991	18 years & 165 days	Southampton
Alan A'Court	14th March 1953	18 years & 165 days	Sunderland
Robbie Fowler	22nd September 1993	18 years & 166 days	Fulham
John McLaughlin	22nd August 1970	18 years & 178 days	Huddersfield Town
Phil Taylor	28th March 1936	18 years & 192 days	Derby County
Brian Jackson	10th November 1951	18 years & 223 days	Bolton Wanderers
Gordon Wallace	8th May 1963	18 years & 329 days	Birmingham City
Jamie Carragher	18th January 1997	18 years & 356 days	Aston Villa

PLAYER HONOURS

FOOTBALL WRITERS' FOOTBALLER OF THE YEAR			
SEASON	**PLAYER**	**APPS**	**GOALS**	**HONOURS WON**
1973/74	Ian Callaghan	61	3	FA Cup
1975/76	Kevin Keegan	57	16	League, UEFA Cup
1976/77	Emlyn Hughes	62	1	League, European Cup, FA Charity Shield
1978/79	Kenny Dalglish	54	25	League
1979/80	Terry McDermott	53	16	League, FA Charity Shield
1982/83	Kenny Dalglish	58	20	League, League Cup, FA Charity Shield
1983/84	Ian Rush	65	47	League, League Cup, European Cup
1987/88	John Barnes	48	17	League
1988/89	Steve Nicol	50	2	FA Cup, FA Charity Shield
1989/90	John Barnes	45	28	League, FA Charity Shield
2008/09	Steven Gerrard	44	24	–

PFA PLAYER OF THE YEAR			
SEASON	**PLAYER**	**APPS**	**GOALS**	**HONOURS WON**
1979/80	Terry McDermott	53	16	League, FA Charity Shield
1982/83	Kenny Dalglish	58	20	League, League Cup, FA Charity Shield
1983/84	Ian Rush	65	47	League, League Cup, European Cup
1987/88	John Barnes	48	17	League
2005/06	Steven Gerrard	53	23	FA Cup, European Super Cup

PFA YOUNG PLAYER OF THE YEAR			
SEASON	**PLAYER**	**APPS**	**GOALS**	**HONOURS WON**
1982/83	Ian Rush	51	31	League, League Cup, FA Charity Shield
1994/95	Robbie Fowler	57	31	League Cup
1995/96	Robbie Fowler	53	36	–
1997/98	Michael Owen	44	23	–
2000/01	Steven Gerrard	50	10	FA Cup, League Cup, UEFA Cup

MANAGER OF THE YEAR			
SEASON	**PLAYER**	**GAMES**	**WIN %**	**HONOURS WON**
1972/73	Bill Shankly	66	56.06	League, UEFA Cup
1975/76	Bob Paisley	59	55.93	League, UEFA Cup
1976/77	Bob Paisley	62	58.06	League, European Cup, European Super Cup, FA Charity Shield
1978/79	Bob Paisley	54	64.81	League
1979/80	Bob Paisley	60	58.33	League, FA Charity Shield
1981/82	Bob Paisley	62	62.90	League, League Cup
1982/83	Bob Paisley	60	63.33	League, League Cup, FA Charity Shield
1983/84	Joe Fagan	67	55.22	League, League Cup, European Cup
1985/86	Kenny Dalglish	63	65.08	League, FA Cup
1987/88	Kenny Dalglish	50	64.00	League
1989/90	Kenny Dalglish	50	60.00	League, FA Charity Shield

EUROPEAN FOOTBALLER OF THE YEAR			
YEAR	**PLAYER**	**APPS**	**GOALS**	**HONOURS WON**
2001	Michael Owen	49	31	FA Cup, League Cup, UEFA Cup, European Super Cup, FA Charity Shield

LONG-SERVING

Steven Gerrard joined the 11-season club in 2009/10 – and having found the net in 2010/11, he is only another three seasons from joining the legendary Billy Liddell at the top of the seasons' scoring charts.

Jamie Carragher is poised to join the top 10 of Liverpool's longest-serving players in 2011. The defender made his first-team debut as a substitute at Middlesbrough in the League Cup in January 1997 – only three months after signing his first pro contract with the club. He will surpass Billy Dunlop and Ian Rush should he remain a part of the first-team picture during the campaign.

PLAYERS TO SCORE FOR LIVERPOOL IN AT LEAST 10 SUCCESSIVE SEASONS

PLAYER	NO. OF SEASONS	SEASONS
Billy Liddell	15	1946-1960
Ronnie Whelan	14	1981-1994
Jack Cox	12	1898-1909
Arthur Goddard	12	1902-1913
Emlyn Hughes	12	1968-1979
Gordon Hodgson	11	1926-1936
Alan A'Court	11	1953-1963
Steven Gerrard	11	2000-2010
Roger Hunt	11	1960-1970
Donald MacKinlay	11	1913-1927
Phil Neal	11	1976-1986
Jack Parkinson	11	1904-1914
Tommy Smith	11	1965-1975
Jack Balmer	10	1936-1951
John Barnes	10	1988-1997
Kenny Dalglish	10	1978-1987
Chris Lawler	10	1965-1974
Ian St John	10	1962-1971
Sami Hyypia	10	2000-2009

Billy Liddell – 15 seasons of goals

LONGEST-SERVING LIVERPOOL PLAYERS

PLAYER	LFC CAREER	TIME SPAN
Elisha Scott	1913-1934	21 yrs, 51 days
Donald MacKinlay	1910-1928	18 yrs, 134 days
Ian Callaghan	1960-1978	17 yrs, 347 days
Phil Taylor	1936-1954	17 yrs, 287 days
Ephraim Longworth	1910-1928	17 yrs, 215 days
Jack Balmer	1935-1952	16 yrs, 155 days
Tommy Smith	1963-1978	14 yrs, 352 days
Billy Liddell	1946-1960	14 yrs, 239 days
Ian Rush	1980-1987	14 yrs, 40 days
	1988-1996	
Billy Dunlop	1895-1909	14 yrs, 23 days

Elisha Scott – 21 years' service

CLEAN SHEETS – GOALKEEPERS

Pepe Reina's success since becoming Liverpool's No.1 in 2005 can be rated by his percentage of clean sheets. He edges out Ray Clemence in terms of clean sheets kept, although Clemence does have a slightly better average goals conceded per game record. A direct comparison of the players over their first 200 LFC games shows that Reina was ahead in terms of how many goals he conceded after 200 games (138 compared to Clemence's 145) and the clean sheets kept over that period (102 to 100).

LIVERPOOL CAREER STATISTICS – AT END OF 2009/10 SEASON					
PLAYER	GAMES PLAYED	GOALS CONCEDED	GOALS PER GAME	CLEAN SHEETS	CLEAN SHEET %
Pepe Reina	259	198	0.76	126	48.65
Ray Clemence	665	488	0.73	323	48.57
Bruce Grobbelaar	628	532	0.85	266	42.36
David James	275	273	0.99	102	37.09
Tommy Lawrence	390	404	1.04	133	34.10
Elisha Scott	468	647	1.38	137	29.27
Sam Hardy	239	340	1.42	63	26.36
Arthur Riley	338	608	1.80	69	20.41

CLUB RECORDS

LIVERPOOL FC SINGLES IN THE UK CHARTS			
SONG TITLE	DATE CHARTED	HIGHEST CHART POSITION	NO. OF WEEKS
We Can Do It	28/05/1977	15	4
Liverpool (We're Never Gonna...)	23/04/1983	54	4
Sitting On Top Of The World	17/05/1986	50	2
Anfield Rap (Red Machine In Full Effect)	14/05/1988	3	6
Pass And Move (It's The Liverpool Groove)	18/05/1996	4	5
The Fields Of Anfield Road	12/04/2009	14	3*

*Weeks spent in top 40

Liverpool's Anfield Rap stars in 1988

PLAYER RECORDS

These pages showcase every 'noughties' Liverpool first-team player.

LIVERPOOL APPEARANCES IN 2000s											
PLAYER	**J-M 2000**	**2000-2001**	**2001-2002**	**2002-2003**	**2003-2004**	**2004-2005**	**2005-2006**	**2006-2007**	**2007-2008**	**2008-2009**	**A-D 2009**	**TOTAL**
Agger	-	-	-	-	-	-	4	43	6	26	15	94
Alonso	-	-	-	-	-	32	53	51	27	47	-	210
Anelka	-	-	22	-	-	-	-	-	-	-	-	22
Aquilani	-	-	-	-	-	-	-	-	-	-	8	8
Arbeloa	-	-	-	-	-	-	-	14	41	43	-	98
Arphexad	-	2	4	-	-	-	-	-	-	-	-	6
Aurelio	-	-	-	-	-	-	-	25	29	33	17	104
Ayala	-	-	-	-	-	-	-	-	-	-	3	3
Babbel	-	60	6	7	-	-	-	-	-	-	-	73
Babel	-	-	-	-	-	-	-	-	49	42	15	106
Barmby	-	46	12	-	-	-	-	-	-	-	-	58
Baros	-	-	1	42	18	45	2	-	-	-	-	108
Barragan	-	-	-	-	-	-	1	-	-	-	-	1
Bellamy	-	-	-	-	-	-	-	42	-	-	-	42
Benayoun	-	-	-	-	-	-	-	-	47	42	27	116
Berger	19	21	31	4	-	-	-	-	-	-	-	75
Biscan	-	21	10	13	39	35	-	-	-	-	-	118
Camara	17	-	-	-	-	-	-	-	-	-	-	17
Carragher	19	58	53	54	29	56	57	51	55	54	25	511
Carson	-	-	-	-	-	5	4	-	-	-	-	9
Cavalieri	-	-	-	-	-	-	-	-	-	4	3	7
Cheyrou	-	-	-	29	19	-	-	-	-	-	-	48
Cisse	-	-	-	-	-	25	54	-	-	-	-	79
Crouch	-	-	-	-	-	-	49	49	36	-	-	134
Darby	-	-	-	-	-	-	-	-	-	2	1	3
Degen	-	-	-	-	-	-	-	-	-	2	5	7
Diao	-	-	-	40	7	14	-	-	-	-	-	61
Diomede	-	4	1	-	-	-	-	-	-	-	-	5
Diouf	-	-	-	47	33	-	-	-	-	-	-	80
Dossena	-	-	-	-	-	-	-	-	-	26	5	31
Dudek	-	-	49	46	38	41	6	6	-	-	-	186
Eccleston	-	-	-	-	-	-	-	-	-	-	2	2
El Zhar	-	-	-	-	-	-	3	3	19	1	-	26
Finnan	-	-	-	-	31	52	52	47	35	-	-	217
Fowler	4	48	17	-	-	-	16	23	-	-	-	108
Garcia	-	-	-	-	-	44	50	27	-	-	-	121
Gerrard	15	50	45	54	47	43	53	51	52	44	23	477
Gonzalez	-	-	-	-	-	-	36	-	-	-	-	36
Guthrie	-	-	-	-	-	-	7	-	-	-	-	7
Hamann	19	53	48	42	35	43	32	-	-	-	-	272
Heggem	5	4	-	-	-	-	-	-	-	-	-	9
Henchoz	19	53	56	32	27	4	-	-	-	-	-	191
Heskey	12	56	56	52	47	-	-	-	-	-	-	223
Hobbs	-	-	-	-	-	-	-	-	5	-	-	5
Hyypia	19	58	57	56	51	49	59	29	44	19	-	441
Insua	-	-	-	-	-	-	-	2	3	13	25	43
Itandje	-	-	-	-	-	-	-	-	7	-	-	7
Johnson	-	-	-	-	-	-	-	-	-	-	21	21
Jones	-	-	-	-	2	-	-	-	-	-	-	2
Josemi	-	-	-	-	-	23	12	-	-	-	-	35
Keane	-	-	-	-	-	-	-	-	-	28	-	28
Kelly	-	-	-	-	-	-	-	-	-	1	1	2
Kewell	-	-	-	-	49	31	41	3	15	-	-	139
Kippe	-	-	1	-	-	-	-	-	-	-	-	1
Kirkland	-	-	4	15	12	14	-	-	-	-	-	45

PLAYER RECORDS

LIVERPOOL APPEARANCES IN 2000s											
PLAYER	J-M 2000	2000-2001	2001-2002	2002-2003	2003-2004	2004-2005	2005-2006	2006-2007	2007-2008	2008-2009	A-D 2009	TOTAL
Kromkamp	-	-	-	-	-	-	17	1	-	-	-	18
Kuyt	-	-	-	-	-	-	-	48	48	51	27	174
Kyrgiakos	-	-	-	-	-	-	-	-	-	-	6	6
Le Tallec	-	-	-	-	23	7	2	-	-	-	-	32
Leto	-	-	-	-	-	-	-	-	4	-	-	4
Litmanen	-	11	32	-	-	-	-	-	-	-	-	43
Lucas	-	-	-	-	-	-	-	-	32	39	25	96
Luzi	-	-	-	-	1	-	-	-	-	-	-	1
McAllister	-	49	38	-	-	-	-	-	-	-	-	87
Mascherano	-	-	-	-	-	-	-	11	41	38	23	113
Matteo	19	-	-	-	-	-	-	-	-	-	-	19
Meijer	9	3	-	-	-	-	-	-	-	-	-	12
Mellor	-	-	-	6	-	16	-	-	-	-	-	22
Morientes	-	-	-	-	-	15	46	-	-	-	-	61
Murphy	14	47	56	56	42	-	-	-	-	-	-	215
Newby	2	-	-	-	-	-	-	-	-	-	-	2
Ngog	-	-	-	-	-	-	-	-	-	19	15	34
Nunez	-	-	-	-	-	27	-	-	-	-	-	27
Otsemobor	-	-	-	1	5	-	-	-	-	-	-	6
Owen	13	46	43	54	38	-	-	-	-	-	-	194
Pacheco	-	-	-	-	-	-	-	-	-	-	2	2
Padelli	-	-	-	-	-	-	-	1	-	-	-	1
Paletta	-	-	-	-	-	-	-	8	-	-	-	8
Partridge	-	1	-	-	-	2	-	-	-	-	-	3
Pellegrino	-	-	-	-	-	13	-	-	-	-	-	13
Peltier	-	-	-	-	-	-	-	4	-	-	-	4
Pennant	-	-	-	-	-	-	-	52	25	4	-	81
Plessis	-	-	-	-	-	-	-	-	2	5	1	8
Potter	-	-	-	-	-	10	7	-	-	-	-	17
Raven	-	-	-	-	-	3	1	-	-	-	-	4
Redknapp	7	-	8	-	-	-	-	-	-	-	-	15
Reina	-	-	-	-	-	-	53	51	52	51	25	232
Riera	-	-	-	-	-	-	-	-	-	40	11	51
Riise	-	-	56	56	35	57	52	48	44	-	-	348
Roque	-	-	-	-	-	-	-	1	-	-	-	1
S-Pongolle	-	-	-	-	23	26	16	1	-	-	-	66
Sissoko	-	-	-	-	-	-	45	28	14	-	-	87
Skrtel	-	-	-	-	-	-	-	-	20	30	18	68
Smicer	10	49	35	34	25	16	-	-	-	-	-	169
Smith	-	-	-	-	-	-	-	1	-	-	-	1
Smyth	-	-	-	-	-	1	-	-	-	-	-	1
Song	4	4	-	-	-	-	-	-	-	-	-	8
Spearing	-	-	-	-	-	-	-	-	2	5	-	7
Staunton	2	2	-	-	-	-	-	-	-	-	-	4
Thompson	13	-	-	-	-	-	-	-	-	-	-	13
Torres	-	-	-	-	-	-	-	-	46	38	19	103
Traore	-	12	1	49	11	42	24	-	-	-	-	139
Vignal	-	7	9	4	-	-	-	-	-	-	-	20
Voronin	-	-	-	-	-	-	-	-	28	-	12	40
Warnock	-	-	-	-	-	30	30	7	-	-	-	67
Welsh	-	-	-	1	2	7	-	-	-	-	-	10
Westerveld	19	61	3	-	-	-	-	-	-	-	-	83
Whitbread	-	-	-	-	-	4	3	-	-	-	-	7
Wright	-	4	17	-	-	-	-	-	-	-	-	21
Xavier	-	-	15	6	-	-	-	-	-	-	-	21
Zenden	-	-	-	-	-	-	17	30	-	-	-	47
Ziege	-	32	-	-	-	-	-	-	-	-	-	32

PLAYER RECORDS

The following players all found the back of the net at least once during the 2000s for Liverpool in first-team games – with two players hitting over a century of goals.

LIVERPOOL GOALS IN 2000s											
PLAYER	J-M 2000	2000-2001	2001-2002	2002-2003	2003-2004	2004-2005	2005-2006	2006-2007	2007-2008	2008-2009	A-D 2009	TOTAL
Agger	-	-	-	-	-	-	-	4	-	2	-	6
Alonso	-	-	-	-	-	3	5	4	2	5	-	19
Anelka	-	-	5	-	-	-	-	-	-	-	-	5
Arbeloa	-	-	-	-	-	-	-	1	-	1	-	2
Aurelio	-	-	-	-	-	-	-	-	1	3	-	4
Babbel	-	6	-	-	-	-	-	-	-	-	-	6
Babel	-	-	-	-	-	-	-	-	10	4	3	17
Barmby	-	8	-	-	-	-	-	-	-	-	-	8
Baros	-	-	-	12	2	13	-	-	-	-	-	27
Bellamy	-	-	-	-	-	-	-	9	-	-	-	9
Benayoun	-	-	-	-	-	-	-	-	11	9	7	27
Berger	5	2	1	1	-	-	-	-	-	-	-	9
Biscan	-	1	-	-	-	2	-	-	-	-	-	3
Camara	3	-	-	-	-	-	-	-	-	-	-	3
Carragher	-	-	-	-	-	-	1	1	-	1	-	3
Cheyrou	-	-	-	1	4	-	-	-	-	-	-	5
Cisse	-	-	-	-	-	5	19	-	-	-	-	24
Crouch	-	-	-	-	-	-	13	18	11	-	-	42
Diao	-	-	-	2	-	1	-	-	-	-	-	3
Diouf	-	-	-	6	-	-	-	-	-	-	-	6
Dossena	-	-	-	-	-	-	-	-	-	2	-	2
El Zhar	-	-	-	-	-	-	-	-	1	-	-	1
Finnan	-	-	-	-	-	1	-	-	-	-	-	1
Fowler	-	17	4	-	-	-	5	7	-	-	-	33
Garcia	-	-	-	-	-	13	11	6	-	-	-	30
Gerrard	-	10	4	7	6	13	23	11	21	24	5	124
Gonzalez	-	-	-	-	-	-	-	3	-	-	-	3
Hamann	1	3	1	2	3	1	-	-	-	-	-	11
Heskey	3	22	14	9	12	-	-	-	-	-	-	60
Hyypia	-	4	5	5	5	3	2	3	4	2	-	33
Insua	-	-	-	-	-	-	-	-	-	1	-	1
Johnson	-	-	-	-	-	-	-	-	-	-	2	2
Keane	-	-	-	-	-	-	-	-	7	-	-	7
Kewell	-	-	-	-	11	1	3	1	-	-	-	16
Kuyt	-	-	-	-	-	-	-	14	11	15	6	46
Le Tallec	-	-	-	-	1	-	-	-	-	-	-	1
Litmanen	-	2	7	-	-	-	-	-	-	-	-	9
Lucas	-	-	-	-	-	-	-	-	1	3	-	4
McAllister	-	7	2	-	-	-	-	-	-	-	-	9
Mascherano	-	-	-	-	-	-	-	-	1	-	1	2
Mellor	-	-	-	1	-	5	-	-	-	-	-	6
Morientes	-	-	-	-	-	3	9	-	-	-	-	12
Murphy	1	10	8	12	8	-	-	-	-	-	-	39
Ngog	-	-	-	-	-	-	-	-	-	3	6	9
Nunez	-	-	-	-	-	1	-	-	-	-	-	1

PLAYER RECORDS

PLAYER	J-M 2000	2000-2001	2001-2002	2002-2003	2003-2004	2004-2005	2005-2006	2006-2007	2007-2008	2008-2009	A-D 2009	TOTAL
LIVERPOOL GOALS IN 2000s												
Owen	4	24	28	28	19	-	-	-	-	-	-	103
Paletta	-	-	-	-	-	-	-	1	-	-	-	1
Pennant	-	-	-	-	-	-	-	1	2	-	-	3
Plessis	-	-	-	-	-	-	-	-	-	1	-	1
Redknapp	1	-	2	-	-	-	-	-	-	-	-	3
Riera	-	-	-	-	-	-	-	-	-	5	-	5
Riise	-	-	8	6	-	8	4	5	-	-	-	31
S-Pongolle	-	-	-	-	2	4	3	-	-	-	-	9
Sissoko	-	-	-	-	-	-	-	-	1	-	-	1
Skrtel	-	-	-	-	-	-	-	-	-	-	1	1
Smicer	1	7	5	1	4	1	-	-	-	-	-	19
Thompson	1	-	-	-	-	-	-	-	-	-	-	1
Torres	-	-	-	-	-	-	-	-	33	17	12	62
Traore	-	-	-	-	1	-	-	-	-	-	-	1
Voronin	-	-	-	-	-	-	-	-	6	-	-	6
Warnock	-	-	-	-	-	-	1	-	-	-	-	1
Wright	-	-	1	-	-	-	-	-	-	-	-	1
Xavier	-	-	2	-	-	-	-	-	-	-	-	2
Zenden	-	-	-	-	-	-	2	-	-	-	-	2
Ziege	-	2	-	-	-	-	-	-	-	-	-	2

Steven Gerrard – Top goalscorer in the 2000s

OPPOSITION

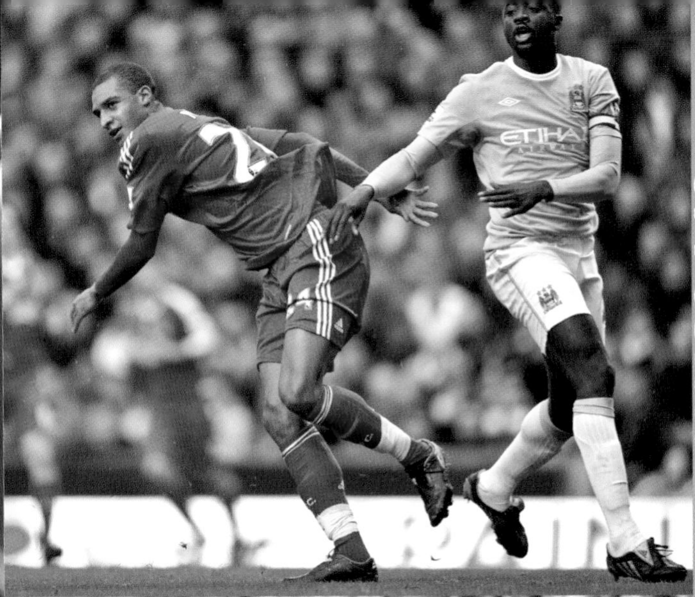

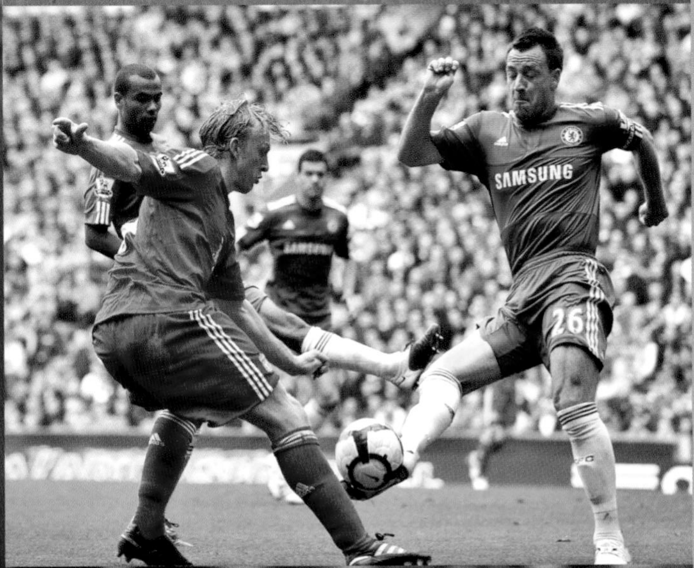

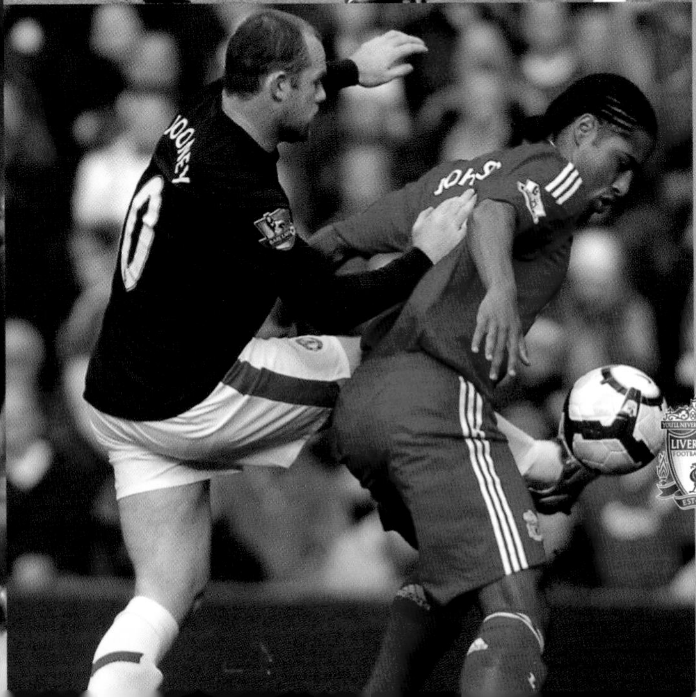

ARSENAL

2009/10 OVERVIEW

Final position: 3rd, Premier League
Best cup runs: QF, Champions Lge, Lge Cup
Player of season: Cesc Fabregas
Top scorer (all): 19, Cesc Fabregas

ALL-TIME RECORD

(League matches only)

	PL	W	D	L
Home:	86	48	16	22
Away:	86	20	28	38
Overall:	172	68	44	60

LAST 2 MEETINGS (LEAGUE)

10/02/2010

Arsenal	1-0	Liverpool
Diaby 72		

13/12/2009

Liverpool	1-2	Arsenal
Kuyt 41		Johnson 50 (o.g.),
		Arshavin 58

CLUB DETAILS

Nickname: The Gunners
Ground: Emirates Stadium, capacity 60,432 (09/10 away alloc. 2,956)
Manager: Arsene Wenger (app. 01/10/96)
Major signing: Marouane Chamakh
Year formed: 1886

USEFUL INFORMATION

Website: www.arsenal.com
Address: Emirates Stadium, Highbury House, 75 Drayton Park N5 1BU
Switchboard: 0207 619 5003

TRAVEL INFORMATION

By Car (from Anfield): 209 miles/3 hours 45 mins.
By Tube: Arsenal (Piccadilly Line) is a three-minute walk. Finsbury Park and Highbury & Islington are also within 10 minutes of the stadium.
By Bus: Main bus stops are located on Holloway Road, Nag's Head, Seven Sisters Road, Blackstock Road and Highbury Corner. Regular services will take you to within 10 minutes walk of the ground.

ASTON VILLA

2009/10 OVERVIEW

Final position: 6th, Premier League
Best cup runs: F, League Cup; SF, FA Cup
Player of season: James Milner
Top scorer (all): 17, John Carew

ALL-TIME RECORD

(League matches only)

	PL	W	D	L
Home:	85	53	17	15
Away:	85	27	21	37
Overall:	170	80	38	52

LAST 2 MEETINGS

29/12/2009

Aston Villa	0-1	Liverpool
		Torres 90

24/08/2009

Liverpool	1-3	Aston Villa
Torres 72		Lucas 34 (o.g.),
		Davies 45,
		A. Young 75 (p)

CLUB DETAILS

Nickname: The Villans
Ground: Villa Park, capacity 42,573 (09/10 away allocation 2,771)
Manager: Gerard Houllier (app. 08/09/10)
Major signing: Stephen Ireland
Year formed: 1874

USEFUL INFORMATION

Website: www.avfc.co.uk
Address: Villa Park, Trinity Road, Birmingham B6 6HE
Switchboard: 0121 327 2299

TRAVEL INFORMATION

By Car (from Anfield): 96 miles/1 hour 50 mins.
By Train: Witton station is a five-minute walk, while Aston is 15 minutes away. From New Street Station, a taxi should take 15 minutes.
By Bus: The number 7 West Midlands Travel Bus runs from Birmingham City Centre to the stadium (Witton). For services check www.travelwm.co.uk

BIRMINGHAM CITY

2009/10 OVERVIEW

Final position: 9th, Premier League
Best cup runs: QF, FA Cup; R3, League Cup
Player of season: Joe Hart
Top scorer (all): 11, Cameron Jerome

ALL-TIME RECORD

(League matches only)

	PL	W	D	L
Home:	49	31	11	7
Away:	49	15	13	21
Overall:	98	46	24	28

LAST 2 MEETINGS

04/04/2010

Birmingham City	1-1	Liverpool
Ridgewell 56		Gerrard 47

09/11/2009

Liverpool	2-2	Birmingham City
Ngog 13,		Benitez 26, Jerome 45
Gerrard 71 (p)		

CLUB DETAILS

Nickname: Blues
Ground: St Andrew's, capacity 30,009 (09/10 away allocation 3,000)
Manager: Alex McLeish (app. 28/11/07)
Major signing: Alexander Hleb
Year formed: 1875

USEFUL INFORMATION

Website: www.bcfc.com
Address: St Andrew's Stadium, Birmingham, West Midlands B9 4RL
Switchboard: 0844 557 1875

TRAVEL INFORMATION

By Car (from Anfield): 99 miles/1 hour 55 mins.
By Train: From Birmingham New Street, you can take a five-minute walk to Moor Street station. Take a train to Bordesley, which is 10 minutes from the stadium.
By Bus: The following services serve the stadium from Birmingham city centre – near Moor Street station on Queensway: 57A, 58, 60. Look for bus stop MF.

BLACKBURN ROVERS

2009/10 OVERVIEW

Final position: 10th, Premier League
Best cup runs: SF, League Cup; R3, FA Cup
Player of season: Steven N'Zonzi
Top scorer (all): 10, David Dunn

ALL-TIME RECORD

(League matches only)

	PL	W	D	L
Home:	62	37	16	9
Away:	62	15	22	25
Overall:	124	52	38	34

LAST 2 MEETINGS

28/02/2010

Liverpool	2-1	Blackburn Rovers
Gerrard 20, Torres 44		Andrews 40 (p)

05/12/2009

Blackburn Rovers 0-0		Liverpool

CLUB DETAILS

Nickname: Rovers
Ground: Ewood Park, capacity 31,367 (09/10 away allocation 7,095)
Manager: Sam Allardyce (app. 17/12/08)
Major signing: Mame Biram Diouf
Year formed: 1875

USEFUL INFORMATION

Website: www.rovers.co.uk
Address: Ewood Park, Bolton Road, Blackburn, Lancashire BB2 4JF
Switchboard: 0871 702 1875

TRAVEL INFORMATION

By Car (from Anfield): 40 miles/45 minutes.
By Train: Blackburn station is a mile and a half away, Mill Hill is one mile. Direct trains run from Manchester Victoria, Salford Crescent and Preston.
By Bus: The central bus station is next to the railway station. Services 3, 3A, 3B, 46, and 346 all go from Blackburn to Darwen. Ewood Park is a mile and a half along the journey.

BLACKPOOL

2009/10 OVERVIEW

Final position: 6th, Championship
Best cup runs: R3, FA Cup; R3, League Cup
Player of season: Charlie Adam
Top scorer (all): 19, Charlie Adam

ALL-TIME RECORD

(League matches only)

	PL	W	D	L
Home:	20	10	5	5
Away:	20	8	4	8
Overall:	40	18	9	13

LAST 2 MEETINGS

09/01/1971

Liverpool	2-2	Blackpool
Heighway 38,		Burns
Craven 82 (o.g.)		Pickering

17/08/1970

Blackpool	0-0	Liverpool

CLUB DETAILS

Nickname: The Tangerines/Seasiders
Ground: Bloomfield Road, capacity 17,600 (10/11 away alloc. 2,500)
Manager: Ian Holloway (app. 21/05/09)
Major signing: DJ Campbell
Year formed: 1887

USEFUL INFORMATION

Website: www.blackpoolfc.co.uk
Address: Bloomfield Road, Seasiders Way, Blackpool FY1 6JJ
Switchboard: 0871 622 1953

TRAVEL INFORMATION

By Car (from Anfield): 53 miles/55 minutes.
By Train: Blackpool North station is around 2 miles away. Trains run every hour from Liverpool Lime Street direct – although check the service is running for the Boxing Day league fixture.
By Bus: The regular No. 11 bus to Lytham St Annes runs from the bus station across the road from Blackpool North, passing the stadium.

BOLTON WANDERERS

2009/10 OVERVIEW

Final position: 14th, Premier League
Best cup runs: R5, FA Cup; R4, League Cup
Player of season: Lee Chung Yong
Top scorer (all): 9, Kevin Davies

ALL-TIME RECORD

(League matches only)

	PL	W	D	L
Home:	57	31	16	10
Away:	57	19	13	25
Overall:	114	50	29	35

LAST 2 MEETINGS

30/01/2010

Liverpool	2-0	Bolton Wanderers
Kuyt 37,		
Davies 70 (o.g.)		

29/08/2009

Bolton Wanderers 2-3	Liverpool
Davies 33, Cohen 47	Johnson 41, Torres 56, Gerrard 83

CLUB DETAILS

Nickname: The Trotters
Ground: Reebok Stadium, capacity 28,000 (09/10 away alloc. 4,635)
Manager: Owen Coyle (app. 08/01/10)
Major signing: Martin Petrov
Year formed: 1874

USEFUL INFORMATION

Website: www.bwfc.co.uk
Address: Reebok Stadium, Burnden Way, Lostock, Bolton BL6 6JW
Switchboard: 0844 871 2932

TRAVEL INFORMATION

By Car (from Anfield): 27 miles/40 minutes.
By Train: Horwich Parkway station is a few minutes walk from the stadium. Regular trains run from Bolton, while from Liverpool you can change at Manchester Oxford Road.
By Bus: The club operate regular buses to and from Bolton town centre.

CHELSEA

2009/10 OVERVIEW

Final position: 1st, Premier League
Best cup runs: W, FA Cup; L16, Ch. League
Player of season: Didier Drogba
Top scorer (all): 37, Didier Drogba

ALL-TIME RECORD

(League matches only)

	PL	W	D	L
Home:	67	44	14	9
Away:	67	16	14	37
Overall:	134	60	28	46

LAST 2 MEETINGS (LEAGUE)

02/05/2010

Liverpool	0-2	Chelsea
		Drogba 33, Lampard 54

04/10/2009

Chelsea	2-0	Liverpool
Anelka 60,		
Malouda 90		

CLUB DETAILS

Nickname: The Blues
Ground: Stamford Bridge, capacity 41,841 (09/10 away alloc. 3,190)
Manager: Carlo Ancelotti (app. 01/07/09)
Major signing: Ramires
Year formed: 1905

USEFUL INFORMATION

Website: www.chelseafc.com
Address: Stamford Bridge, Fulham Road, London SW6 1HS
Switchboard: 0871 984 1955

TRAVEL INFORMATION

By Car (from Anfield): 216 miles/4 hours.
By Tube: Fulham Broadway (District Line) is five minutes' walk away. Take a tube to Earls Court and change for Wimbledon-bound tubes. West Brompton overground station is 15 minutes away.
By Bus: Numbers 14, 211 and 414 go along Fulham Road from central London via West Brompton station.

EVERTON

2009/10 OVERVIEW

Final position: 8th, Premier League
Best cup runs: R4, FA Cup; L32, Europa Cup
Player of season: Steven Pienaar
Top scorer (all): 15, Louis Saha

ALL-TIME RECORD

(League matches only)

	PL	W	D	L
Home:	91	39	29	23
Away:	91	31	27	33
Overall:	182	70	56	56

LAST 2 MEETINGS

06/02/2010

Liverpool	1-0	Everton
Kuyt 55		

29/11/2009

Everton	0-2	Liverpool
		Mascherano 12, Kuyt 80

CLUB DETAILS

Nickname: The Toffees
Ground: Goodison Park, capacity 40,260 (09/10 away allocation 2,881)
Manager: David Moyes (app. 14/03/02)
Major signing: Jermaine Beckford
Year formed: 1878

USEFUL INFORMATION

Website: www.evertonfc.com
Address: Goodison Park, Goodison Road, Liverpool L4 4EL
Switchboard: 0871 663 1878

TRAVEL INFORMATION

By Car (from Anfield): 0.8 miles/3 minutes.
By Train: From Liverpool Central, take any train heading for Ormskirk or Kirkby and get off at Kirkdale - from there it is a 10-minute walk.
By Bus: From Queen's Square Bus Station in Liverpool city centre, numbers 1, 2, 19, 20, 21, 311, 345 and 350 go past or near the stadium.

FULHAM

2009/10 OVERVIEW

Final position: 12th, Premier League
Best cup runs: F, Europa League; QF, FA Cup
Player of season: Bobby Zamora
Top scorers (all): 19, Bobby Zamora

ALL-TIME RECORD

(League matches only)

	PL	W	D	L
Home:	23	16	7	0
Away:	23	9	6	8
Overall:	46	25	13	8

LAST 2 MEETINGS

11/04/2010

Liverpool	0-0	Fulham

31/10/2009

Fulham	3-1	Liverpool
Zamora 24,		Torres 42
Nevland 73, Dempsey 87		

CLUB DETAILS

Nickname: Cottagers
Ground: Craven Cottage, capacity 25,678
(09/10 away allocation 2,911)
Manager: Mark Hughes (app. 29/07/10)
Major signing: Carlos Salcido
Year formed: 1879

USEFUL INFORMATION

Website: www.fulhamfc.com
Address: Craven Cottage, Stevenage
Road, Fulham, London SW6 6HH
Switchboard: 0870 442 1222

TRAVEL INFORMATION

By Car (from Anfield): 216 miles/4 hours.
By Tube: Alight at Putney Bridge (District Line),
from central London. The stadium is a 10-minute
walk. Bishop's Park, along the Thames is the
quickest route – note it's closed after night games.
By Bus: The following run down nearby Fulham
Palace Road: 74, 190, 211, 220, 295. London
Transport's website is www.tfl.gov.uk

MANCHESTER CITY

2009/10 OVERVIEW

Final position: 5th, Premier League
Best cup runs: SF, League Cup; R5 FA Cup
Player of season: Carlos Tevez
Top scorer (all): 29, Carlos Tevez

ALL-TIME RECORD

(League matches only)

	PL	W	D	L
Home:	74	45	16	13
Away:	74	29	21	24
Overall:	148	74	37	37

LAST 2 MEETINGS

21/02/2010

Manchester City	0-0	Liverpool

21/11/2009

Liverpool	2-2	Manchester City
Skrtel 50,		Adebayor 69,
Benayoun 77		Ireland 76

CLUB DETAILS

Nickname: Blues/The Citizens
Ground: City of Manchester Stadium,
capacity 48,000
(09/10 away allocation 2,644)
Manager: Roberto Mancini (app. 20/12/09)
Major signing: Mario Balotelli
Year formed: 1887

USEFUL INFORMATION

Website: www.mcfc.co.uk
Address: City of Manchester Stadium,
SportCity, Rowsley Street,
Manchester M11 3FF
Switchboard: 0870 062 1894

TRAVEL INFORMATION

By Car (from Anfield): 36 miles/50 minutes.
By Train: Ashburys station is a 15-minute walk, a
five-minute train journey from Manchester
Piccadilly (20-25 minutes on foot).
By Bus: The following services run direct from
Piccadilly Gardens: 216, 217, 218, 231, 236 and 237.
See www.gmpte.com for more information.

MANCHESTER UNITED

2009/10 OVERVIEW

Final position: 2nd, Premier League
Best cup runs: W, League Cup; QF, Ch. League
Player of season: Wayne Rooney
Top scorer (all): 34, Wayne Rooney

ALL-TIME RECORD

(League matches only)

	PL	W	D	L
Home:	77	37	18	22
Away:	77	15	25	37
Overall:	154	52	43	59

LAST 2 MEETINGS

21/03/2010

Manchester Utd	2-1	Liverpool
Rooney 12, Park 60		Torres 5

25/10/2009

Liverpool	2-0	Manchester Utd
Torres 65, Ngog 90		

CLUB DETAILS

Nickname: Red Devils
Ground: Old Trafford, capacity 76,312
(08/09 away allocation 3,026)
Manager: Sir Alex Ferguson (app. 06/11/1986)
Major signing: Javier Hernandez
Year formed: 1878

USEFUL INFORMATION

Website: www.manutd.com
Address: Old Trafford, Manchester M16 0RA
Switchboard: 0161 868 8000

TRAVEL INFORMATION

By Car (from Anfield): 33 miles/45 minutes.
By Train: Services run from Piccadilly to the club's railway station. There is also a Metrolink service, with the station located next to Lancashire CCC on Warwick Road, which leads to Sir Matt Busby Way.
By Bus: The 250, 255, 256, 263, 290 and 291 run from Piccadilly Gardens in the city centre.

NEWCASTLE UNITED

2009/10 OVERVIEW

Final position: 1st, Championship
Best cup runs: R4, FA Cup; R3, League Cup
Player of season: Kevin Nolan
Top scorers (all): 19, Andy Carroll

ALL-TIME RECORD

(League matches only)

	PL	W	D	L
Home:	74	49	14	11
Away:	74	22	23	29
Overall:	148	71	37	40

LAST 2 MEETINGS

03/05/2009

Liverpool	3-0	Newcastle United
Benayoun 22, Kuyt 28, Lucas 87		

28/12/2008

Newcastle United	1-5	Liverpool
Edgar 45		Gerrard 31, 66, Hyypia 36, Babel 50, Alonso 77 (p)

CLUB DETAILS

Nickname: Magpies
Ground: St James' Park, capacity 52,387
(08/09 away allocation 2,749)
Manager: Chris Hughton (app. 01/06/09)
Major signing: Hatem Ben Arfa
Year formed: 1881

USEFUL INFORMATION

Website: www.nufc.co.uk
Address: St James' Park, Newcastle-upon-Tyne NE1 4ST
Switchboard: 0844 372 1892

TRAVEL INFORMATION

By Car (from Anfield): 173 miles/3 hours.
By Train: The stadium is a 10-minute walk from Newcastle Central Station. It is also served by its own Metro station (St James' Metro).
By Road: Any bus from the town centre heading towards Gallowgate takes you past St James' Park.

STOKE CITY

2009/10 OVERVIEW

Final position: 11th, Premier League
Best cup runs: QF, FA Cup; R4, League Cup
Player of season: Matthew Etherington
Top scorers (all): 8, Ricardo Fuller

ALL-TIME RECORD

(League matches only)

	PL	W	D	L
Home:	55	42	10	3
Away:	55	12	20	23
Overall:	110	54	30	26

LAST 2 MEETINGS

16/01/2010

Stoke City	1-1	Liverpool
Huth 90		Kyrgiakos 57

19/08/2009

Liverpool	4-0	Stoke City
Torres 4, Johnson 45, Kuyt 78, Ngog 90		

CLUB DETAILS

Nickname: The Potters
Ground: Britannia Stadium, capacity 27,500 (09/10 away all'tion 2,871)
Manager: Tony Pulis (app. 13/06/06)
Major signing: Kenwyne Jones
Year formed: 1863

USEFUL INFORMATION

Website: www.stokecityfc.com
Address: Stanley Matthews Way, Stoke-on-Trent ST4 4EG
Switchboard: 0871 663 2008

TRAVEL INFORMATION

By Car (from Anfield): 60 miles/1 hour 10 minutes.
By Train: Stoke-on-Trent is two minutes from Glebe Street, where buses to the stadium run. Turn right out of the station and then next right. Follow the road to the end then turn left, down a bank into Glebe Street.
By Bus: From Hanley Bus Station take the 23 to Glebe Street where shuttle bus services to the stadium depart. Service is at 15-minute intervals.

SUNDERLAND

2009/10 OVERVIEW

Final position: 13th, Premier League
Best cup runs: R4, FA Cup & League Cup
Player of season: Darren Bent
Top scorer (all): 25, Darren Bent

ALL-TIME RECORD

(League matches only)

	PL	W	D	L
Home:	73	37	18	18
Away:	73	28	13	32
Overall:	146	65	31	50

LAST 2 MEETINGS

28/03/2010

Liverpool	3-0	Sunderland
Torres 3, 60, Johnson 32		

17/10/2009

Sunderland	1-0	Liverpool
Bent 5		

CLUB DETAILS

Nickname: The Black Cats
Ground: Stadium of Light, capacity 49,000 (08/09 away alloc. 2,361)
Manager: Steve Bruce (app. 03/06/09)
Major signing: Asamoah Gyan
Year formed: 1879

USEFUL INFORMATION

Website: www.safc.com
Address: The Sunderland Stadium of Light, Sunderland SR5 1SU
Switchboard: 0871 911 1200

TRAVEL INFORMATION

By Car (from Anfield): 169 miles/3 hours.
By Train: Sunderland mainline station is a 10-15 minute walk. The Metro service also runs from here, with St Peter's or the Stadium of Light stations nearest the stadium.
By Bus: Numbers 2, 3, 4, 12, 13, 15 and 16 all stop within a few minutes walk of the ground. All routes connect to the central bus station, Park Lane Interchange.

TOTTENHAM HOTSPUR

2009/10 OVERVIEW

Final position: 4th, Premier League
Best cup runs: SF, FA Cup; QF, League Cup
Player of season: Michael Dawson
Top scorers (all): 24, Jermain Defoe

ALL-TIME RECORD

(League matches only)

	PL	W	D	L
Home:	67	43	19	5
Away:	67	20	15	32
Overall:	134	63	34	37

LAST 2 MEETINGS (LEAGUE)

20/01/2010
Liverpool 2-0 Tottenham H.
Kuyt 6, 90 (p)

16/08/2009
Tottenham H. 2-1 Liverpool
Assou-Ekotto 44, Gerrard 56 (p)
Bassong 59

CLUB DETAILS

Nickname: Spurs
Ground: White Hart Lane, capacity 36,240 (08/09 away alloc. 2,929)
Manager: Harry Redknapp (app. 26/10/08)
Major signing: Rafael van der Vaart
Year formed: 1882

USEFUL INFORMATION

Website: www.tottenhamhotspur.com
Address: 748 High Road, Tottenham, London N17 0AP
Switchboard: 0844 499 5000

TRAVEL INFORMATION

By Car (from Anfield): 214 miles/3 hours 45 mins.
By Tube: The nearest tube station is Seven Sisters (Victoria - a 25-minute walk), with trains running to Liverpool Street. The nearest mainline station is White Hart Lane, approx 5 minutes walk.
By Bus: A regular service runs from Seven Sisters past the stadium entrance (numbers 149, 259, 279).

WEST BROMWICH ALBION

2009/10 OVERVIEW

Final position: 2nd, Championship
Best cup runs: R5, FA Cup; R3, League Cup
Player of season: Graham Dorrans
Top scorer (all): 18, Graham Dorrans

ALL-TIME RECORD

(League matches only)

	PL	W	D	L
Home:	58	32	17	9
Away:	58	23	16	19
Overall:	116	55	33	28

LAST 2 MEETINGS

17/05/2009
West Brom 0-2 Liverpool
Gerrard 28, Kuyt 63

08/11/2008
Liverpool 3-0 West Brom
Keane 34, 43,
Arbeloa 90

CLUB DETAILS

Nickname: Baggies
Ground: The Hawthorns, capacity 26,500 (08/09 away allocation 3,000)
Manager: Roberto Di Matteo (app. 30/06/09)
Major signing: Marc-Antoine Fortune
Year formed: 1878

USEFUL INFORMATION

Website: www.wba.co.uk
Address: The Hawthorns, West Bromwich, West Midlands B71 4LF
Switchboard: 0871 271 1100

TRAVEL INFORMATION

By Car (from Anfield): 94 miles/1 hour 45 mins.
By Train: The Hawthorns Metro stop is 10 minutes away, served by a service from Birmingham Snow Hill. Smethwick Rolf Street is 15 minutes from the stadium, served by Birmingham New Street trains.
By Bus: The 74 (between Birmingham and Dudley), 79 (Birmingham and Wolverhampton) and 450 (Bearwood and West Bromwich) stop nearby.

WEST HAM UNITED

2009/10 OVERVIEW

Final position: 17th, Premier League
Best cup runs: R3, FA Cup & League Cup
Player of season: Scott Parker
Top scorer (all): 10, Carlton Cole

ALL-TIME RECORD

(League matches only)

	PL	W	D	L
Home:	53	36	14	3
Away:	53	20	15	18
Overall:	106	56	29	21

LAST 2 MEETINGS

19/04/2010

Liverpool	3-0	West Ham

Benayoun 19,
Ngog 29, Green 59 (o.g.)

19/09/2009

West Ham	2-3	Liverpool

Diamanti 29 (p),   Torres 20, 75, Kuyt 41
Cole 45

CLUB DETAILS

Nickname: The Hammers
Ground: Upton Park, capacity 35,647
(09/10 away allocation 2,912)
Manager: Avram Grant (app. 03/06/10)
Major signing: Frederic Piquionne
Year formed: 1895

USEFUL INFORMATION

Website: www.whufc.com
Address: Boleyn Ground, Green Street,
Upton Park, London E13 9AZ
Switchboard: 0208 548 2748

TRAVEL INFORMATION

By Car (from Anfield): 224 miles/4 hours 5 mins.
By Tube: Upton Park is the closest tube station, around 45 minutes from Central London (District Line). When you exit the station turn right, the stadium is then a two-minute walk. East Ham and Plaistow Stations, which are further away, may also be worth using to avoid match congestion.
By Bus: Routes 5, 15, 15A, 58, 58A, 104, 147 and 238 all serve Upton Park.

WIGAN ATHLETIC

2009/10 OVERVIEW

Final position: 16th, Premier League
Best cup runs: R4, FA Cup; R2, League Cup
Player of season: Charles N'Zogbia
Top scorer (all): 10, Hugo Rodallega

ALL-TIME RECORD

(League matches only)

	PL	W	D	L
Home:	5	4	1	0
Away:	5	3	1	1
Overall:	10	7	2	1

LAST 2 MEETINGS

08/03/2010

Wigan Athletic	1-0	Liverpool

Rodallega 35

16/12/2009

Liverpool	2-1	Wigan Athletic

Ngog 9, Torres 79   N'Zogbia 90

CLUB DETAILS

Nickname: The Latics
Ground: DW Stadium,
capacity 25,023
(09/10 away allocation 3,983)
Manager: Roberto Martinez (app. 15/06/09)
Major signing: Mauro Boselli
Year formed: 1932

USEFUL INFORMATION

Website: www.wiganlatics.co.uk
Address: DW Stadium, Robin Park,
Newtown, Wigan WN5 0UZ
Switchboard: 01942 774000

TRAVEL INFORMATION

By Car (from Anfield): 21 miles/30 minutes.
By Train: Wigan Wallgate and Wigan North Western are a 15-minute walk. From either station head under the railway bridge and keep to the right – following the road (A49) for 10 minutes.
By Bus: No particular route, as the venue is within easy distance of the station.

WOLVERHAMPTON WANDERERS

2009/10 OVERVIEW

Final position: 15th, Premier League
Best cup runs: R4, FA Cup; R3, League Cup
Player of season: Kevin Doyle
Top scorer (all): 9, Kevin Doyle

ALL-TIME RECORD

(League matches only)

	PL	W	D	L
Home:	45	30	7	8
Away:	45	14	10	21
Overall:	90	44	17	29

LAST 2 MEETINGS

26/01/2010
Wolves	0-0	Liverpool

26/12/2009
Liverpool	2-0	Wolves

Gerrard 62,
Benayoun 70

CLUB DETAILS

Nickname: Wolves
Ground: Molineux, capacity 29,400
(09/10 away allocation 2,447)
Manager: Mick McCarthy (app. 21/07/06)
Major signing: Steven Fletcher
Year formed: 1877

USEFUL INFORMATION

Website: www.wolves.co.uk
Address: Waterloo Road, Wolverhampton,
West Midlands WV1 4QR
Switchboard: 0871 222 2220

TRAVEL INFORMATION

By Car (from Anfield): 88 miles/1 hour 35 minutes.
By Train: The stadium is a 15-minute walk from Wolverhampton station. Follow the Ring Road, walking down the side of the Chubb buildings. At the crossroads you will see the stadium on your left.
By Bus: The 503 and 504 from stand R in the city centre bus station stop at the stadium – this is opposite the railway station, in easy walking distance.

Fernando Torres in action against Wolves – the Reds are due to visit Molineux in January 2011

TICKETS

ADDRESS

Ticket Office,
PO Box 204,
Liverpool
L69 3JF

TELEPHONE NUMBERS/WEBSITE

0843 170 5555 (24-Hour Ticket Information Line)
++44 (0)151 907 9399 (International)
www.liverpoolfc.tv/tickets

TICKET OFFICE HOURS

Monday-Friday 8.15am-3.45pm
Matchdays 8.15am to kick-off (weekday), 9.15am to kick-off (weekend)
Non Match Saturdays 9.15am-1.00pm

PRICES

	Category A	Category B	Category C
Kop			
Adult	£43	£39	£37
Over 65	£32.50	£29.50	£28
Disabled and Visually Impaired	£32.50	£29.50	£28
Main Stand			
Adult	£45	£41	£39
Over 65	£34.50	£31	£29.50
Centenary Stand			
Adult	£45	£41	£39
Over 65	£34.50	£31	£29.50
Paddock Enclosure			
Adult	£45	£41	£39
Over 65	£34.50	£31	£29.50
Disabled and Visually Impaired	£34	£31	£29.50
Anfield Road			
Adult	£45	£41	£39
Over 65	£34.50	£31	£29.50
Combined 1 Adult/1 Child (16 or under)	£67.50	£61.50	£58.50
Disabled and Visually Impaired	£34	£31	£29.50
Personal Assistants	FREE	FREE	FREE

CATEGORY A MATCHES

Arsenal, Chelsea, Everton, Manchester City, Manchester United, Tottenham Hotspur.

CATEGORY B MATCHES

Aston Villa, Blackburn Rovers, Bolton Wanderers, Newcastle United, West Ham United.

CATEGORY C MATCHES

Birmingham City, Blackpool, Fulham, Stoke City, Sunderland, West Brom, Wigan, Wolves.

BUYING TICKETS – BARCLAYS PREMIER LEAGUE HOME GAMES

Match tickets will go on sale first to members. If you are not already a member you can join NOW at **www.liverpoolfc.tv/ALLRED**

The Members Sale lasts for 2 days. Remaining tickets will be available to all fans through Late Availability (previously known as General Sale). Late Availability will be open until all remaining tickets are sold.

TICKETS

BUYING TICKETS – BARCLAYS PREMIER LEAGUE HOME GAMES

In order to offer fans the best opportunity to apply for tickets, any tickets returned through the Ticket Exchange will also be available through Late Availability so keep checking the online ticketing system as tickets may become available to purchase.

You can apply for tickets online at **liverpoolfc.tv** or via 0843 170 5555 (Overseas (0044) 843 170 5555). If tickets are still available 3 days before the match, supporters can apply to purchase tickets in person from the Ticket Office. For further details please visit **www.liverpoolfc.tv/tickets**

Please note: Postal applications are no longer accepted.

Disabled fans, please visit our Accessibility section on the website for details on aplying for tickets – **www.liverpoolfc.tv/tickets/accessibility**

BUYING TICKETS – BARCLAYS PREMIER LEAGUE AWAY GAMES

Tickets to away games are only available to season-ticket holders and members, with priority given according to the number of Barclays Premier League away fixtures attended during the 2009/10 season.

For any available tickets following the Season Ticket and Members Sale, further announcement will be made at **www.liverpoolfc.tv/tickets**

BUYING TICKETS – DOMESTIC CUP AND EUROPEAN GAMES

For information on cup and European games, please see the fixture's selling notice under 'Latest Ticket News' on **www.liverpoolfc.tv**

TICKET OFFICE INFORMATION

Ticket stubs should be retained as they may be required for future ticket allocation or in the event a match is abandoned.

For latest ticket information visit **www.liverpoolfc.tv/tickets**

ABOUT ANFIELD

ADDRESS

Liverpool Football Club
Anfield Road
Liverpool
L4 0TH

ABOUT

First used in 1884 to house Everton FC, the Reds have called Anfield their home since 1892. Originally owned by John Orrell, fellow brewer and friend John Houlding bought the ground in 1891, soon after Everton won the league title. His proposed increase in rent to Everton – some records state a four-fold increase on their original agreement with Orrell – saw the club leave. With an empty ground and no team, Houlding formed his own club – and so Liverpool FC were born. Their first match at Anfield saw a 7-0 victory over Rotherham Town on September 1 1892, with the first Football League match played a year later, the Reds seeing off Lincoln City 4-0 on September 8, 1893 in front of an estimated 5,000 spectators.

On its original inauguration in 1884 Anfield housed 20,000. Extensive redevelopment has seen Anfield hold upwards of 60,000, the stadium's record attendance of 61,905 coming against Wolves on February 2, 1952.

The ground, which hosted European Championship games in 1996 and is rated a 4-star stadium by UEFA, holds 45,522 – with this figure taking into account the Press and disabled areas and all seating, some of which is not used due to segregation. Anfield, or a new stadium, is also due to host games during the 2015 rugby union World Cup, while Liverpool has been pencilled in as a host for games should England win the right to stage the 2018 World Cup.

THE KOP GRANDSTAND

Built in 1906, after the Reds won the league championship for a second time. It was named 'The Spion Kop' after a South African hill in Natal which was the scene of a bloody Boer War battle. In 1928 it was rebuilt and a roof was added with the capacity reaching close to 30,000 – the largest covered terrace in the Football League at that time. It was rebuilt in summer 1994 to its current splendour after an emotional send-off against Norwich City at the end of the 1993/94 campaign.

CENTENARY STAND

The original Kemlyn Road Stand incorporated a barrel roof and was fronted by an uncovered paddock. It was demolished in 1963 to make way for a new cantilever stand. In 1992 a second tier was added, and the stand was renamed to mark the club's 100th anniversary.

MAIN STAND/PADDOCK

The original structure was erected in the late 19th century, a 3,000-capacity stand with a distinctive red and white tudor style with the club's name in the centre. In 1973 it was redeveloped with a new roof and officially opened by HRH the Duke of Kent. Seats were added to the Paddock in 1980.

ANFIELD ROAD STAND

In 1903 the first Anfield Road stand was built. Once a simple one-tier stand which contained a covered standing enclosure (the roof was first added in 1965), it was demolished to make way for a two-tier development in 1998 – the stand having been originally altered to accomodate multi-coloured seating in the early 1980s.

GETTING TO ANFIELD

HOW TO GET THERE - BY CAR

Follow the M62 until you reach the end of the motorway. Then follow the A5058 towards Liverpool for 3 miles, then turn left at the traffic lights into Utting Avenue (there is a McDonald's on the corner of this junction). Proceed for one mile and then turn right at The Arkles pub for the ground. It is recommended that you arrive at least 2 hours before kick-off in order to secure your parking space. Otherwise, you can park in the streets around Goodison Park and walk across Stanley Park to Anfield, or you can park in a secure parking area at Goodison.

HOW TO GET THERE - BY TRAIN

Kirkdale Station is the closest to Anfield (about a mile away), although Sandhills Station the stop before has the benefit of a bus service to the ground (Soccerbus). Both stations can be reached by first getting a train from Liverpool Lime Street (which is over 3 miles from the ground) to Liverpool Central (Merseyrail Northern Line), and then changing there for trains to Sandhills (2 stops away) or Kirkdale (3 stops). Note: only trains to Ormskirk or Kirkby go to Kirkdale station. A taxi from Liverpool Lime Street should cost between £5 and £7.

HOW TO GET THERE - SOCCERBUS

There are frequent shuttle buses from Sandhills Station to Anfield for all Liverpool home Premiership and Cup matches. Soccerbus will run for 2 hours before each match (last bus from Sandhills Station is approximately 15 minutes before kick-off) and for 50 minutes after the final whistle (subject to availability). You can pay as you board the bus. Soccerbus is FREE for those who hold a valid TRIO, SOLO or SAVEAWAY ticket, or a Merseytravel Free Travel Pass.

HOW TO GET THERE - BY BUS

Take a 26 (or 27) from Paradise Street Bus Station or a 17B, 17C, 17D or 217 from Queen Square bus station directly to the ground. The 68 and 168 which operate between Bootle and Aigburth and the 14 (from Queen Square) and 19 stop a short walk away.

HOW TO GET THERE - BY AIR

Liverpool John Lennon Airport is around 10 miles from the ground, and taxis should be easily obtainable. Alternatively, you can catch the 80A bus to Garston Station and change at Sandhills for the Soccerbus service.

HOW TO GET THERE - ON FOOT

From Kirkdale Station, turn right and then cross the railway bridge, where you will see the Melrose Abbey pub. Walk past up Westminster Road for around 1/3 of a mile before you arrive at the Elm Tree pub. Follow the road around the right-hand bend and then turn left into Bradwell Street. At the end of the road you will come to County Road (A59). Cross over at the traffic lights and then go down the road to the left of the Aldi superstore. At the end of this road you will reach Walton Lane (A580). You should be able to see Goodison Park on your left and Stanley Park in front of you. Cross Walton Lane and either enter Stanley Park, following the footpath through the park (keeping to the right) which will exit into Anfield Road. As an alternative to going through Stanley Park, bear right down Walton Lane and then turn left down the road at the end of Stanley Park to the ground.

TO CHECK BUS AND TRAIN TIMES (8AM-8PM, 7 DAYS A WEEK):

Traveline Merseyside   0871 200 22 33
Soccerbus   0151 330 1066

STADIUM & LEGENDS TOUR

ABOUT

The all new LFC Stadium Tour is a must for any Liverpool FC fan.

Anfield – the name alone conjures up a million memories; many associated with success. It is one of the oldest and most famous football grounds in the world. Originally the home of Everton Football Club between 1884 and 1892, Anfield has long since become synonymous with Liverpool Football Club and the amazing success achieved by the Reds.

Over the years some of football's greatest names have graced the hallowed turf and contributed to some of the most memorable matches ever played.

LFC STADIUM TOUR

- Gain exclusive access behind the scenes at one of the world's true sporting cathedrals, soaking up the peerless heritage of England's most successful football club.
- Watch and learn as our passionate tour guides provide fascinating insights into Anfield's celebrated past and Liverpool FC's bright future, taking in rarely seen stadium areas.
- Take a look at the view from the best seats in the stadium.
- Enjoy an interactive experience in the Anfield Press Room.
- Follow in the footsteps of legends like Shankly, Paisley and Dalglish in a stadium steeped in glory.
- Sit in the same dressing room as modern day icons, Gerrard, Torres and Carragher.
- To the backdrop of spine-tingling sound effects, walk down the tunnel, touch the world famous "THIS IS ANFIELD" sign and emerge to the roar of the Anfield faithful.
- Marvel at the Spion Kop – the most illustrious terrace in world football.
- Treat yourself to an unforgettable trip for all the family.
- Fantastic photo opportunities at every turn – don't forget your cameras!

Book now to take advantage of increased tour availability (leaving every 15 minutes during peak periods). In addition to treating yourself, you can now purchase a stadium tour as a gift, allowing the recipient to book within a 12-month period.

Price (includes LFC Museum entrance):

Adults	£14
Children	£8
Family ticket	£38 (2 adults and 2 children)

Open everyday from 9am onwards, running later during summer and finishing earlier in winter. Please see **www.liverpoolfc.tv/tours** for up-to-date availability.

LFC LEGENDS TOUR

This nostalgic stadium tour takes you behind the scenes at Anfield with insights and dressing room tales never told before in this way.
Visit the dressing room, finding out how things have changed whilst reminiscing on the memories and highlights – hearing at first hand what playing at Anfield meant to them.
Go down the tunnel to the sound of the crowd and touch the famous "This Is Anfield" sign, before taking your seat in the dugout to hear how they received their instructions from the touchline.
Hear what affect the roar from the world-famous Kop had on the players with tales of their greatest goal scored, defence-splitting pass or crunching tackle before you finish off with a fun and entertaining question and answer session.
A Legends Tour of Anfield is the perfect day out for you or could make the perfect gift, as gift vouchers are available.

Price:

Adults	£35
Children and Concessions	£18

MUSEUM TOUR

LIVERPOOL FC MUSEUM

The Liverpool FC Museum captures the glory and catalogues the success of one of Britain's most successful football clubs. Amongst many other notable collections it is home to 5 European Cups, including the original trophy won for the fifth time against AC Milan in 2005.

You can soak up the memories of the many legends to have worn the famous red strip, relive many of our famous triumphs and get lost in the nostalgia.

Price:

Adults	£6
Children	£4
Family ticket	£18 (2 adults and 2 children)

Opening times:
9am-5pm (with last admission at 4pm).
Matchdays – Last admission is 1 hour before kick-off.
Please note, when we have later tours the museum will remain open in conjunction with them.

Booking information:
Please see **www.liverpoolfc.tv/tours** for up-to-date opening times, promotions or other important booking information, or call 0151 260 6677.

Mini stadium tours:
Before some home games when we are preparing the stadium, there are restrictions with some of the areas we can visit. These tours will still give you limited access to the stadium and the LFC Museum (at a reduced cost).

The Liverpool dressing room – Available to visit on the LFC Stadium Tour

THE ANFIELD EXPERIENCE

Liverpool Football Club offers you the perfect opportunity to treat yourself or anybody else to a choice of two exclusive VIP days. These can be purchased either as an open voucher, giving you the flexibility to redeem the day over the next nine months (subject to availability), or on a specific date.

As they come in a stylish presentation pack which can be personalised for the lucky recipient, they make the perfect gift for any Liverpool fan.

The stadium tour takes you behind the scenes at Anfield, visiting the dressing rooms, down the tunnel to the sound of the crowd, a chance to touch the famous "This Is Anfield" sign and sit in the team dugout. A knowledgeable tour guide will tell you about the historic Anfield Stadium and escort you on to The Kop – the most famous terrace in world football. Bring your cameras and hand-held video recorders to take those precious pictures of the stadium and museum.

You'll enjoy a luxurious three-course lunch in one of our executive boxes overlooking the pitch – expect one of our Legends to drop in and make a special personal appearance. Before you leave with your limited edition gift, join the rest of the guests for a fun question and answer session with your Liverpool Legend. A great day out for all Liverpool fans!

THE ULTIMATE ANFIELD EXPERIENCE

What if you could live a life in the day of a Liverpool Legend? Take a nostalgic tour around Anfield Stadium and Museum, and revel in the club's great history. Then play with Reds' Legends at the Liverpool Academy in a unique training session before dining with them in one of our luxury suites.

The Ultimate Anfield Experience is truly unique.

You'll be spending a day at the club you love...meeting past greats, collecting autographs and accessing areas of Liverpool FC that few fans are privileged to see. It's a real once-in-a-lifetime VIP experience.

For more information please call **0151 263 7744** or visit **www.theanfieldexperience.com**

CLUB STORES

Selling everything from the new replica kits to the latest toys and games, the club stores provide Reds fans with a wealth of souvenirs. With the new adidas range having been unveiled, there remains a wealth of choice for the 2010/2011 season.
Addresses and contact details are as follows:

WILLIAMSON SQUARE OFFICIAL CLUB STORE

11 Williamson Square, Liverpool, L1 1EQ
United Kingdom
Tel +44 (0)151 330 3077
Opening times: Mon-Wed 9am - 5.30pm;
Thursday 9am - 7pm; Fri-Sat 9am - 5.30pm;
Sundays 10am - 4pm; the day before and on a matchday 9am - 7pm (Except Sunday).

ANFIELD OFFICIAL CLUB STORE

Telephone +44 (0)151 264 2368
Opening times Mon-Sat 9am - 5pm;
Sundays 10am - 4pm.
The store will have varying opening hours on match days, depending on kick-off times.
Please call for details.

LIVERPOOL ONE SUPERSTORE

7 South John Street, Liverpool, L1 8BU
United Kingdom
Tel +44 (0)151 709 4345
Opening times: Mon-Fri 9.30am - 8pm;
Saturdays 9am - 7pm;
Sundays 11am - 5pm.

CHESTER OFFICIAL CLUB STORE

48 Eastgate Street, Chester, CH1 1LE
United Kingdom
Tel +44 (0)1244 344 608
Opening times: Mon-Sat 9am - 5.30pm;
Sundays 10am - 4pm.

ONLINE STORE

www.liverpoolfc.tv/store

ORDERING BY PHONE

0844 800 4239
(International calls) 00 44 138 684 8247
Lines open: Monday-Friday 8.00am - 9.00pm
Saturday 8.00am - 7.00pm
Sunday 9.00am - 6.00pm

Liverpool One, in the heart of the city

OFFICIAL WEBSITE

WWW.LIVERPOOLFC.TV

ABOUT

Anfield may be the world-famous home of Liverpool FC but when it comes to visiting the club online, there's only one place called 'home' and that's **www.liverpoolfc.tv**

Launched in April 2001 – and relaunched in December 2009 – the official website of Liverpool Football Club has proved an incredible success for the Reds and is now one of the most popular sports sites on the web.

Within 12 months of launch the website, run by passionate supporters employed by the club, was recognised as the most visited football club website in the world – with fans from 139 countries viewing 13.3 million pages a month.

In May 2005, **www.liverpoolfc.tv** set a new record as 2.8 million fans viewed 48 million pages in a single month as Reds fans all over the world logged on to bask in the glory of Rafael Benitez's remarkable comeback in Istanbul. But even those incredible numbers were dwarfed in July 2007, the month Fernando Torres swapped Madrid for Merseyside, as 2.9 million supporters from 238 different countries visited the site to read all about the Spaniard's move to Anfield with an incredible 65 million pages viewed within 31 days.

Three years on and **www.liverpoolfc.tv** has been totally relaunched to ensure the website stays ahead of the chasing pack in delivering the best possible online service to fans desperate to interact with the football club they love. Since the relaunch, more fans are visiting the site every day and viewing more pages than ever before.

In July 2010 – the month which saw Roy Hodgson and Joe Cole arrive on Merseyside – another website record was set as more than four million fans logged on to view over 85 million pages on **www.liverpoolfc.tv**. With exclusive first interviews with the new manager and his first signings, behind-the-scenes footage of Cole's medical, daily updates from the training camp in Switzerland and live coverage of our pre-season friendly games, it was a momentous month for the Reds both on and off the field.

Whether you visit the website to read the latest official news as it breaks, watch goals, highlights and interviews with Roy Hodgson and his players, buy the new kit from the online store, comment on the news as it happens or share your opinions on the ever-vibrant discussion forums, **www.liverpoolfc.tv** offers something for every supporter.

No wonder millions of Reds all over the world consider it the club's online home.

Website homepage, August 2010

LFC TV ONLINE

ABOUT

LFC TV Online is the club website's on-demand video service.

- Watch LFC TV, the club's TV channel LIVE or catch up with the best bits, at your leisure;
- Watch selected pre-season matches LIVE;
- Enjoy web-friendly and bite-sized videos of the best LFC video content anywhere;
- LIVE match commentary and picture slideshow of every LFC game;
- Goal clips and video highlights of all our Premier League and Europa League matches;
- Live and exclusive coverage of every Reserve match Liverpool FC play;
- Exclusive video interviews with players, managers and legends;
- The only place to watch every Reds press conference – IN FULL;
- Relive KOP classics – live and breathe Liverpool's history;
- Enter our exclusive match ticket ballot;
- Edit your own match highlights and watch your own creations.

Watch what you want, where you want and when you want!

For a FREE PREVIEW, visit **www.liverpoolfc.tv/preview**

LFC TV

ABOUT

The only place on TV to savour every minute of every Barclays Premier League and Europa League game Liverpool play, LFC TV is a must-watch for supporters in the UK.

Bringing you unrivalled access to Roy Hodgson's Liverpool FC on and off the pitch, LFC TV allows you to follow the team like never before from the comfort of your own home.

'LFC Now' is our daily news show, 'The Match' features every kick of every game while 'A Closer Look' sees LFC TV's resident expert Gary Gillespie analyse every game we play in detail.

'This is Anfield' is your chance to have your say on the issues that matter – whether by phone, email, Facebook or Twitter – while 'The Academy' follows the progress of the kids just starting out.

If 'The Academy' is all about what promises to be a fantastic future for the club, 'Cup Kings' is about our glorious past and allows fans everywhere to wallow in the glory of the moments that made this football club what it is today.

Whatever your age, you'll always find something worth watching on LFC TV and what's more, we won't charge you a penny for tuning in every day on your TV!

LFC TV can be viewed online via LFC TV Online, (**www.liverpoolfc.tv/eseason**), on Sky Channel 434 or Virgin Media Channel 544.

Visit **www.liverpoolfc.tv/tv**

LIVERPOOL FC MOBILE ZONE

ABOUT

The Liverpool FC Mobile Zone is your one-stop shop to decorate your phone with the latest apps, ringtones, animations or wallpapers from Anfield.

With regular updates to this ever popular area on **www.liverpoolfc.tv**, we have a wide array of the very latest downloads to give the chance of bringing your favourite club to your mobile phone.

IPHONE APPLICATIONS – LIVERPOOL MATCH AND NEWS CENTRE

Kopites can now follow the team they love wherever they go with the LFC Match and News Centre on the iPhone.

Whether it's breaking news, exclusive interviews or in-game scores and commentary you're after, you won't miss a thing with this innovative application.

Features include:

- In-game scores for all UK league and Europa League games;
- Text commentary for LFC games;
- Match reports and stats;
- All breaking news from the club;
- Interviews with players and management;
- Player profiles;
- Player wallpapers.

IPHONE APPLICATIONS – ISTANBUL 05 + OTHERS...

One of our most famous European nights ever is now available to relive over and over again with the fantastic Istanbul iPhone app.

'Istanbul '05: LFC glory' is your must-have souvenir from the night we overcame the greatest of odds to secure the most famous comeback in sporting history to land the Champions League trophy for the fifth time.

There are more Applications to be launched throughout the season.
Look out for new and exciting apps launching across the season...and not just for the iPhone.

For iPhone apps, search for Liverpool FC in the App Store to see what's on offer...

MOBILE MEMBERSHIP

You can now download as many wallpapers and videos as you like with LFC Mobile Membership. For £1.50 a week, you will have access to match action, features, interviews and the latest news videos plus wallpapers of your favourite players and the famous crest.
Text CLUB to 61718 for info. Text will cost standard network rate. Phone must be WAP enabled.

TEXT ALERTS AND DOWNLOADS

Whether it's news of the latest goal to your mobile or a You'll Never Walk Alone ringtone, we've got it all.

Text Alerts: Choose from goals, teamsheets, latest news and more straight to your mobile as it happens.

Downloads: Animations of your favourite players, ringtones to get your phone jumping and wallpapers of the team in action. Show your allegiance to the Reds on your mobile...

LIVERPOOL SOCCER SCHOOL

ABOUT

Take your natural skills onto the next level...

This 3-day specialist programme for both outfield players and goalkeepers is designed to develop the potential of every child that attends by enhancing their confidence and improving their skills, whilst ensuring they are fun and rewarding in every sense.

It is available to children of all abilities from the ages of 5 to 14 – from beginner to superstar!
By taking part you'll benefit from:

- Professional and dedicated coaching from Academy staff in all areas of the game;
- Expertly designed practices, activities and skill sessions;
- Learning new tactics and techniques;
- Improving your ball skills, passing, balance and co-ordination;
- Mini-tournaments and penalty shoot-outs.

And who knows? If our coaches spot your talent you could be the next Academy protégé to make it through to the first team.

So whether you want to show off your skills or improve your techniques, why not take the opportunity to play like your heroes and book your place.

For more information or to book please visit **www.liverpoolfc.tv/soccerschools**

ALL RED – THE LFC OFFICIAL MEMBERSHIP SCHEME

ABOUT

Become a member of ALL RED, the LFC Official Membership Scheme and you'll enjoy a whole host of benefits:

ADULTS

- Priority ticket access for up to 8,000 seats at every Barclays Premier League home game, that's up to 3,000 more than last season!
- Exclusive ALL RED embossed card wallet and members card;
- 10% retail discount in our online shop or in any LFC official club store;
- 3 months free LFC TV online trial;
- 20% off the new Anfield Stadium Tour;
- 40% off the LFC Magazine subscription;
- Exclusive club competitions and prize draws;
- Exclusive offers from LFC Partners.

JUNIORS

- Priority ticket access for up to 8,000 seats at every Barclays Premier League home game, that's up to 3,000 more than last season!
- Exclusive ALL RED Merchandise which includes a kit bag, wallet, stickers, poster, wrist bands and members card;
- The opportunity to attend an exclusive ALL RED junior member's Soccer School at the Academy;
- The chance to be an LFC mascot and walk out with your LFC heroes;
- 10% retail discount in our online shop or in any LFC official club store;
- 3 months free LFC TV online trial;
- 20% off the new Anfield Stadium Tour;
- 40% off the LFC Magazine subscription;
- Exclusive club competitions and prize draws;
- Exclusive offers from LFC Partners.

PRICES

Adult Members: £29 (Inc P&P)
Junior Members: £11.99 (Inc P&P)

HOW TO JOIN

Visit **www.liverpoolfc.tv/ALLRED** or telephone **0843 170 5000**.
International calls **+44 151 261 1444**.

OFFICIAL PUBLICATIONS

Official Matchday Programme

The award-winning 84-page souvenir matchday publication, available every Anfield matchday, is the perfect accompaniment for Reds fans. Exclusive interviews with players and management, club news, columns, quizzes, facts and statistics remain, while a new feature includes the Kids' Zone pull-out with a player poster. Regulars like Kop 'n' Goal Years, Files of Anfield Road and LFC Uncut have been joined by a Memorabilia section in 2010/11.

How to subscribe

Phone: 0845 143 0001 (Monday-Friday 9am-5pm)
Website: www.liverpoolfc.tv/match/magazine
(Also available in braille and other formats - contact community department on 0151 264 2316 for details)

LFC Weekly

Established as the only weekly publication produced by a Barclays Premier League club in 2002, the club magazine continues to inform and entertain fans of all ages. Packed with fresh content and analysis, the magazine offers greater interaction with fans and liverpoolfc.tv. Going behind the scenes at Melwood, we speak to the stars while offering the very best match previews, reports, on-field action, interviews and statistics – while columnists Kenny Dalglish and Alan Hansen deliver their expert opinion.

How to subscribe

Phone: 0845 143 0001 (Monday-Friday 9am-5pm)
Website: www.liverpoolfc.tv/match/magazine

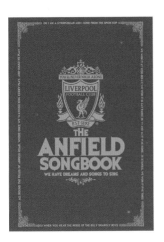

The Anfield Songbook

When it comes to inventing funny and inspirational songs for their team, no other set of fans can compare with Liverpool FC's. Now, for the first time, comes this definitive compilation of Kop songs and chants from the heart of the club. The book is a complete collection of the timeless anthems, traditional classics, player chants and witty one-liners that have made the Kop unique.

How to order

Phone: 0845 143 0001 (Monday-Friday 9am-5pm)
Website: www.liverpoolfc.tv/store

LFC IN THE COMMUNITY

ABOUT

The quality of Liverpool FC's work was recognised in 2009/2010 with a "Team Achievement Award" from the Football Foundation; "Safer Knowsley Partnership Award" from Knowsley MBC and a "Youth Recognition Award" from Merseyside Police (for the **Kickz** project). The team also gained the Attorney General's Office "Excellence through Partnership for Young People Award" and through achieving the independently-judged **Community Mark** standard from Business in the Community, one of only 34 companies nationally to do so.

These accolades speak of the Club's values and commitment to the programmes it delivers itself and with partners in the following ways:

CommunityMark
developed by Business in the Community

EDUCATION

* Schools programmes such as the **Truth 4 Youth** assemblies delivering hard-hitting messages about bullying, racism, substance abuse, violence and health. The programme recently received an award from the Attorney General's Office for 'excellence through partnership for young people'.
* **Tactics 4 Families** is an LFC-developed education programme addressed to children in school years 4-6 and their families. It uses footballing language and principles to inspire understanding and mutual support within families. Our family support work also includes family fun days, parent/child activity sessions and 'dads and lads' football coaching.
* For over a decade LFC's rebuilt **Reducate** centre has delivered innovative educational activities for over 37,000 school children in such diverse subjects as English, Maths, IT, Spanish and French. Materials are tailored to the needs of individual schools and updated using current sporting and other events to engage pupils in learning.
* **Citizenship Education** – Young people who display courage, bravery, caring and commitment to others are rewarded at the **Young Persons of the Year Award** event – a prestigious evening attended by a first-team player.
* LFC takes an active part in the national anti-racism campaign, **Kick it Out**, and has sponsored educational films and plays dealing with issues such as hoax calls to emergency services, anti-social behaviour, alcohol abuse and gangs in partnership with the fire service, police and the Anthony Walker Foundation among others.
* **SweeperZone** is a programme whereby each matchday schools will nominate 25 young people who collect litter around Anfield and receive free entry to the match. Each year these youngsters achieve a Liverpool City Council Environmental Citizen of the Year award.
* **Rewards 4 Respect** is about giving children who care for others and act responsibly recognition within their school and community.

SOCIAL INCLUSION

* The Premier League **Social Inclusion** project delivers football coaching for minority ethnic and excluded groups around the city. The programme seeks to bring together the diverse communities within Liverpool regardless of ethnicity, gender, sexuality or background.
* The **Kickz** programme of late-night football for 12 to 18-year-olds has proved very successful in stemming anti-social behaviour. Supported by LFC and the Premier League and run jointly with Everton FC, this project won two national awards in 2010.
* LFC's **Goals 4 Girls** programme is multi-sports based for young women. The programme also delivers messages on well-being, confidence and peer pressure.
* With the Big Issue in the North's **Social Academy**, LFC trains the homeless, unemployed and socially-excluded to coach, putting them through their FA Level 1 coaching badge.
* LFC provides opportunities for those with disabilities to take part in football. Specialist coaches run the **Respect 4 All** centre where impairment specific football sessions are available four evenings per week for children and adults with visual impairment, physical and learning disabilities. Sports sessions are held in up to 40 special schools each month. In addition the **Ability Counts** teams train each week and compete at home and abroad.

LFC IN THE COMMUNITY

PHYSICAL ACTIVITY

- Each week LFC coaches run sessions in schools as well as after-school and holiday sessions in community centres. In 2009 this amounted to almost 3,000 hours of coaching.
- LFC, in partnership with Everton FC, also offers sessions in multi-sports activities including table tennis, badminton, judo and volleyball as part of the Premier League's **PL4Sport** programme linked to the 2012 Olympics.
- Each week LFC coaches deliver coaching sessions in 10 special schools in Liverpool.
- Working in partnership with the **Princes Trust**, LFC delivers a week-long 'Get Started with Football' course to young people and all earn an FA Junior Football Organisers certificate. The course encourages teenagers to participate and lead coaching to younger children.

HEALTH

- The **Action for Health** programme includes activities, publications and lifestyle information through its website, kiosks and exhibitions. Managed by public health professionals, it has enabled over 6,000 health checks in community venues, sponsored an exercise song book/CD for Under-5s, established a men's health programme (**PL Health**) and sessions for the over 50s (**PL Extra Time** and **PL Imagine Your Goals**). LFC works with the Primary Care Trust, Liverpool City Council, Mersey Care NHS Trust, the Premier League and community partners to make a difference. Other sponsors include Sport Relief and Time to Change.
- As a member of the **European Healthy Stadia Network** LFC has focused upon the range of food choices for fans and employees, offered health checks for its employees and initiated the Cycle2Work scheme. It shares good practice with other stadia across Europe.

LFC IN ANFIELD

- LFC has worked with Liverpool City Council and the community on the Anfield Breckfield Regeneration Strategy. This partnership has meant the restoration of Stanley Park and the Isla Gladstone Conservatory, new community centres, improved highways infrastructure, new schools, new and restored housing and a planned health centre.
- LFC contributed over £9 million towards local regeneration projects to match the public funding through the city council. Its contribution to the economic life of North Liverpool is essential to the area's recovery through tourism, employment and business support.
- LFC is a key member of numerous community networks including Stronger Communities (with LCC Neighbourhood Management, Merseyside Police, Merseyside Fire and Rescue Service, etc.), the Anfield Breckfield Partnership Forum and Stanley Park Events Forum.

SUPPORT FOR OTHER CHARITIES

- LFC helps communicate with its huge national and international fan base through the Charity section, where thousands of letters are received and answered each year.
- The department receives huge demand for players' signatures and charitable donations. These requests are then individually assessed, with those who have special needs with registered charities taking priority. Similarly, visits to meet players at Melwood are prioritised for those individuals who are, unfortunately, seriously or terminally ill.
- LFC supports **Football Aid** and **Alder Hey Children's Hospital**. The players visit the hospital every Christmas, with the squad chatting and giving out gifts to approximately 300 children on every ward. Community coaches also visit hospitals at this time of year.

INTERNATIONAL COMMUNITY WORK

- LFC has a long track record in working within poor areas throughout the world. In 2009/10, LFC's Community Coaches were in Northern Ireland, the Sudan and South Africa. The most recent trip to South Africa was in May 2010 with Oxfam coaching as part of their "Fair Play for Africa" programme.
- LFC donates hundreds of kits to third-world countries via bona fide charities.
- LFC were a sponsor of Liverpool's pavilion at the Shanghai Expo in 2010, sharing experiences in regeneration and public health, and solidifying its Chinese links.

REDUC@TE

ABOUT

Reduc@te delivers innovative educational activities to school children in Liverpool from across the key stages by inspiring and motivating children with a wide range of specially made curriculum materials. All these materials are available on the Reduc@te website for young people to access anywhere in the world.

Visits to the centre for schools can be arranged by contacting the centre manager, Keith White:

Phone: **0151 263 1313**
Email: **krwhite.lfc.study@talk21.com** or **keith.white@liverpoolfc.tv**

For more details please visit:

www.liverpoolfc.tv/community

ASSOCIATION OF INTERNATIONAL BRANCHES

ABOUT

There are currently over 200 official branches registered to Liverpool Football Club and these are located both in the UK and internationally. It is an opportunity for fellow Reds to meet on a local level to show their loyalty and dedication to LFC.
All registered branches are listed at **www.liverpoolfc.tv/club/aib**

LIVERPOOL DISABLED SUPPORTERS' ASSOCIATION

AIMS AND OBJECTIVES

To act in partnership with Liverpool Football Club to promote inclusiveness for the disabled fans of the club, the disabled fans of visiting clubs as well as those individuals who support disabled people and those with impairments.

This association recognises that all fans should have an equal opportunity to participate in an enjoyable matchday experience and that people with disabilities and/or impairments must have their interests recognised and promoted by LFC with equal status to that of all other Liverpool fans.

CONTACT DETAILS

Disability liaison officer Colin McCall continues to develop the LDSA, acting as a link between the club and its supporters. The LDSA committee is made up of 10 members who are all Liverpool supporters and they meet once a month with the liaison officer to discuss disability issues at LFC.

If you would like any more information about the LDSA then please email **LDSA@liverpoolfc.tv** or write to **LDSA, Liverpool Football Club, Anfield Road, Liverpool, L4 0TH**.

OFFICIAL CLUB PARTNERS

Standard Chartered
www.standardchartered.com

adidas
www.adidas.com/liverpoolfc

Carlsberg
www.partofthegame.tv

Thomas Cook
www.thomascooksport.com/liverpoolfc

188Bet
www.188promo.com/liverpool

Jack Wolfskin
www.jack-wolfskin.com/en/

LFC Credit Card
www.liverpoolfc.tv/corporate/lfc-credit-card

Maxxis
www.maxxis.co.uk

Lucozade Sport
www.lucozade.com/sport/football

Visit Spain
www.spain.info

2011	Jan	Feb	March	April	May	June
Monday						
Tuesday		1	1			
Wednesday		2	2			1
Thursday		3	3			2
Friday		4	4	1		3
Saturday	1	5	5	2		4
Sunday	2	6	6	3	1	5
Monday	3	7	7	4	2	6
Tuesday	4	8	8	5	3	7
Wednesday	5	9	9	6	4	8
Thursday	6	10	10	7	5	9
Friday	7	11	11	8	6	10
Saturday	8	12	12	9	7	11
Sunday	9	13	13	10	8	12
Monday	10	14	14	11	9	13
Tuesday	11	15	15	12	10	14
Wednesday	12	16	16	13	11	15
Thursday	13	17	17	14	12	16
Friday	14	18	18	15	13	17
Saturday	15	18	18	16	14	18
Sunday	16	20	20	17	15	18
Monday	17	21	21	18	16	20
Tuesday	18	22	22	18	17	21
Wednesday	18	23	23	20	18	22
Thursday	20	24	24	21	18	23
Friday	21	25	25	22	20	24
Saturday	22	26	26	23	21	25
Sunday	23	27	27	24	22	26
Monday	24	28	28	25	23	27
Tuesday	25		29	26	24	28
Wednesday	26		30	27	25	29
Thursday	27		31	28	26	30
Friday	28			29	27	
Saturday	29			30	28	
Sunday	30				29	
Monday	31				30	
Tuesday					31	

July	Aug	Sept	Oct	Nov	Dec	
1						Monday
2				1		Tuesday
3				2		Wednesday
4	1			3	1	Thursday
5	2			4	2	Friday
6	3		1	5	3	Saturday
7	4		2	6	4	Sunday
8	5		3	7	5	Monday
9	6		4	8	6	Tuesday
10	7		5	9	7	Wednesday
11	8		6	10	8	Thursday
12	9		7	11	9	Friday
13	10		8	12	10	Saturday
14	11		9	13	11	Sunday
15	12		10	14	12	Monday
16	13		11	15	13	Tuesday
17	14		12	16	14	Wednesday
18	15		13	17	15	Thursday
18	16		14	18	16	Friday
20	17		15	18	17	Saturday
21	18		16	20	18	Sunday
22	18		17	21	18	Monday
23	20		18	22	20	Tuesday
24	21		18	23	21	Wednesday
25	22		20	24	22	Thursday
26	23		21	25	23	Friday
27	24		22	26	24	Saturday
28	25		23	27	25	Sunday
29	26		24	28	26	Monday
30	27		25	29	27	Tuesday
31	28		26	30	28	Wednesday
	29		27		29	Thursday
	30		28		30	Friday
			29		31	Saturday
			30			Sunday
			31			Monday
						Tuesday

OTHER USEFUL CONTACTS

The Premier League
30 Gloucester Place,
London W1U 8PL
Phone: 0207 864 9000
Email: **info@premierleague.com**

The Football Association
Wembley Stadium,
PO Box 1966,
London SW1P 9EQ
Phone: 0844 980 8200

The Football League
Edward VII Quay, Navigation Way,
Preston PR2 2YF
Email: **fl@football-league.co.uk**

Professional Footballers' Association
2 Oxford Court,
Bishopsgate,
Off Lower Mosley Street,
Manchester M2 3WQ
Phone: 0161 236 0575
Email: **info@thepfa.co.uk**

Hillsborough Family
Support Group
c/o Liverpool FC,
Anfield Road,
Liverpool L4 0TH
Email: **hfsg@worthside.co.uk**

Liverpool FC logo and name are registered trademarks of
The Liverpool Football Club and Athletics Grounds Ltd and are reproduced under license.
Published in Great Britain in 2010 by: Trinity Mirror Sport Media, PO Box 48, Old Hall Street, Liverpool, L69 3EB

All Rights Reserved. No part of this publication may be reproduced, stored in a retrieval system, or transmitted in any form, or by
any means, electronic, mechanical, photocopying, recording or otherwise without the prior permission in writing of the copyright
holders, nor be otherwise circulated in any form of binding or cover other than in which it is published and without a similar
condition being imposed on the subsequent publisher.

ISBN: 1 9068 0254 7
978 1 9068 0254 7

Photographs: PA Photos, Trinity Mirror, Liverpool FC & AG Ltd
Printed and finished by Korotan